Intelligent Health Policy

Petri Virtanen • Jari Stenvall

Intelligent Health Policy

Theory, Concept and Practice

 Springer

Petri Virtanen
The Finnish Innovation Fund SITRA
Helsinki, Finland

Jari Stenvall
School of Management
University of Tampere
Tampere, Finland

ISBN 978-3-319-69595-2   ISBN 978-3-319-69596-9   (eBook)
https://doi.org/10.1007/978-3-319-69596-9

Library of Congress Control Number: 2017957622

Printed on acid-free paper

This Springer imprint is published by Springer Nature
The registered company is Springer International Publishing AG
The registered company address is: Gewerbestrasse 11, 6330 Cham, Switzerland

Preface

Health matters to everyone. It is an essential ingredient in our lives. If you do not have good or adequate health, you most likely suffer somehow in your life. Good health promotes your activities in life and brings you happiness and good spirit. This is why we have chosen health as a policy subject in this book.

Moreover, public policies and organisations are important—or, to be more precise, essential. Every one of us is affected by public policies and uses the services provided by public, private or non-governmental organisations.

In this book, we have combined these important topics—health, public policy and organisations—and written about health policy from a perspective that we consider to be novel. Throughout this book, we maintain that the future of health policies and healthcare service delivery pretty much depends on how intelligently they are planned, implemented and evaluated. In our thinking, public policy constitutes a learning cycle that aims at the betterment of the society. Intelligence is an important ingredient, based on client-centred thinking, systematic data-driven leadership mechanisms and good leadership, for future health policies and services—and service ecosystems.

We approach public health policy from a comprehensive public policy viewpoint. In doing so, we deliberately focus on healthcare organisations as they exist in the current and future service space by not making a distinction between the roles of the service purchaser and the service producer. If we had decided to include this topic, the manuscript would have been twice as long. Other interesting and important topics are also out of reach of this manuscript for the same reason—topics such as democracy issues and topics related to co-creation models at the public policy level.

A word of warning. We are not trained doctors or representatives of any healthcare profession. We have written this book as public governance, public policy and public administration experts and enthusiasts with a joint professional and academic track record on these topics totalling more than 50 years.

This is our fifth book together along with numerous academic and semi-academic papers written together over the last 15 years. With regard to monographs, we have previously written about change leadership (published in 2007), public sector leadership (2010), development models in health and social services (2012) and intelligent public organisation (2014). There are also numerous spin-off academic and semi-academic articles from our books.

Without exception, our writing missions have been a great fun, and this has been the case with this book as well. For us, the writing process is fun when we learn something together. Parts of this book have been written in Finland, our home country, and also in China, the Netherlands, Qatar, Indonesia, the USA, the United Arab Emirates, the UK and Singapore.

Finally, Petri wants to thank Johanna for her love, understanding and patience during the writing process of this book. Jari is deeply thankful to Kirsi for her all-encompassing support and love over the years.

Helsinki, Finland   Petri Virtanen
Tampere, Finland   Jari Stenvall
September 2017

Contents

Chapter 1
Introduction

Abstract Generally speaking, the basic topics of organisation theories have not changed much over the decades. Finding a balance between the rational and non-rational elements of human behaviour is still a cardinal issue of modern life, society and thinking. The basic question is how to best coordinate human activities in order to make up a highly rational unit and, at the same time, maintain social integration, the normative commitments of participants and their motivation to participate. This is one of the key questions in intelligent organisations as well. Comprehensive models of organisational intelligence, which bring together relevant assumptions and concepts, are lacking in literature. For this reason, the purpose of this chapter is to present an integrative approach to organisational intelligence research. We emphasise that organisations need intelligence if they want to find ways to survive in complex environments. Our starting point is that healthcare organisations can learn from the literature on organisational intelligence.

1.1 A Quest for Well-Being

The city of Hämeenlinna is a small city with 70,000 habitants near to Helsinki in Finland. Hence, it has been one of the prime movers in developing healthcare in the Nordic countries. The city has reformed its healthcare system over the last 10 years. The turning point was the insight that there was a need for a paradigm change in the healthcare system. It required service users to have a stronger position in the service system. They are more and more capable to evaluate and take responsibility for health-related issues by themselves. Hence, there are service users who need a lot of services as well. For this reason, Hämeenlinna established the so-called channel model for the most demanding service users. Technology constantly gives new possibilities in developing health services. Healthcare professionals' attitudes, competencies and working methods should change in the new environments. Hämeenlinna has moved towards the paradigm of health intelligence. This is a comprehensive approach for developing health policy with service users and using new technological possibilities. Developing health-intelligent policy is a process. The content and methods of health policy change all the time.

The city of Hämeenlinna is not alone. Many countries—like Finland, the UK and the Netherlands—have faced significant challenges that concern healthcare systems

© Springer International Publishing AG 2018   1
P. Virtanen, J. Stenvall, *Intelligent Health Policy*,
https://doi.org/10.1007/978-3-319-69596-9_1

and services. Healthcare systems and policies are under considerable strain owing to population ageing, fiscal consolidation, migration, increasing inequality and both Europeanisation and globalisation. Here, decision-makers face a quandary: how can one constrain healthcare spending and yet satisfy public demands in the health system? The question is how to outline and implement healthcare policy, how organisations operate, how they are managed and how to provide services for service users. The welfare-state crisis means discussions on how to maintain—if it is possible to maintain—welfare in society.

In the context of health policy, new kinds of intelligent technologies have been considered as solutions for reinventing health policy. The European Union has, for instance, put forward a digital agenda to improve every citizen's health by making health data available to everyone using eHealth tools. However, eHealth is only one issue on the digitalisation agenda. All sociotechnical systems operate on a technical base. This means that email, chat, bulletin boards, blogs, Wikipedia, eBay, Twitter, Facebook, YouTube and other health-related sensors, apps and web services are all sociotechnical systems, which millions of people use. The question, then, is how do these systems affect health and shape the way we understand, experience, develop and maintain our health?

Given the transformational change in the field of health, policy instruments need to be mobilised in order to make sustainable and health promotion-based changes in people's way of life, well-being and health, both experience- and diagnosis-based. Health policies ought to be more coherent (between policy areas, taking into account the emergence of nexus policy problems), evidence-based and intelligent. Digitalisation plays an important role in how traditional concepts of health and well-being are currently changing. The role of the individual in the process of sustaining health and enhancing well-being plays a crucial role here as well.

The contribution of this book is to note that austerity, personalisation and service integration are driving the new governances of services beyond interorganisational coordination into more closely coupled service systems in which service users (as co-producers) play an active role. In this book, what we seek here is a better understanding of the intelligence in public health policies, healthcare organisations and healthcare service systems. We also want to show why contemporary public policy making, leadership and planning within the field of health should be replaced and with what.

1.2   Why Does Intelligence Matter?

In this book, our approach is to link the concept of intelligence with public health policy and healthcare organisations. At the outset, we think that nobody wants to be silly or dumb, nor do we think that anybody would want to work in a ridiculous, moronic or stupid organisation. People don't want to use their time to implement a useless policy that is so stupid that it does not help people. The fact is that not only human beings but also organisations or even the system of policy making can be intelligent or stupid. In some cases, intelligent people might even make stupid decisions due to their working environment.

In recent years, researchers have increasingly started to talk about requirements for more intelligence in public activities and public administration and generally about more intelligent service interventions and service ecosystems (Stenvall and Virtanen 2015; Virtanen and Vakkuri 2015). This kind of discussion tells us that it is possible to increase intelligence in organisations, policy making as well as implementation. There are technological possibilities to develop organisational intelligence.

There are many books about intelligence and many more about health policy. Without a doubt, intelligence is a popular topic in management and organisational research and attracts many researchers and practitioners from different fields (Akgün et al. 2007). In the organisational and policy context, it is possible to approach intelligence, as an example, from the perspective of professions (Abbott 1988), teams (Hackman 2011), key persons' retention to organisation (Goffee and Jones 2009) and policy making (Lindblom 1965). The literature on public policy includes little discussion on the relationship between policy and intelligence.

Although the term *intelligence* is quite unknown in public policy literature, there are a lot of themes that are relevant for us. One of the traditional discussion topics is what the relationship between politicians and experts in policy making and implementation is. This is related to the discussion raised by Max Weber (1978). We can ask what makes administrative systems and actions rational. There is a lot of discussion on evidence-based policy in the literature. It is public policy informed by a rigorously established objective (Head 2008). Learning is also an important aspect in intelligence-led public policy (Hall 1993).

The essential purpose of this book is to clarify the conceptual relationship between public policy and intelligence in the context of health. This requires both practical examples on health policy and theoretical discussions. We agree with Guy Peters's (2015) argument that public policy must strike a balance between academic, theory-driven work and the practitioner-oriented, real world of public policy.

There is a lack of coherent studies that put together the system perspective, intelligence and health policy. Our intellectual goal in this book is to cover this pitfall by making explicit the organisational activities that generate organisational intelligence within health policy. This is a challenging task because there are many forms and levels of intelligence.

1.3 Intelligence and Health Policy

It is reasonable to raise the question of why intelligence is a relevant issue in health policy. Why should organisations be intelligent in the health system? One of the main arguments for why intelligence is an important aspect can be seen in the findings of studies which show that intelligent organisations and policy making are more successful than so-called non-intelligent organisations and policy making (cf. Matheson and Matheson 2001; Virtanen and Stenvall 2014).

There are several definitions of public policy. For instance, Gerston (2015) defines public policy as the combination of basic decisions, commitments and actions made by those who hold or have an influence on government positions of authority. In general, public policy includes which policy ideas are embedded and the basis on which policies are framed, articulated and implemented (Hall 1993; Peters 2015). In a broader sense, public policy can be described as the overall framework within which government actions are undertaken to achieve public goals. The framework of public policy covers policy objectives, policy instruments, government's implementation structure and implications for reform. Public policies—like health policy—are filtered through a specific policy process, adopted and implemented through laws, regulatory measures, courses of government action and funding priorities and are enforced by a public agency.

Actors, practices and processes either make or do not make public policy intelligent. In this book, health policy intelligence is understood as the capability of health policy actors to bring about the outcomes they desire—both internally and in the environment.

This leads to the following definition:

> In our approach, the intelligence of health policy relates to better deployment of knowledge in planning and supervising service production, better involvement of co-creation mechanisms in developing healthcare services and better evaluation of health policies. Overall, intelligence in the domain of health policy involves better adaptiveness and change management as drivers for organisational change.

There are several factors that are the cornerstones of intelligent health policy. First, intelligent public policy is related to the discussion on how to use expertise or evidence in public policy. Intelligence as a part of policy making means wisely managing in a complex environment. In this context, different kinds of think tanks can produce better policy making by creating new ideas for policy making. According to Sanderson (2009), intelligent policy making rests on two pillars: our developing knowledge about complexity and ideas from a pragmatist philosophical position. He argues that, at the heart of intelligent policy making, people should be committed to experimentation and learning.

Second, the cornerstones of intelligent health policy are precise and ambitious objectives. Intelligent policy making means that the actors of policy making have the ability to identify weak signals from the environment and the factors of change in the operating environment. They have a better capacity to change, and they utilise resources better than non-intelligent organisations (Virtanen and Stenvall 2014). Intelligence means the capacity to manage complex and constantly changing environments.

Public policies interact with their environments. In this context, health policy and service systems appear to become even more complex. Intelligence is necessary due to, for instance, ongoing changes, increasing complexity and technological development. The number of actors involved in the formulation, implementation and evaluation of health policy continues to expand, which means that the full calibre of all traditional policy instruments (i.e. regulation, financial resources and information) should be mobilised.

The need to be innovative in the design architectures, service designs and the implementation of health policy calls for new adaptive capacities in organisations in the field of health. Health service systems appear to have become even more complex. Even the service users' life situations are much more complex, which emphasises new kinds of service-delivery systems and practices like co-production (Tuurnas 2016). Intelligence in health policies means better and more qualitative services for service users.

In Table 1.1, we have summarised the main components of intelligent health policy.

Without a doubt—as Travica (2015) has noted—intelligence produces several necessary outcomes for organisations. An intelligent organisation is capable of making the right decisions. Intelligence can produce the capabilities of creating successful and innovative products, impacting the environment and mobilising creative people and other resources.

In this book, we focus our attention on intelligence and intelligent solutions within health policy, especially within comprehensive health policy. This means that we pay attention to the value of health and intelligence at the levels of both policy and the service users.

Summarising our viewpoints, intelligence can be considered a potential pathway for developed health policy. In practice, policies create the context for intelligence. Intelligence in health policy and health services interacts at various interfaces and levels within organisations in relation to political decision-making, service users and cooperating partners. The demand for intelligence involves all aspects of an operation.

Table 1.1 The main proponents of intelligence in health policy

	Non-intelligent health policy	Intelligent health policy
The role of knowledge creation and deployment in decision-making	Sporadic	A mechanism for constant strategic insight
The role of patient involvement in service development	Co-production	Co-creation
The role of evaluation	Ex post, looking for scapegoats	Ex ante and ex nunc, looking for betterment in services
The role of management changes	Reactional	Built-in adaptivity to change
The role of technology	A threat or innovation imposed from environment	A mechanism for change
The role of healthcare professionals	Dominant	Co-creation tribes
The role of quality of healthcare services	Organisational secret	Based on open data, a mechanism to improve

1.4   The Concept of Organisational Intelligence

There exists a plethora of research literature on intelligence and healthcare organisations related to knowledge creation, leadership, the role of the patients and technology. Hence, there is not just one practice—like good leadership and processes—that produces organisational intelligence. Actually, organisational intelligence is a comprehensive phenomenon (Stenvall and Virtanen 2015). Our conclusion is that the research literature that is missing at the moment is, in fact, those that combine the above-mentioned elements. This book tries to fill this gap in the research literature.

In this book, our starting point is—like Wilensky (1967) and March (1991) have noted—that organisational intelligence is the key element in complex systems and environments. At an organisational level, intelligence is understood as the capability of an organisation to bring about the outcomes it desires, both internally and in the environment. Both structural and human aspects are important in creating intelligence in organisations.

There are several human-based factors in organisations that have an effect on intelligence. Employees have different kinds of intelligence due to their backgrounds, experiences and abilities. Different actors have, for example, divergent abilities to observe external events like developments in health problems. Some experts might emphasise the importance of people's personal lifestyles, while others take into consideration the quality of the service system in solving health problems.

The structures of organisations affect intelligence as well. Wilensky (1967) made the ground-breaking observation concerning this issue in the 1960s. Due to their structures, organisations show a similar tendency to believe what they want to believe, to become the victims of their own slogans and propaganda and to resist or to silence warning voices that challenge their assumptions. This decreases intelligence in organisations.

Generally speaking, the concept of organisational intelligence can be approached in two ways. First, intelligence can be based on individual employees' or professionals' intelligence. This approach emphasises people's competence, skills and talent. Generally, an intelligent person can learn from experience, understand abstract thought, resolve novel problems and adapt to and manipulate a given environment (Travica 2015). From this point of view, health policy is intelligent if individual employees have the ability to solve customers' problems and implement health policies purposefully. An organisation's intelligence is the sum of its employees' intelligence. We call this type of intelligence individual intelligence.

Traditionally, social scientists often make use of variables to describe not only individual persons but also groups, communities or other collectives. The second form of intelligence is collective intelligence. Conceptually, it is a phenomenon where a group of initially independent agents develop a collective approach to tackle a shared problem, and this is a more powerful approach than any of them might have developed individually, which can be called collective intelligence (Heyloghen 2013). Knowledge creation, sharing and use can take place in a group context (Travica 2015).

On the other hand, organisational intelligence may be invisible and unnoticeable for people who work in organisations. This is related to the idea presented by Dreyfus and Dreyfus (1980). According to them, experts have the ability to solve complex problems, but they do not necessarily know themselves which aspects their working methods are based on.

Our starting point is therefore not that healthcare organisations do not represent a high level of intelligence. Actually, if we compare typical healthcare organisations with any number of organisations in other sectors, they, quite often, stand out as the most intelligent organisations. The employees are well educated, and the organisations in the healthcare sector work in very rational ways. In the existing research literature, healthcare organisations are described using the concept of an expert or professional organisation. This indicates that healthcare organisations have a lot of intelligence.

There are several common characteristics in professional organisations. The following aspects have been used in describing professional organisations (Abbott 1988; Sveiby 1997; Alvesson 1993; Brock 2006). These aspects are typical in healthcare organisations as well:

- Organisations' core activities are based on knowledge.
- Knowledge creation is an important aspect in organisations.
- Organisations use employees' expertise in solving complex problems.
- Organisations have complex structures.
- Outputs are created by the activities in relation to customers.
- A key part of the staff consists of highly educated employees.
- There are a lot of non-material outcomes in organisations (like services).
- Experts have strong autonomy in organisations. Their autonomy covers not only planning work but operational aspects as well.
- Experts have a lot of power in organisations.
- Professions and their ethical codes have an effect on work in organisations.

Healthcare organisations are typically professional organisations that concentrate especially on treatments concerning human health and diseases. Their intelligence is based on the capacity of individual experts, doctors in particular, but, increasingly, other medical staff too. The actions of healthcare organisations are based on theoretical knowledge. The key experts often have quite extensive experience in their respective fields.

Experts' work is based on the values and ethics of their profession (Sveiby 1997). In practice, healthcare experts are guided by stronger ethics than many other professions. From this perspective, healthcare organisations are not independent from their professional community.

Highly educated experts quite often use a language of their own. For example, doctors would use their professional jargon—medical terms, etc.—which is very difficult for outsiders to understand. This may have an adverse effect on a healthcare organisation's collaboration with other professional organisations or with service users.

In healthcare, the autonomy of professionals is very high within organisations. Professionals—for example, doctors—have a lot of control over their work. To a high extent, this power covers the planning of work as well as operational aspects, such as decision-making concerning customers. In many organisations, healthcare experts have a lot of resource power due to their knowledge. They know what kinds of equipment are needed in successful medical treatment, etc. In practice, it would be very hard to create coercive healthcare organisations in which, for instance, 'policy makers had power over professional employees'.

Professionals have an important role in creating, sharing and using knowledge. To some extent, professional principles have an effect on producing collective intelligence in healthcare organisations. This is related to collegial practices. For instance, it is possible that doctors consult each other concerning the treatment of a patient. Different kinds of collegial meetings at hospitals are another example of organisational practices that create collective intelligence.

In addition, the various professions are not equal in healthcare organisations. Doctors, especially, have traditionally had a lot of power and special roles in healthcare organisations (Freidson 1988). This has created hierarchical structures and tensions that have an effect on the contents of intelligence.

There are a lot of professional coercive practices in healthcare organisations as well. Typically, the processes have to be reliable and rational, which is a guarantee of quality in treatments. People would have defined roles—like in surgeries—in healthcare practices.

Summing up then, healthcare organisational intelligence is largely determined by the archetype of a professional organisation. Intelligence is highly personalised and employees quite often have different job descriptions as experts. Hence, healthcare organisations have plenty of practices that shape collective intelligence. Some of them are quite often enabling (like collegiality) practices, but there are coercive practices (like well-defined processes) as well. If healthcare organisations represent a high level of intelligence, one may ask: What is the problem? Why is it still important to think about how to make changes in organisational intelligence?

The problem of healthcare organisations' intelligence is related to changing environments. When organisational environments are rapidly changing, how can organisations sustain the capabilities of adapting to and shaping their environments? This problem has been addressed by, for instance, the contextually dynamic capabilities (Teece et al. 1997; Teece 2007). In a constantly changing society, the starting point is that organisations need the abilities to learn, evolve and adapt more and more. In this framework, an organisation can maintain a high level of intelligence if it is dynamic and reflective.

Actually, healthcare organisations have been criticised for the fact that they are not able to implement changes. According to these arguments, healthcare organisations are too rigid. For example, Baker and Denis (2011) have paid attention to the fact that there is a lot of resistance to changes in hospitals due to institutionalised habits and beliefs. Traditionally, they act steadily, slowly and predictably in a changing environment and produce products and services that are based on experts' standardised working methods. According to Baker and Denis, this is a problem because hospital environments are facing changes and increasing turbulence. Various studies have found problems with unchangeable intelligence in the healthcare sector. Professional communities, for example, have a higher tendency to maintain the existing order than to make rapid changes. Rigidity is even higher if the changes are a threat to the hierarchical power relations that, for instance, give doctors the position of the key profession in healthcare organisations. If there are problems in customer relationships, healthcare organisations may only react by developing new, standardised services. This has happened even when the customers' changing values have been the main reasons for service delivery. Yet, it is an exaggeration to claim that healthcare organisations are totally lacking adaptability. For example, new treatments, medicines and technologies are normal business in healthcare organisations.

Hence, the main challenge is how to change the framework within which health organisations try to solve emerging and complex problems in a changing environment. The intelligent health policy is a comprehensive framework for developing of healthcare organisations' management system, activities and services.

1.5 Synthesis

This book is not intended to be a so-called 'traditional' book on health policy in which the authors go through the literature and discussions on health management and health policy. Our framework of intelligent health policy is based on the literature of public management, organisation theories and public policy, which we put into context of health. Our purpose is to describe the present comprehensive framework for the development of health policy and organisations. In particular, we have the following four cornerstones in the book: the evolution of well-being, technology and digitalisation, knowledge-based policy making and service production and intelligent management and leadership systems (Fig. 1.1).

First, we emphasise the evolution of the concept of well-being. The intelligent policy means that we are moving to a more comprehensive understanding about health. This is related to technology and digitalisation, which are affect healthcare services. There is more and more co-creation of value, quality and efficiency. The third cornerstone is intelligent management and leadership of services. The outcomes are more agile organisation structures, cultures and professions. The last cornerstone of intelligent health policy includes knowledge-based policy making and service implementation.

The book consists of eight main chapters. Following this chapter, we continue on contemporary systemic governance challenges due to the technological revolution. Harvey points out that technology is defined as the use of natural processes and things to make products (and services, we would like to add) for human purposes (2015, pp. 92–93). The twentieth century and the turn of the millennium changed the

Fig. 1.1 Main elements in this book

evolution of generic technologies into a totally new era: technological innovations became big business. Today, the rapidly changing technological context—particularly the progress of robotisation, artificial intelligence, the Internet of Things (IoT)—has radically altered the kinds of skills that are advantageous to labour, and educational systems have often lumbered awkwardly to keep up with the new demands.

Chapter 3 of this book is especially grounded on the newest literature concerning policy analysis. This chapter broadly discusses current challenges in organising and running public policies and health policy in particular. In this part of the book, we argue that there is a lot of talk about complexity in society—but eventually little evidence about what actually constitutes this complexity and how public policies deal with the complexity domain. This part of the book deals with what the promotion of intelligence presupposes from the perspectives of public policy, decision-making, implementation and evaluation. The starting point is especially the knowledge management and decision-making procedures at the level of health policy. This chapter deals with issues such as forecasting and the urgent need to develop specific ex ante evaluation methods and procedures and underlines putting an emphasis on forecasting societal and health policy-related problems instead of ex post trials. Moreover, this chapter analyses the emergence of new information bases for health policy and the role of big data and the Internet of (Intelligent) Things in particular.

The topic of Chap. 4 is the conceptual roots of organisational intelligence. This chapter explores the nature of the intelligence and organisational learning of public policy and healthcare organisations with regard to both individual organisations and multiple organisational ecosystems. The main ideas behind modern systems theory

(MST) and the logic developed by MST theorists in the domain of organisational intelligence are pinpointed in the chapter.

Chapter 5 includes a discussion on organisational knowledge and service users at the heart of modern organisational intelligence. Knowledge management has attracted considerable attention in recent years in the fields of public management and health policies. Nonetheless, there are few widely shared views according to which the term itself is defined, much less a consensus on how best to apply it in business. In this chapter, the role of organisational knowledge in the field of health is scrutinised (by making a distinction, for instance, between the use and exchange value of information). The chapter discusses how to manage knowledge internally and externally in order to achieve organisational success in health-related services.

Chapter 6 examines the characteristics of intelligent healthcare organisations (i.e. the organisation-level forms of intelligence). An intelligent organisation is, for instance, able to operate interactively, share its expertise, cross professional silos, learn from mistakes and act adaptively in relation to changes in the operating environment. This part of the book makes a new interpretation of organisational theories from the perspective of intelligence with special emphasis on research concerning the crossing of interfaces. In addition, this part of the book introduces the concept of the 'service space', developed and theorised by the authors for this book and our earlier publications.

The content of the seventh chapter is intelligent leadership in the field of health. The chapter sets out to explore debates within the field of leadership studies. The basic argument is that traditional leadership paradigms do not suffice anymore in healthcare organisations. Intelligent people–like doctors, nurses and other healthcare professionals–behave differently. The leader's role is to point the direction, act as the coach and develop the personnel. This approach challenges and confronts the contemporary models of clinical leadership in healthcare in multiple ways.

Chapter 8 of the book discusses the role of accountability and performance management within the framework of intelligent health policy. In this chapter, we discuss first—from the service-systems perspective—how accountabilities differ from a hierarchic and organisational perspective within the domain of new public management (NPM) and new public governance (NPG), looking to shed new light upon accountability as a management topic. This chapter scrutinises the concept of service systems and their accountabilities, and the role of integrated social and healthcare services is discussed in particular. This chapter also explores the implications of this transformation for evaluation, performance monitoring and accountability, and it emphasises that horizontal accountability, which references a wide democratic footprint, is likely to become more explicit. To this end, this chapter develops the idea of the transformation of public sector performance management from the viewpoint of organisational intelligence.

The synthesis part of the book draws together the main ideas of the book—theoretically, conceptually and in terms of practice. This part of the book sets out practical and managerial implications as well—for policy, organisational and service-user level. It also discusses the landscape of future health policies and asks what is the modus

operandi of public policy after the emergence of organisational intelligence. The essential purpose of this chapter is to provide everyday actors with insights and ideas to reform policies and services in the field of health towards the direction of intelligent organisation.

References

Abbott A (1988) The system of professions. An essay on the division of expert labour. University of Chicago Press, Chicago

Akgün AE, Byrne JC, Keskin H (2007) Organizational intelligence: a structuration view. J Organ Chang Manag 3:272–289

Alvesson M (1993) Organizations as rhetoric: knowledge-intensive firms and the struggle with ambiguity. J Manag Stud 30(6):997–1015

Baker RG, Denis J-L (2011) Medical leadership in health care systems: from professional authority to organizational leadership. Public Money Manag 31(5):355–362

Brock DM (2006) The changing professional organization: a review of competingarchetypes. Int J Manag Rev 8(3):157–174

Dreyfus SE, Dreyfus HL (1980) A five-stage model of the mental activities involved in directed skill acquisition. Operations Research Center, ORC-80-2. University of California, Berkeley, CA

Freidson E (1988) Profession of medicine: a study of the sociology of applied knowledge. University of Chicago Press, Chicago

Gerston L (2015) Public policy making: process and principles. Routledge, London

Goffee R, Jones G (2009) Clever: leading your smartest, most creative people. Harvard Business Press, Boston

Hackman JR (2011) Collaborative intelligence: using teams to solve hard problems. Berrett-Koehler, San Francisco

Hall P (1993) Policy paradigms, social learning, and the state: the case of economic policymaking in Britain. Comp Polit 25(3):275–296

Harvey D (2015) Seventeen contradictions and the end of capitalism. Profile books, London

Head BW (2008) Wicked policy problems. Public Policy 3(2):101–118

Heyloghen F (2013) Self-organization in communicating groups: the emergence of coordination, shared references and collective intelligence. In: Massip-Bonet A, Bastardas-Boadas A (eds) Complexity perspectives on language, communication and society. Springer, Berlin, pp 117–139

Lindblom C (1965) The intelligence of democracy: decision making through mutual adjustment. The Free Press, New York

March JG (1991) Exploration and exploitation in organizational learning. Organ Sci 2(1):71–87

Matheson D, Matheson JE (2001) Smart organizations perform better. Res Technol Manag 44:49–54

Peters GB (2015) Advanced Introduction to public policy. Edward Elgar, Cheltenham

Sanderson I (2009) Intelligent policy making for a complex world: pragmatism, evidence and learning. Polit Stud 57(4):699–719

Stenvall J, Virtanen P (2015) Intelligent public organizations? Public Organ Rev, published on-line 2.12.2015. https://doi.org/10.1007/s11115-015-0331-1

Sveiby KE (1997) The new organizational wealth: managing and measuring knowledge-based assets. Berrett-Koehler, San Francisco

Teece D (2007) Explicating dynamic capabilities: The nature and microfoundations of (sustainable) enterprise performance. Strateg Manag J 28:1319–1350

Teece D, Pisano G, Shuen A (1997) Dynamic capabilities and strategic management. Strateg Manag J 18(7):509–533

Travica B (2015) Modeling organizational intelligence: nothing googles like Google. J Appl Knowl Manag 3(2):1–18. http://www.iiakm.org/ojakm/articles/2015/volume3_2/OJAKM_Volume3_2pp1-18.pdf

Tuurnas S (2016) The professional side of co-production. Acta Universitatis Tamperensis 2163, Tampere

Virtanen P, Stenvall J (2014) The evolution of public services from co-production to co-creation and beyond – an unfinished trajectory for the New Public Management? Int J Leadersh Public Serv 10(2):91–107

Virtanen P, Vakkuri J (2015) Searching for organizational intelligence in the evolution of public sector performance management. NISPAcee J Public Adm Policy 8(2):89–99

Weber M (1978) Economy and society. University of California Press, Berkeley

Wilensky H (1967) Organizational intelligence: knowledge and policy in government and industry. Quid Pro Books, New Orleans, LA

Chapter 2
Systemic Governance Challenges and Well-Being

Abstract This chapter discusses the role of contemporary systemic governance challenges in society. Of particular interest is the question of how these challenges affect human health and well-being. By definition, health is a rather difficult concept since it contains many elements and dimensions. In this chapter, we argue that today we need a much broader understanding about human well-being than the 'mere' definition of health. Well-being addresses human life more comprehensively. Systemic governance challenges, based on the ongoing and pervasive technology revolution, exist as a result of changes in the quality and quantity of human beings, the stock of human knowledge particularly as applied to human command over nature and the institutional framework that defines the deliberate incentive structure of a society. These changes have an effect on the way we think, our ability to understand societal problems and our health and well-being. Governance challenges redefine the role of governance. We suggest that there are definitely limits for governing because of the complexity of society. Consequently, this affects how health policies and healthcare organisations operate in local, regional, national and transnational service spaces—service ecosystems consisting of public, private and non-governmental healthcare service providers. This also means that public sector management paradigms transform towards a new framework—a framework in which the role of government is to coordinate, integrate and set guidelines and meta-level societal objectives. This view holds that the current public sector management paradigms of the NPM and NPG have not only reached their maturity but will eventually come to an end. The complexity of society calls for complex public policies and a new understanding and analysis of the integrative role of the government. This, in turn, requires the competence to carry out a system-level redesign of healthcare.

2.1 The Evolution from Health to Well-Being

In this section, our main argument relates to the changes in society, which mainly occur through digitalisation, and the connections between health and society. Health and society are definitely linked with each other. Marrot (2015, pp. 42–43) stated not long ago that there are two definite ways that societies can affect health in multiple ways—there are two definite variables in society that can affect health in multiple

P. Virtanen, J. Stenvall, *Intelligent Health Policy*,
https://doi.org/10.1007/978-3-319-69596-9_2

ways. In this chapter, we take the position that the concept of health is a bit old-fashioned in today's society. We propose that the concept of well-being would be a better concept to deploy in the future health policy since it covers more explicitly the citizens' subjective views. Health is thus not only a symptom; it is also a subjective feeling of well-being.

This is because we think it is important to understand that society's new systemic governance challenges test digitalisation as a framework for approaching the question of health as well as the changing context of public policy making in society. At the heart of these conceptual dimensions is health itself. In the following, we ask how the concept of health evolves in a society where governance challenges are pervasive and vast.

It should be noted that health itself is a problematic, multidimensional and also controversial concept. The concept of health refers, first, to a narrow medico-technical definition. Take, for instance, the degree of bodily functioning, which is a measurable procedure at hospitals. Second, there are descriptions of health in the framework of generic descriptive systems, which make it possible to measure health, for instance, in clinical trials and evaluative studies (such as the health-related quality of life [HRQL] by using the metrics of HRQL).

Finally, we can think of health—as the famous World Health Organization definition suggests—as a state of complete physical, mental and social well-being and not merely the absence of disease or infirmity. This kind of approach defines health in a broader perspective by taking into account more aspects in regard to health than the above-mentioned medico-technical definitions do. What is important to notice is that the World Health Organization definition takes a perspective towards the well-being of individuals and communities, which incorporates the idea of comprehensive well-being (Evans et al. 2013; Dye et al. 2013; Olsen 2009).

One important aspect is to make a distinction between diagnosed and experiential health. Both of these aspects are relevant since they correlate with each other. For instance, the health module in the European Union Statistics on Income and Living Conditions (EU-SILC) survey allows respondents to report on their general health status, whether they have a chronic illness and whether they are limited in usual activities because of a health problem. Despite the subjective nature of these questions, indicators of perceived general health have been found to be a good predictor of people's future healthcare use and mortality (DeSalvo et al. 2005; Bond et al. 2006).

Based on the evolving nature of the concept of health and the discussion related to combining the government's role, the objectives of health policy and the means of implementation in terms of health have emerged gradually during the last years. Michaelson and Hämäläinen (2014), to take one example, made a substantial achievement by rethinking the role of health and social deprivation in the current policy discourse. They suggest that policy makers should consider this question seriously in the real-world business of public policy making because they most likely might start to think that a more comprehensive understanding of health is actually the primary focus of modern societies. The simple reason for this is the fact that, today, only a gradually decreasing minority of the global population suffer from material and financial deprivation problems. This is not to deny that the poverty would not exist but is to make argument that for a majority of global population, poverty-related questions are not relevant anymore.

The main problem behind the criticism presented by Michaelson and Hämäläinen (2014) is that the current headlines of health-related policy measures are outdated because they rest too much on pathogenic paradigms of health, overemphasise economic models and do not take into account subjective measures of well-being. Therefore, there is a need for an approach in government priority and goal setting in health policy that would be anchored in more multidisciplinary approaches, ideas and practice. Public policies should take a more comprehensive view of individual- and community-based health and conceive of human beings as biological, psychological, social, political and economic creatures (Hämäläinen 2014). Then, the crucial question is where to look science-wise if the approach includes multidisciplinary elements. According to Michaelson and Hämäläinen (2014), a window of opportunity is open, but it is based on rethinking economic growth in relation to human happiness, positive psychology and the emerged contributions of well-being theory (Seligman and Csiksentmihalyi 2000; Seligman 2011; Virtanen and Sinokki 2014).

One might think that happiness and well-being cannot be on government agendas because it is such a new idea without a long history of conceptual theory building, and it has never been thought to be included in the government's tasks. Just think what the German philosopher Gottfried Wilhelm Leibnitz wrote in his *Codex Juris Gentium* over 300 years ago. He claimed that the careful and constant pursuit of happiness is a natural right of human beings, and this is a right the government has to protect. The same idea is replicated in the writings of John Locke and Thomas Jefferson (as cited in Csiksentmihalyi 2014).

To conceive well-being as a policy goal is not without problems, though, far from it, as Hämäläinen suggests (2014). One of the main problems around the subject is the measurement aspect or the lack of theory building behind the existing well-being measures. Hämäläinen (2014) suggests that the key determinants of well-being in everyday life are composed of five separate dimensions: the environment; the individual's capacities and resources, everyday activities and roles and sense of coherence; and Maslowian needs categories. This combination of fundaments is of importance since it incorporates the multidimensional approach towards well-being. As far as how we read Hämäläinen (2014), the notion of everyday activity is of special importance since it focusses on individual's memberships in several communities and social tribes.

Alongside with well-being, what is also important is the sense of coherence aspect—based on the famous work by Antonovsky—since it approaches the subjective dimensions of well-being, which constitute the basic elements of happiness in the everyday life of individuals. This salutogenic approach (see Eriksson and Lindström 2014) underlines the importance of structured and empowering environments where people are able not only to satisfy their basic needs and to get access to health services but are also able to identify their internal and external resources and to deploy them in order to realise their aspirations, to experience meaningfulness and to cope with their lives by taking into account health promotion aspects in the framework of societal determinants of health.

There are also downsides to well-being, which are also highlighted by Hämäläinen (2014). They include 'short-termism' (individuals' preferences vary over time), selfishness (which eradicates socially harmonious and unselfish behaviour) and path dependence (individuals' decisions in certain situations are predestined by earlier decisions individuals took in the earlier phases of their life's course). Path dependence reportedly applies also to health policy (Weissert and Weissert 2012). This means that policy decisions easily become self-reinforcing: earlier decisions quite often 'lock up' policy options that decision-makers would not now choose to initiate. This leads to the situation in which future policy decisions are, in a word, path-dependent on past decisions with regard to health policy.

Our suggestion is that the concept of health evolves towards a more comprehensive concept of well-being, and this process will consequently affect policy making in the field of public policies related to health and well-being issues. What is important to notice is that the complexity of policy making changes also parallels changing understanding in regard to health. We do not suggest, however, that health policies (content-wise) undergo radical re-engineering process. Instead, we stress that the innovation aspect should be incorporated within the health policy domain and framework. This means that there is definitely a new agenda for issues related to well-being in the government agenda. Our assumption is that well-being is, more or less, transformed from the austerity agenda to a framework, which manifests health- and well-being-related issues as a mechanism to enhance local-, regional-, national- and transnational-level competitiveness.

This paradigm shift takes place where systemic governance challenges prevail and penetrate current societies and all horizontal and vertical levels of public policy and administration. In the following, we will discuss what these challenges are and how they affect public policies in terms of planning, implementation and evaluation. Moreover, the changing contents of health (or well-being, for that matter) are not the only key issues of importance at stake here—it is also interesting to focus on and scrutinise how the role of policy making and how the government and market contribute complex policy setting.

Finally, this changing role will seriously affect the traditional way of understanding decision-making at the level of public policy, which, as Saltman has described, is a morally responsible process where decision-makers are ethically constrained to 'begin from the Hippocratic premise of "first, do not harm"' (2015, p. 23). We argue that not only are moral and ethics important; it is equally (or more important) to understand modern societies through the lenses of digitalisation and 'the second machine age', as Brynjolfsson and McAfee (2014) labelled this phenomenon. Before we can focus on systemic governance challenges, we'll have to formulate an understanding about the concept of governance itself. That is where our story continues from here.

2.2 Elusive Governance

Governance is definitely a concept with multiple definitions as well as connotations. Kuhlmann et al. define the concept simply by describing it as 'governing without government' (2015a, b, pp. 4–5). According to them, the field of health governance includes qualitatively new dimensions of policy making that attempt to connect institutional governance (e.g. regulation) and operational governance (e.g. leadership, management and organisational varieties of coordination, networking and control). According to Kuhlmann et al. 2015a, b), this definition links the concept of governance to NPM and to the debates of accountability, performance and leadership.

Kuhlmann et al. (2015a, b) are, of course, right when defining the role of meso-level governance powers as consisting of a variety of healthcare organisations, stakeholder institutions and professional actors. What is also important in their conceptual framework is, in fact, the role of transnationalism and how it has created multidimensional tensions between local, regional, national and transnational dimensions of governing. Goodin et al. (2008; see also Young 2008) point out that there have always been various limits to command and control in the public policy framework. This causes the government to give way to 'governance', suggesting that governing actually is less and less a matter of ruling by power and hierarchical authority structures and more and more a matter of negotiating through a series of various floating alliances and networks.

Governance is fundamental as a framework for complex public policies and service space constituted by public, private and non-governmental organisations. Moreover, it is deployable in the framework of open systems as interpreted from the point of view of MST. Governance can address, to take an example, interdependencies and network relations of different factors (such as determinants, stakeholders, institutional actors, settings, reciprocal cooperation and coordination mechanisms and the power relations in between principals and their subordinate agents).

In this book, however, we hold the ambitious view that governance relates—as a phenomenon—both to theories and models. Theoretically, governance refers to a conceptual framework (what constitutes governing) adapted to the public policy domain, and, as a model, it is more or less a process (how governing actually is carried out). With theory, we refer to Giere (1998), who argues that theories are generalised theoretical hypotheses. This means that justifying a theory is actually about justifying a theoretical hypothesis or a set of hypotheses. Models, then, in our analytical dictionary, refer to kinds of conceptual and partly theoretical frameworks, which help to conceptually understand the topic under scrutiny and also give guidance to the actual implementation of governing. Popper (1963) calls this a discovery of axiomatic systems—models, which consist of a set of things, relations, operations or functions.

Before turning to discussing the emergence of new systemic governance challenges, it is appropriate to look at different theories and models of governance and its conceptual framework through interpreting and reinterpreting the contemporary management and public policy literature about governance. Governance has played a pivotal role in the semantic toolbox of public policy and public administration for decades (Asaduzzaman and Virtanen 2017). In the wise words of Pollitt (2005), there are certain 'hardy perennials' of contemporary public policy and public management. According to our view, these hardy perennials include conceptual entities such as bureaucracy, network, decentralisation/centralisation, organisation, leadership, management, power and governance. The last one of these, governance, has been an unassailable concept in the management and public policy sciences for decades now.

As a whole, the concept of governance has thus had a long conceptual history with multifaceted meanings. Governance has acted as a counterpart of (often unspoken) alternatives for public sector management, NPG and public sector leadership. Governance has gained popularity in management sciences and in academic public policy discourse because of its multivalency—its ability to link up with many other arguments and theoretical concepts.

Despite the current interest and debates around the concept governance, one should bear in mind that governance is not a new concept but rather is as old as civilisation or human history (Farazman 2015). As a concept, governance is incorporated with the very long history of governing, rule, authority structures and domination. Currently, it not only occupies the central stage of development discourse, but it is also considered as the fundamental component to be incorporated in the development policy of both developed and developing nations. Despite its growing importance to researchers, development practitioners, policy makers and international aid agencies, governance is far from mature as a concept. Rather it is a dynamic concept and worth examining analytically and systematically (Asaduzzaman and Virtanen 2017).

Overall, it seems that the term *governance* is notoriously slippery and for good reason. But maybe this—the conceptual vagueness of the term—is in fact what manifests the secret of its success. By definition, however, we would like to emphasise the trivial starting point that the terms *government* and *governance* are not same. They are not synonymous terms, although both share goal-oriented objectives, activities (interventions), networking practices and expected (or unexpected) outcomes.

Government is about legally and formally derived authority and policing power to execute and implement activities. De Vries (2016, pp. 19–20), for instance, describes government as a constituting element of a nation-state, which is about the totality of political and administrative organisations and institutions within that nation and which is authorised to allocate collectively binding values and services—i.e. public values and services. Government, thus, is about bureaucracy, legislation, financial control, regulation and power, whereas governance refers to the creation, execution and implementation of activities backed by the shared goals of citizens and organisations, who may or may not have formal authority or policing power (Bourgon 2007). Consequently, governance refers more to a growing use of non-regulatory policy instruments, which focus the attention towards proposed, designed and implemented cooperation by government and non-state actors working together within the same framework of policy agenda.

By definition, our approach treats governance as a system of multiple governments, other institutions and organisations working together in the form of formal and informal networks focusing on strengthening effective and accountable institutions, democratic principles, electoral processes and representation and responsible structures of government agencies in order to ensure an open and legitimate relationship between civil society and the state. This definition emphasises the relationship between civil society and the state, which is a very fundamental aspect in the origins of the governance concept. This means that this setting differentiates the study of governance from the study of government. This view holds that the credibility and legitimacy of government can be achieved effectively and efficiently through decentralisation, sharing, people's participation, accountability, transparency and responsiveness (Asaduzzaman and Virtanen 2017). This definition also takes pretty much into account how, for instance, the Organisation for Economic Cooperation and Development (OECD) (1995) defines governance, including public administration; the institutions, methods and instruments of governing; the relationships between the government and citizen (including businesses and other citizen groupings); and the role of the state.

In terms of health and well-being, governance is an important mechanism in transforming the objectives of public policies into concrete measures, transnationally. This is due to the fact that healthcare policy has long been impacted by actors and governance processes outside of the control of national jurisdictions and single governments. Ruckert et al. (2015, 37–38, 49–50), to take an example, argue that, in the wake of neoliberal reform processes during the 1980s and 1990s by various multilateral organisations, especially international finance institutions (such as the World Bank and the International Monetary Fund), social and health policy choices and agendas have been increasingly circumscribed by various adjustment programmes, which, in turn, have strengthened the role of these international finance institutions as agenda-setters in terms of global social and healthcare policies. Ruckert et al. say that this development is not to be treated as a positive transition, and they suggest that the global 'health policy community' should greet the return of these international finance institutions as the principal crisis fighters with suspicion because of the loss of policy space, commodification of health systems, austere budget environments and tightening fiscal policies.

To summarise then, we can say that the concept of governance applies to multiple forms of collective action. However, it is about more strategic aspects of steering a society: the larger decisions about direction and roles. That is, governance is not only about where to go but also about who should be involved in deciding and in what capacity. Therefore, we would like to address five deployment areas where governance is manifested with special reference to public policy making in the field of health (on this typology, see Asaduzzaman and Virtanen 2017).

First, *governance in global space*, or *global governance*, deals with issues outside the purview of individual governments, as suggested above with examples of international finance institutions' new role in defining the transnational and global health policy agendas. Global governance occurs at a global scale, and one consequence of this is that nation-states become more or less powerless, as Castells already indicated two decades ago. According to him, the instrumental capacity of the nation-state is '. . .exclusively undermined by globalisation of core economic activities, by globalisation of media and electronic communication, and by globalisation of crime. . .' (1997, pp. 245–246).

Secondly, there is *governance in national space*, i.e. within a country, which is sometimes understood as the exclusive preserve of government of which there may be several distinctive administrative—public policy—levels: national, provincial or state, indigenous, urban or local. However, governance is concerned with how other actors, such as civil society organisations, may play a role in taking decisions on matters of public concern.

Thirdly, *organisational governance* (governance in 'organisation space') is comprised of the activities of organisations that are usually accountable to a board of directors. Some will be privately owned and operated, e.g. business corporations. Others may be publicly owned, e.g. hospitals, schools, government corporations and so on. This type of governance takes organisations per se as starting points of analysis for governing. Then the interest and focus lies on leadership, strategy formulation, personnel policy, financial resources, organisational processes and service-user co-production and co-creation mechanisms.

Fourthly, a *service space governance mechanism* emerges at different levels of local and regional governing and also at the national and transnational levels. It reflects the idea of governing local, regional and national service spaces, consisting of various service providers from the private, the public and the third sectors, working together for the same purpose of providing the best possible service for the service users. In this multi-hybrid organisational framework, the role of cooperation networks and joint business models is of importance.

Finally, there is *community governance* (governance in 'community space'), which includes activities at a local level where the organising body may or may not assume a legal form and where there may not be a formally constituted governing board. These community-based governance bodies are mostly ad hoc and informal. One example can be an ad hoc construction of cooperation and informal organising of (medical) help because of natural disasters such as floods, forest fires and the like.

Overall, it seems that the concept of governance is often referred to for more rhetorical rather than substantive reasons. An interesting test laboratory question for the term governance is to ask what makes governance good. Asaduzzaman and Virtanen (2017) have emphasised that there actually is not a straightforward definition available for good governance. They argue that, in general, good governance is associated with efficient and effective administration in a democratic framework: in short, and especially when looked at from the local government point of view, it is a citizen-friendly, citizen-caring, responsive, decentralised local government system comprised of an autonomous political society, an efficient and accountable bureaucracy, strong civil society and a free media. Co-production of services in between public service providers and service users has been quite often noted as a relevant newcomer as an ingredient in the making of good governance (Tuurnas 2016).

The dynamic nature of society is one of the reasons why the concept of governance has remained blurry and elusive. If the context is constantly evolving and radically changing—global economy, institutional changes, military status quo, global trade agreements, societal values and so on—no wonder that the theories and models of governance have constantly lagged somewhat behind. The complexity of society, for instance, has emerged as a distinctive (and partly buzzword) topic within management, political and social sciences. Still very little is actually known about what actually constitutes this complexity, how public policies deal with the complexity issue, how the domain of governance fits into this picture and what this has to do with the policy making in the field of health.

It seems that the problem of existing public policy evaluation paradigms and programme evaluation models in particular are that they do not fit in with the current societal challenges, the emergent nexus problems and the explicated models and theories for governance. Therefore, it is easy to foresee that the academic as well as the practical discussion around the concept of governance will continue as a polyphonic exercise. This means that the complexity of society is predominantly affected by challenges, which are pervasive and affect practically all human beings regardless of nation, culture, education or wealth. We refer to these challenges as systemic governance challenges due to the nature of their capability to change humanity and the way people have lived their lives up until now. Technology, as we will see, has been at the heart of this revolution and will continue to be. The point is that this digital revolution alters practically every facet of human life—health included.

2.3 Technology Revolution

Contemporary systemic governance challenges are mainly due to the technological revolution. According to Castells, we are living through one of the rare intervals in human history. It is 'an interval characterised by the transformation of our material culture by the works of a new technological paradigm organised around information technologies' (1996, p. 29). The difference between the current technology revolution with its historical predecessors (and especially the Industrial Revolution of the eighteenth and nineteenth century) is the speed of adopted innovations and the comprehensiveness of the change. The Industrial Revolution, for example, did extend to most of the globe from Europe during two centuries, and the expansion was highly selective (expanding in the following decades through colonial domination). The technology revolution of the twentieth century, in contrast, spread throughout the globe in two decades between the mid-1970s and the mid-1990s (Castells 1996).

Harvey (2015, pp. 92–93) notes that technology is defined as the use of natural processes and things to make products (and public services and healthcare, we would like to add) for human purposes. However, the processes of technological change have altered their character over time. In the age of technological revolution in the eighteenth and nineteenth century, generic technologies were developed in a way that could be applied across multiple industries.

Computers and computerisation were key drivers in the technology revolution in the latter half of the twentieth century. Microelectronics, however, changed everything at the 1970s. According to Castells, it was a 'revolution within the revolution' (1996, pp. 43–44). The advent of the microprocessor (in a word: the capacity to put a computer on a chip) in 1971 turned the world of computers upside down. This meant the birth of what we refer to today as the digitalisation of the society. This was also the launch of digitalised healthcare.

Even though DNA's double helix had already been discovered in 1953, it was the early 1970s that changed the domain of medicine and health. This was caused by the fact that gene splicing and recombinant DNA as well as the technological foundation of genetic engineering made the application and deployment of cumulative knowledge in the field of medicine possible. Thereafter, everything in this branch of science happened fast; in 1975, Harvard University researchers isolated the first mammalian gene out of the rabbit haemoglobin, and, in 1977, the first human gene was finally cloned. This paved the way for advanced genetic technologies for medical applications and the development of healthcare.

Consequently, from the 1980s and 1990s onwards, the search for generic technologies that could be applied almost everywhere became important. The twentieth century and the turn of the millennium changed the evolution of generic technologies into the new era; technological innovations became big business. Today, the rapidly changing technological context—particularly the progress of robotisation, artificial intelligence and the IoT—has radically altered the kinds of skills that are advantageous to labour and educational systems that have often lumbered awkwardly to keep up with the new demands (1996).

Castells (1996) makes an important argument with five distinctive features of the technology revolution of the late twentieth century. His argument is relevant in terms of health, well-being and the related services. His first point is that information is raw material—i.e. new technologies act on information. This view holds that new technologies radically alter the ways we produce, channel and deploy information. In terms of healthcare, this means radical changes to how health-related services—public, private or semi-public—are there to help people.

Second, the effects of the deployment of the new technologies are pervasive. For health, a good example of this is the emergence of system-based proactive predictive, preventive, personalised and participatory (P4) medicine and health, combining systems biology and the digital revolution (Hood and Flores 2012).

Third, there is the networking logic of any system or set of relationship using the new information technologies. This logic is fundamental when we analyse the service space of healthcare, constituted of public, private, semi-public or non-governmental healthcare organisations. This service space is a space of relations and networks of service providers, embedded as integral parts in service (eco)systems, among agencies (personal, organisational) acting through communication (flows), making use/utilising the possibilities of ubiquitous technologies and providing customer-driven services by deploying service-dominant logic (Virtanen and Kaivo-oja 2015; Virtanen et al. 2016a; Kaivo-oja et al. 2015).

Fourth, the technology revolution brings about flexibility, which penetrates everything—in the field of health, this refers to the changing role of public health policies and healthcare organisations. Technology affects organisations. Reforms abound, so to say.

Fifth, there is the growing convergence of specific technologies into a highly integrated system within which old and separate technological trajectories become indistinguishable. In terms of healthcare, this means that all parts of the technology system—consisting of digitalised services, new business models, advanced technologies, service protocols and charters and the like—are integrated into larger service systems, networks and models, operating on different administrative layers and sectors (both horizontal and vertical).

Finally, it is appropriate to ask whether technology—or technological innovations—is equal to systemic governance challenges. We feel this sort of conclusion is an oversimplification. It is necessary to ask why systemic governance challenges exist in the first place. The technology revolution is one explanation for them, but it does not, however, provide a full explanation. Systemic governance challenges exist as the results of changes in the quality and quantity of human beings, the stock of human knowledge as applied to human command over nature in particular and the institutional framework that defines that deliberate incentive structure of a society: the global population is increasing, its educational level is reaching new levels and techno-economic control over nature has developed dramatically. This development has brought about new scientific and technological development waves in society, which, according to Garreau (2005), are so-called GRIN waves, consisting of gene technology (G), robotics (R), informatics (I) and nanotechnology (N).

GRIN waves penetrate all levels of society, vertically and horizontally, and particularly the field of health policies and healthcare organisations. For example, gene technology will affect demographic development and population structures. People simply live longer and are healthier. Second, robotics influence organisations both in public and private sectors in terms of the nature of work, division of labour, leadership and the management of processes in healthcare organisations. Also emerging public service systems are affected by the emergence of cooperation and coordination mechanisms. Human motivation systems will likely also change because of robotics, automation and artificial intelligence: work motivation inevitably changes and transforms when new robotic inventions and innovations replace work places.

Simultaneously, society itself changes and transforms towards what has been labelled as the birth of ubiquitous society, which is an umbrella term for the next generation of information and communications technology. This view holds that new information technology will intrude all the time and everywhere. New kinds of content will be created, distributed and consumed digitally. One of the biggest sociotechnical changes, and this is a very relevant point from the health policy and healthcare point of view, is that all kinds of objects, goods and even places will be integrated into the network with the help of ubiquitous electronic sensors. This process takes place in the framework of the IoT emphasising machine-to-machine communication and learning in service production (Virtanen and Kaivo-oja 2015; Virtanen et al. 2016a).

It is appropriate to address here the fact that perhaps technology itself was not, after all, the sole driver of the current societal revolution, but the revolution started when technology became vested in the daily lives of human beings. This is caused by the fact that a ubiquitous society and its technology opens up new opportunities in all areas of life, including public services, in terms of production, delivery, distribution, delivery and learning. Considering health, this creates new ground for upgrading current service models and introducing elements of digitally created platforms and forums for individuals and communities to enhance their well-being and health. Healthcare- and health service-related new technical possibilities include cloud computing, big data, smart technologies and crowdsourcing techniques, which will increase inherent possibilities associated with e-democracy and deliberative democracy.

To summarise, even though there is a worldwide debate over the social, economic and cultural consequences of the Internet, the framework and contents of digitalised life and the birth of the digital citizen have been in full swing for more than two decades (Isin and Ruppert 2015); the academic debate regarding the effects of ubiquitous technologies on organisations, services and healthcare services in particular is far from fertile. This means that there has been a remarkably limited discussion, let alone theorisation, on the relation between ubiquitous technologies vis-á-vis organisational matters such as change management, knowledge creation and utilisation, organisational learning theories, the status and role of the service users and patients as well as the possibility of transnational utilisation of knowledge management processes (Holden and Glisby 2014). This underutilisation is somewhat surprising since the effects of these technologies to organisations and organisational cultures are already evident today—even though the scale of the effects is not known today (Kaivo-oja et al. 2015). The ubiquitous technologies affect how health policies function, how healthcare organisations exist, how the information for these evolves, how the organisations run their processes and how they treat service users and patients. As Rigby (2007) underlines from the healthcare services' point of view, these new-generation, ubiquitous technologies present a major opportunity for the use of health informatics in health and healthcare, underlining that a paradigm shift is about to happen. It is about moving the ongoing monitoring of the vulnerable or at-risk patient from the health facility (usually hospital) to the patient's daily living environment.

2.4 Digitalised Health

The main driver in the emergence of systemic governance challenges is the digitalisation of society. It is not an event, which occurs as a totality, but as waves or as a process (Kaivo-oja et al. 2016). During the 1990s, the first wave of digitalisation offered consumers and service users new channels to access the market and service spaces (through, for instance, homepages, ecommerce and net marketing). The second wave of digitalisation, which took place roughly at the turn of the millennium, brought about new marketing logic for services to the private sector and also to the public sector (including disruptive agents, new kinds of network trading and new business models in the field of healthcare). The third wave of the current decade introduced new action logic for digitalised services and service production (driven by the IoT and robotics in particular).

The role of big data is of particular importance here because everything we do increasingly leaves a digital trace or data, which we can deploy and analyse to strengthen our well-being and perceived and diagnosed health. Because the EU faces significant challenges that concern healthcare systems and services, the EU has put forward a digital agenda to improve every citizen's health by making health data available to everyone using eHealth tools (Currie and Seddon 2015; Murdoch and Detsky 2013). At the end of the day, eHealth is only one issue on the digitalisation agenda. All sociotechnical systems operate on a technical base. This means that email, chat, bulletin boards, blogs, Wikipedia, eBay, Twitter, Facebook, YouTube and other health-related sensors, apps and web services are all sociotechnical systems, which millions of people use. The question is how do these systems affect health and shape the way we understand, experience, develop and maintain our health?

Digitalisation impacts healthcare at all levels: ways of working and processes, resource allocations, policies and the ways through which health is understood, experienced and measured. Take the health impact assessment (HIA), for instance. Traditionally, the HIA has influenced decision-making in many ways: by raising awareness, by helping to iterate policy options between different means and by helping those affected by policies to take part in decision-making (Kemm et al. 2004). The traditional HIA does not suffice anymore in exploring the health and well-being effects of digitalised society. Thus, there is a need for a new way to define and conduct the HIA. Furthermore, digitalisation offers the possibility to include completely new types of measures to the HIA, such as automatic analysis of general sentiments and opinions about health, based on social media text analysis.

Another example is P4 medicine. The vision of health measures that are predictive, preventive, personalised and participatory (P4) is not a new one. Systems approaches to biology, health and medicine are now beginning to provide patients, consumers and healthcare professionals with personalised information about each individual's unique health experience of both health and disease at the molecular, cellular and organ levels. This information will make disease care radically more cost-effective by personalising care to each person's unique biology and by treating the causes rather than the symptoms of disease (Flores et al. 2013; Murdoch and Detsky 2013). Consequently, the concept of health evolves as we discussed earlier in this chapter. Modern definitions of health and well-being connect the individual's psychophysical health and wellness to the wider social and environmental context and remove the traditional and very artificial division between health and other areas of human living/conditions. This calls for a new, more holistic and comprehensive measurement of well-being.

How, then, does digitalisation affect our health and well-being? First, digitalisation enables citizens to take a more active role in developing and maintaining their health using various sensing devices, mobile apps and web services. If a citizen's motivation to maintain and improve health gets higher, significant cost savings also become possible. Second, an individual's everyday behaviour and actions can be tracked by using various data sources and modelled and learned using predictive analytics methodologies and mathematical modelling. Third, combining lifestyle-related behavioural data and digital footprint data with clinical data and genomics provides vast possibilities for highly personalised and tailored care and for disease prevention (Kish and Topol 2015). Finally, behavioural data, when combined with population-level health statistics, could be utilised for profiling the health attitudes and everyday behaviours of both individuals and groups of people.

Of course, the digital divide challenge can be a big potential problem for health services of the future because of serious inequalities in access to and use of ICT among the categories of persons in a given population and across countries. The conditions of motivation, access and skills (so-called MAS competences) vary among citizens and create serious digital divides. Socio-economic situation, personal values and psychological profiles strongly affect personal conceptions of health and the motivation to actively improve it.

To summarise, the changing role of health in society is profoundly related to the society-wide phase of transformation brought about by digitalisation. The manifestation of a complex society is not a new phenomenon, but digitalisation has brought about the evolution of certain new, interesting topics with regard to the complexity of society. One of these topics is the notion of nexus problems. These are societal problems that aren't anchored in existing policy agendas or public policy structures but exist somewhere in between existing policy structures and domains. Nexus problems refer to new kinds of societal problems affecting multiple public policy areas and domains—they are difficult to pinpoint and are often challenging to measure and tackle. In the field of health, they concern phenomena such as loneliness, psychiatric symptoms, unemployment, lack of financial resources, alcohol misuse and so on. These nexus problems challenge health policies in many ways and require intelligent public policy making and evaluation systems. The emphasis on multiplex societal issues and nexus policy detecting, forecasting and developmental evaluation are milestones in the governance of health-related nexus problems.

Healthcare services, for their part, are amidst the ongoing digitalisation revolution. The agility of service organisations and the competence to manage changes has become pivotal. Technology awareness, the understanding related to the digitalised reform context and the sensitivity of customer policies as well as the adoption of service-dominant logic as a leadership paradigm, more or less dictates the success of health service systems in the future. We argue that austerity, personalisation and service integration require a new form of governance beyond interorganisational coordination. There is a need for more closely coupled health service systems in which service users/patients (as co-producers) play an active role. This active role of the citizens manifests itself in the chronic care model in health services. From the perspective of public and semi-public healthcare service managers, this development also challenges accountability systems.

Adopting a service systems perspective, which we propose to incorporate in our argument, allows us to view accountability as processual flows within service systems; flows between agents the content of which, we argue, includes knowledge, value, empathy and accountability. Centring co-producing users (including informal careers) in services that are delivered by a consortium of public, private and third-sector agents (including networks) invites a new perspective on local service design and delivery: the service system (including individual users and organisations) replaces organisations as the unit of analysis in healthcare (Virtanen et al. 2016b).

2.5 Reforms and Intelligent Health Policy

Health policies and healthcare organisations as they used to exist do not suffice anymore. Reforming and redesigning policies and organisations are necessary to meet the challenges of systemic governance challenges and complex society. It is important to notice that there is a need for a system-level reorganising of healthcare. As this is the case, a closer look at what public sector reforms are and how they function is appropriate. Christensen and Laegreid (2016) stress that public sector reforms are typically hybrid, meaning that complexity is compounded by inconsistency. Moreover, public sector reforms usually address permanent tensions between certain key elements in public policy, that of the juxtaposition between centralisation and decentralisation, between coordination and specialisation, between integration and fragmentation and among efficiency, fairness and resilience.

Bad news comes here. It is much easier to speak and write about system-level changes and public sector reforms than to carry them out. The proof of this is the plethora of research literature related to difficulties, bottlenecks and pitfalls about changing public policies (Weissert and Weissert 2012), institutions (Mahoney and Thelen 2010), organisations (Holbeche 2006) and organisational cultures (Argyris 2010).

Concerning implementing changes in health policy, Weissert and Weissert (2012) provide a lengthy list of lessons learned from the USA in reforming health policy during the past decades. We treat their list as policy change challenges. These challenges include, for instance, the diffusion of political party interests, policy making path dependence (earlier policy decisions narrow future policy options) and institutional structures with regard to decision-making and public administration. Also, maintaining the status quo among important and powerful interest groups (such as political parties, health professionals, drug companies, equipment makers, laboratories, social and healthcare service providers, private and non-governmental organisations in the field of health and many more) causes bottlenecks in reforming policies. Finally, there is the budget issue. Reforms normally require funding, i.e. financial resources. Weissert and Weissert conclude with a pessimistic tone: '...given these realities of our healthcare system and our political culture and political institutions, it seems unlikely that we will see comprehensive reform including cost control and quality assurance in the near future' (2012, p. 336).

A very important question is as follows: Do comprehensive healthcare reforms always require additional financial resource? What if additional resources have to be there because the future healthcare system will build upon the existing healthcare system? Does additional financial input always cause a positive impact on the health of the people? The answer to all of these three questions is not necessarily, because the bigger the healthcare system is, the bigger the bureaucratic costs to run the system are.

If so, then it is reasonable to ask what if healthcare systems were built based on the logic that when a new healthcare system is put in place, simultaneously, something from the old system would have to be dismantled and deconstructed? In our previous research, we stressed the fact that changing healthcare actually starts from the bottom. A key point in understanding service integration, achieving cost savings and improving the level of patient service is the development of organisational cultures of the healthcare service providers and front-line professionals as well as the proliferation of partnership and communication across organisational boundaries. We have called this the intelligent mode of service development in healthcare (Stenvall and Virtanen 2012).

Overall, analysing complex and hybrid healthcare reforms—particularly at the level of health systems—is far from straightforward. It is not straightforward or simple because we need analytical tools that can grasp this type of change dynamic. Public sector reforms can be approached from different analytical perspectives consisting of, for instance, an institutional, a transformative, a principal-agent, an innovation, a change management, a cultural theory or an interpretative perspective. These perspectives have an immanent link and point of departure with organisational theory, which encompasses instrumental and institutional elements (Christensen and Laegreid 2016). From the public policy point of view, the transformative perspective or approach to public sector reform offers a solid analytical framework to capture the dynamics of system-level change in healthcare. This is because the organisational and institutional dynamics of reforms can be grasped and interpreted as a complex mixture of environmental pressures, historical institutional context and the public policy dimension (Christensen and Laegreid 2016).

A plethora of research literature exists about the dynamics of organisational change. This referenced academic—and business-oriented, for that matter—literature cover issues such as change dynamics, resistance to change, leading change processes and the evaluation of implemented change projects. If we think healthcare reforms as system changes, however, there is the need to think about system-level changes from the point of culture and public policy/politics. This is because healthcare reforms are primarily a product of the national historical–institutional context and traditions. Healthcare reforms are path-dependent in the sense that national reforms usually (if not always) have unique features that are influenced by the normative and professional contexts that are put in place in healthcare institutions prior to the ongoing reform. Public policy and politics, for their part, refer to the dimensions of political–administrative structures (including, for instance, the form of government, the decision-making within the political–administrative system, financing of healthcare, accountability mechanisms and traditions and the role of the market in healthcare service provision).

In addition, it is necessary to think of the public policy frame as a system-level change mechanism, which raises the question of intelligent public policy making. Let us start with the concept of frame. Goffman (1986), a sociological theorist, made a major claim in his magnum opus, originally written in 1974, by arguing that the concept of *frame* in sociology refers to an inevitably relational dimension of meaning. A frame, in his sense, is a particularly tangible metaphor for the use of concepts such as *background*, *setting* and *context* or a phrase like *in terms of*. These concepts attempt to convey what goes on in interactions, and they are normally governed by unstated rules or principles more or less implicitly set by the character of some larger entity within which the interaction occurs.

In the frame of public policy, then, to convey the semantics set by Goffman (1986), organisational intelligence constitutes rules and principles about policy making and the governance of healthcare organisations. The notion of intelligent public policy making brings about the role of environmental pressure and internal public policy mechanisms based on knowledge management. At the organisational level, this frame applies. We have discussed before the role of environmental pressures, knowledge management processes and service-user-dependant modus operandi function in enhancing or diminishing organisational intelligence (Stenvall and Virtanen 2015). This view holds an important notion on what is the external pressure's role in the forming of adaptation mechanisms for policy and organisations.

Christensen and Laegreid (2016) make a very useful distinction by classifying four types of environmental pressure related to public sector reforms along with two dimensions (the content of the environment and the amount of the pressure). Their typology sets out four adaptation strategies, which are very relevant in understanding healthcare changes at the system level. *Deterministic adaptation* reflects the idea that there is no alternative—the change has to be there no matter what might be the root cause of the change.

An example of this is the radical change towards privatised healthcare organisations orchestrated alongside NPM principles because of the scarcity of budget resources. Another option is *isomorphic adaptation*, which is based on the strong pressure from the operating environment, but the adaptation is more or less informed by myths, symbols, professional mechanisms and fads envisaged in the environment. This adaptation type holds that changes are not necessarily seen as radical when looked at from the outside, but they might and can be very profound when scrutinised from the inside of the healthcare organisation. *Optional adaptation* means negotiating the contents and timing of the change process. This process often involves compromises reached across levels and sectors of healthcare, not necessarily among principals and agents (hierarchically), but also in between actors and institutions across various horizontal and vertical levels (van Thiel 2016). *Pragmatic adaptation* advocates the idea of rather weak pressure from the institutional environment. It also contains the idea of an incremental change process based on rather narrow reform elements from different public policy levels and horizontally and vertically different organisational hierarchies. This pragmatic approach usually encompasses broad families of reform elements with vast internal variety.

Two dimensions of system-level change in reforming and redesigning healthcare organisations and health policy are of utmost importance. First, the adaptive change capacity refers to an organisational-level mechanism that makes it possible to forecast changes in the operating environment, to deploy the idea of organisational learning and unlearning and to strengthen an organisation's capacity to be more resilient (Virtanen and Kaivo-oja 2015). Second, an innovation perspective in reforming public policies brings about the introduction of new elements into public policy, public service and healthcare as a domain. In the words of Osborne and Brown (2005, p. 4), this consequently forms and constitutes new knowledge and new organisational, management-related and process-related skills, which represent discontinuity with the past.

The existing definitions of public policy and public service innovation are very broad. As it is, we have found a very useful categorisation of public sector innovations by Bekkers and Tummers (2016, pp. 64–65), who speak of product and service innovations, process innovations, organisational innovations, governance innovations and conceptual innovations. They all are, according to our view, fundamental in understanding the need for system-level change in the field of healthcare.

System-level analysis of health policy is important. It brings about a comprehensive approach to understand the need of reforms and change dynamics. Next, we will shortly discuss healthcare changes in the Nordic countries from this system-level perspective.

The Nordic countries consist of five countries in northern Europe: Denmark, Sweden, Finland, Norway and Iceland. These countries are commonly perceived as quite similar when analysed and viewed in a broader transnational perspective. No wonder, then, that there has been a standard assumption among European health policy makers and the wider audience that a 'Nordic model' for the healthcare system exists. This perceived 'unity' of the Nordic model lies at the core of the welfare regime principles. These are, for instance, universalism of service production, high taxation (resulting from income distribution), broad public participation as well as funding (predominantly by taxes), decentralised public governance structures (except Norway from 2002 onwards) and public ownership of the service delivery structure (Esping-Andersen 1990; Magnussen et al. 2009b; Böhm et al. 2013; Varabyova and Müller 2016).

With a closer look, healthcare systems in the Nordic countries have undergone a process of major change or, to deploy our earlier semantics, different strategies of adaptation since the early 1990s. Healthcare reforms have reflected shifts in the economic environment and cultural and political development, and they have been subjected to prevailing public sector reforms, commonly termed NPM (Virtanen and Stenvall 2014). Moreover, these reforms have taken place due to rapid development in information technology and patients' improved possibilities to take part themselves in the care processes in the context of the chronic care model. The

Nordic healthcare model has changed at many levels—both systemic and operational. These changes have happened in terms of welfare goals and aspirations (e.g. the principle of equity and the possibility of public participation), structural issues (e.g. funding, governance structures, delivery mechanisms) and policy applications (e.g. decentralisation/centralisation aspects and patient choice mechanisms) (Magnussen et al. 2009a).

In the research literature, there exists a plethora of evidence not only from health system reforms at the level of all Nordic countries (Magnussen et al. 2009a, b). This research concerns Denmark (Christiansen and Petersen 2001; Cox 2001; Greve 2006; Kvist 1999 2003; Larsen and Andersen 2009; Vrangbaek and Christiansen 2005), Sweden (Dahlgren 2014; Fredriksson et al. 2012; Rosen et al. 2014), Norway (Defechereux et al. 2012; Ringard et al. 2013), Finland (Niemelä et al. 2015; Vuorenkoski 2008) and Iceland (Johnsen 2014; Sigurgeirsdóttir et al. 2014).

If we use here, rather loosely, the reform concept to describe the changes that have taken place in the Nordic countries, certain key elements have to be underlined in the context of Nordic healthcare systems. At the outset, it should be noted there are clear differences in the details of the Nordic countries in terms of healthcare reforms, but there are also undisputed similarities. Vrangbaek (2009), for instance, points out that Denmark and Norway have implemented major top-down reforms, whereas Finland and Sweden have chosen more voluntary bottom-up approach. Thus, the political processes in Nordic countries in terms of reforming health systems have been rather different. The Danish and Norwegian changes might be labelled as the 're-engineering' model, which builds upon fast and government-controlled mechanisms, whereas Finland and Sweden have chosen a somewhat slower process based on a longer period of consideration (taking place over many governments and parliamentary elections), information steering by the government and voluntary mergers of the healthcare organisations. With regard to Sweden, for instance, market-oriented healthcare reforms have occurred in phases from 1990 to 2013 (Dahlgren 2014). The first phase of these reforms was the introduction of NPM systems, where public health centres and public hospitals were to act as private firms in an internal healthcare market. A second phase saw an increase of tax-financed, private, for-profit providers. A third phase can be envisaged with the increased private financing of essential health services.

As a whole, the Nordic model for healthcare reforms has been caused by the combination of both external and internal factors (Vrangbaek 2009). The external factors, such as globalisation and Europeanisation, have challenged the field of healthcare in multiple ways. Healthcare systems that have been affected by, for instance, advances in medical technology, the need for new service architectures and the internalisation of the knowledge base for medical practice have been particularly important factors. Moreover, certain societal and population-related factors of the Nordic countries (e.g. the ageing of the population, changing epidemiological profiles and overall increasing demands for individualised services) have boosted reform activity in health policies.

According to Martinussen and Magnussen (2009), specific change pressures have accelerated reforms in the Nordic countries. First, the relative role of the private sector has grown in importance, and this has epitomised the 'state-versus-market debate' in all Nordic countries. The second broad reform theme has been decentralisation, and it has consisted of two separate but interlinked topics such as administrative deconcentration and policy devolution. Third, patient empowerment has emerged as a central theme since the late 1990s, emphasising the growing role of patient choice. Fourth, the role of public health in the national health policy has become a central topic not only in terms of the state-versus-market debate (and the emergence of private sector) but also as a forum for political debates. Fifth, methods for financing and service payments have been the subject of considerable interest in the past decades in the public and political debates in the domain of healthcare systems.

All of these topics mentioned above have had similar effects in all Nordic countries with regard to health policies. It has resulted in, for instance, a trend towards the formalisation of regulation in healthcare (e.g. sanctions concerning waiting times, patients' rights legislation and quality regulation). Also, there has been an increase in the regulation of healthcare, which has been increasingly carried out by the central state as well as a strengthening of national health policy making that has gone hand in hand with the demand for evidence-based health policies and documentation of performance.

As a conclusion, certain observations can be made when looking at the Nordic experience in healthcare systems over the last two decades or so (Vrangbaek 2009; Virtanen et al. 2016b). First, there has been a growing concern for the future sustainability of health systems in terms of funding and the quality of healthcare services as well as competent healthcare professionals. Second, coordination issues should not be underemphasised since they pertain to interaction, power and accountability processes at various administrative and organisational levels both horizontally and vertically. Third, the Nordic countries have witnessed an increasing trend in national steering ambitions in health policies as well as, on the contrary side, the reduced acceptance of geographical differences in service mechanisms and delivery. Fourth, the Nordic experience indicates that circumstances must be right for large-scale structural reform to take place, and there must be an especially relatively strong and committed government in office. Fifth, health organisations and organisation structures have been under critical scrutiny during the last decades in all Nordic countries. This is due to the argument that administrative costs can be reduced by having fewer administrative organisations in terms of hierarchical layers.

To summarise, it would be an oversimplification to argue that healthcare reforms have been implemented in the Nordic countries intelligently. The reform processes in various countries have resulted in adaptations of various kinds: deterministic, isomorphic, optional and pragmatic. The challenge is that none of the Nordic countries have implemented a reform from the system-level perspective. The reforms have been partial reforms even though they might appear as comprehensive ones. What has been missing in the reform frame is a new understanding about the systemic governance challenges and the role of public policy making in a turbulent environment.

2.6   Synthesis

Our first conclusion concerns the understanding of public services as an embedded part of a service system, looking at public service delivery from an organisational point of view and also from the service-user standpoint. Historically, NPM and NPG have shown a distinct lack of interest in these issues, and, thus, it is reasonable to argue that public health services are not at the heart of these ideologies. The healthcare management reforms that are currently taking place in public service systems—and healthcare services in particular—call for service-dominant logic, new participation models as well as co-creation approaches.

Second, the emergent systemic governance changes are pervasive and profound. They are likely to result in changes that simply cannot be understood in economic terms but instead must be judged from a societal viewpoint. These changes, for instance, concern gene technology, robotics, informatics and nanotechnology and cover various technological fields in the framework of health policies. The impacts and cross-impacts of these changes are not predictable and apparently go beyond the scale of human adaptation. Adaptive complex system theory will thus be more relevant than conventional organisational theories, which assume the existence of simple, hierarchical and closed systems without complex or even chaotic systemic interaction.

Third, systemic adaptability to changes requires new kinds of leadership and management styles in public services. Future governance, leadership and management models must be agile and adaptive to complex changes.

There are definitely critical issues at stake here. These include communication and communication capacity, new levels and intensity of machine–machine and machine–human interaction in the fields of ubiquitous robotics, the quality of participatory processes and participative management skills at various levels of healthcare—at the level of policies and organisations.

There is clearly also a need to rethink change management logic, classical motivation theories and leadership models in order to render them better able to cope in a world engulfed by systemic governance challenges. Typically, the new service elements are linked to the development of novel service designs and new service architectures in healthcare. We are sure that disruptive technological changes radically challenge and change the patient-dominant logic of the existing healthcare professions. For instance, there are many promising examples today that incorporate crowdsourcing processes to service development in service planning in the field of healthcare.

New understandings of well-being and systemic governance challenge consequently affect existing healthcare policies and organisations at local, regional, national and transnational levels of governance. This, in turn, will have an effect on healthcare, or, to be more precise, healthcare policies and organisations need to be reformed and redesigned to better meet the service needs of patients and citizens.

References

Argyris C (2010) Organizational traps. Leadership, culture, organizational design. Oxford University Press, Oxford

Asaduzzaman M, Virtanen P (2017) Governance theories and models. In: Farazman A (ed) Global encyclopedia of public administration, public policy and governance. Springer, New York (Forthcoming)

Bekkers V, Tummers L (2016) An innovation perspective. In: Van de Walle S, Groenewald S (eds) Theory and practice of public sector reform. Routledge, Oxford, pp 61–78

Böhm K, Schmid A, Landwehr C, Rothgang H (2013) Five types of OECD healthcare systems: empirical results of a deductive classification. Health Policy 113(3):258–269

Bond J, Dickinson HO, Matthews S, Jagger C, Brayne C (2006) Self-rated health status as a predictor of death, functional and cognitive impairments: a longitudinal cohort study. Eur J Ageing 3(4):193–206

Bourgon J (2007) Responsive, responsible and respected government: towards a new public administration theory. Int Rev Adm Sci 73(1):7–26

Brynjolfsson E, McAfee A (2014) The second machine age. Work, progress and prosperity in a time of brilliant technologies. W.W. Norton, New York

Castells M (1996) The rise of the network society. Blackwell, Oxford

Castells M (1997) The power of identity. Blackwell, Oxford

Christensen T, Laegreid P (2016) A transformative perspective. In: Van de Walle S, Groenewald S (eds) Theory and practice of public sector reform. Routledge, Oxford, pp 27–42

Christiansen NF, Petersen K (2001) The dynamics of social solidarity: the Danish welfare state, 1900–2000. Scand J Hist 26(3):177–196

Cox RH (2001) The social construction of an imperative: why welfare reform happened in Denmark and the Netherlands but not in Germany. World Polit 53(3):463–498

Csiksentmihalyi M (2014) The politics of consciousness. In: Hämäläinen T, Michaelson J (eds) Well-being and beyond. Broadening the public and policy discourse. Edward Elgar/Sitra, Cheltenham/Northampton, pp 271–282

Currie WE, Seddon JJM (2015) E-health policy and benchmarking in the European Union. In: Kuhlmann E et al (eds) The Palgrave international handbook of healthcare policy and governance. Palgrave MacMillan, New York, pp 526–542

Dahlgren G (2014) Why public health services? Experiences from profit-driven health care reforms in Sweden. Int J Health Serv 44(3):507–524

De Vries M (2016) Understanding public administration. Palgrave MacMillan, New York

Defechereux T, Paolucci F, Mirelman A, Youngkong S, Botten G, Hagen T, Niessen LW (2012) Health care priority setting in Norway a multicriteria decision analysis. BMC Health Serv Res. https://doi.org/10.1186/1472-6963-12-39

DeSalvo KB, Fan VS, McDonell MB, Fihn SD (2005) Predicting mortality and healthcare utilization with a single question. Health Serv Res 40(4):1234–1246

Dye C, Reeder JC, Terry RF (2013) Research for universal health coverage. Sci Transl Med 5 (199):1–2

Eriksson M, Lindström B (2014) The salutogenic framework for well-being: implications for public policy. In: Hämäläinen T, Michaelson J (eds) Well-being and beyond. Broadening the public and policy discourse. Edward Elgar/Sitra, Cheltenham/Northampton, pp 68–97

Esping-Andersen G (1990) The three worlds of welfare capitalism. Polity Press, Cambridge

Evans DP, Hsu J, Boerma T (2013) Universal health coverage and universal access. Bull World Health Organ 91:546–546A. https://doi.org/10.2471/BLT.13.125450. http://www.who.int/bulletin/volumes/91/8/13-125450/en/. Accessed 23 Sept 2016

Farazman A (2015) Governance in the age of globalization: challenges and opportunities for south and southeast Asia. In: Jamil I (ed) Governance in south, southeast and east Asia, Volume 15 of the series Public administration, governance and globalization, pp 11–26

Flores M, Glusman G, Brogaard K, Price ND, Hood L (2013) P4 medicine: how systems medicine will transform the healthcare sector and society. Pers Med 10(6):565–576

Fredriksson M, Blomqvist P, Winblad U (2012) Conflict and compliance in Swedish health care governance: soft law in the 'Shadow of Hierarchy'. Scand Polit Stud 35(1):48–70

Garreau J (2005) Radical evolution: the promise and peril of enhancing our minds, our bodies—and what it means to be human. Doubleday, New York

Giere RR (1998) Justifying scientific theories. In: Klemke ED et al (eds) Introductory readings in the philosophy of science. Prometheus Books, New York, pp 415–434

Goffman E (1986) Frame analysis. An essay on the organization of experience. Northwestern University Press, Boston, MA

Goodin RE, Rein M, Moran M (2008) The public and its policies. In: Moran M et al (eds) The Oxford handbook of public policy. Oxford University press, Oxford, pp 3–35

Greve C (2006) Public management reform in Denmark. Public Manag Rev 8(1):161–169

Hämäläinen T (2014) In search of coherence: sketching a theory of sustainable well-being. In: Hämäläinen T, Michaelson J (eds) Well-being and beyond. Broadening the public and policy discourse. Edward Elgar/Sitra, Cheltenham/Northampton, pp 17–67

Harvey D (2015) Seventeen contradictions and the end of capitalism. Profile books, London

Holbeche L (2006) Understanding change. Theory, implementation and success. Elsevier, Oxford

Holden N, Glisby M (2014) The Nonaka-Takeuchi –model of knowledge conversion: a discussion of many contexts of Japanese history and culture. In: Örtenblad A (ed) Handbook on research on knowledge management. Adaptation and context. Edward Elgar, Cheltenham, pp 366–390

Hood L, Flores M (2012) A personal view on systems medicine and the emergence of proactive P4 medicine: predictive, preventive, personalized and participatory. New Biotechnol 29 (6):613–624

Isin EF, Ruppert ES (2015) Being digital citizens. Rowman & Littlefield, London

Johnsen G (2014) Bringing down the banking system. Palgrave MacMillan, New York

Kaivo-oja J, Virtanen P, Jalonen H, Stenvall J (2015) The effects of the internet of things and big data to organizations and their knowledge management practices. In: Luden L et al (eds) Knowledge management in organizations, vol 224. Springer, Heidelberg, pp 495–513

Kaivo-oja J, Virtanen P, Stenvall J, Jalonen H, Wallin J (2016) Future prospects for knowledge management in the field of health. KMO 2016. In: Proceedings of the 11th international knowledge management in organizations, Article no. 40. https://doi.org/10.1145/2925995. 2926006, ACM, New York. http://dl.acm.org/icps.cfm

Kemm J, Parry J, Palmer S (eds) (2004) Health impact assessment. Oxford University Press, Oxford

Kish L, Topol E (2015) Unpatients – why patients should own their medical data. Nat Biotechnol 33(9):921–924

Kuhlmann E, Blank RH, Bourgeault IL, Wendt C (2015a) Healthcare policy and governance in international perspective. In: Kuhlmann E et al (eds) The Palgrave international handbook of healthcare policy and governance. Palgrave MacMillan, New York, pp 3–19

Kuhlmann E, Blank RH, Bourgeault IL, Wendt C (eds) (2015b) The Palgrave international handbook of healthcare policy and governance. Palgrave MacMillan, New York

Kvist J (1999) Welfare reform in the Nordic countries in the 1990s: using fuzzy-set theory to assess conformity to ideal types. Eur J Soc Policy 9(3):231–252

Kvist J (2003) A Danish welfare miracle? Policies and outcomes in the 1990s. Scand J Public Health 31(3):241–245

Larsen CA, Andersen JG (2009) How new economic ideas changed the Danish welfare state: the case of neoliberal ideas and highly organized social democratic interests. Governance 22 (2):239–261

Magnussen J, Vrangbaek K, Saltman RB, Martinussen PE (2009a) Introduction: the Nordic model of health care. In: Magnussen J et al (eds) Nordic health care systems: recent reforms and current policy challenges. McGraw-Hill, New York, pp 3–20

Magnussen J, Vrangbaek K, Saltman RB, Martinussen PE (eds) (2009b) Nordic health care systems: recent reforms and current policy challenges. McGraw-Hill, New York

Mahoney J, Thelen K (eds) (2010) Explaining institutional change. Ambiquity, agency and power. Cambridge University Press, Cambridge

Marrot M (2015) The health gap. The challenge of an unequal world. Bloomsbury, London

Martinussen PE, Magnussen J (2009) Health care reform: the Nordic experience. In: Magnussen J et al (eds) Nordic health care systems: recent reforms and current policy challenges. McGraw-Hill, New York, pp 21–52

Michaelson J, Hämäläinen T (2014) New theories and policies for well-being: introduction. In: Hämäläinen T, Michaelson J (eds) Well-being and beyond. Broadening the public and policy discourse. Edward Elgar/Sitra, Cheltenham/Northampton, pp 1–13

Murdoch TB, Detsky AS (2013) The inevitable application of Big Data to health care. J Am Med Assoc 309(13):1351–1352

Niemelä M, Kokkinen L, Pulkki J, Saarinen A, Tynkkynen LK (2015) Terveydenhuollon muutokset. Politiikka, järjestelmä, seuraukset [Changes in healthcare. Policy, system and consequences, in Finnish]. TAY Press, Tampere

OECD (1995) Governance in transition: public management in OECD Countries. OECD, Paris

Olsen JA (2009) Principles in health economics and policy. Oxford University Press, Oxford

Osborne SP, Brown L (2005) Managing change and innovation in public service organizations. Routledge, London

Pollitt C (2005) Decentralization. A central concept in contemporary public management. In: Ferlie E et al (eds) The Oxford handbook of public management. Oxford University Press, Oxford, pp 371–397

Popper K (1963) Conjectures and refutations. Routledge/Kegan Paul, New York

Rigby M (2007) Applying emergent ubiquitous technologies in health: the need to respond to new challenges of opportunity, expectation, and responsibility. Int J Med Inform 76(4):349–352

Ringard Å, Sagan A, Sperre Saunes I, Lindahl AK (2013) Norway: health system review. Health Syst Transit 15(8):1–162

Rosen P, De Fine Licht J, Ohlsson H (2014) Priority setting in Swedish health care: are the politicians ready? Scand J Public Health. Published online before print February 10, 2014, https://doi.org/10.1177/1403494813520355

Ruckert A, Labonté R, Parker RH (2015) Global healthcare policy and the austerity agenda. In: Kuhlmann E et al (eds) The Palgrave international handbook of healthcare policy and governance. Palgrave MacMillan, New York, pp 37–53

Saltman RB (2015) Healthcare policy and innovation. In: Kuhlmann E et al (eds) The Palgrave international handbook of healthcare policy and governance. Palgrave MacMillan, New York, pp 23–36

Seligman MEP (2011) Flourish. A visionary new understanding and well-being. Free Press, New York

Seligman MEP, Csiksentmihalyi M (2000) Positive psychology: an introduction. Am Psychol 55 (1):5–14

Sigurgeirsdóttir S, Waagfjörð J, Maresso A (2014) Health system review. Health Syst Transit 16 (1):1–182

Stenvall J, Virtanen P (2012) Sosiaali- ja terveyspalvelujen uudistaminen [available only in Finnish, The development of social and healthcare services]. Tietosanoma, Helsinki

Stenvall J, Virtanen P (2015) Intelligent public organizations? Public Organ Rev, published on-line 2.12.2015. https://doi.org/10.1007/s11115-015-0331-1

Tuurnas S (2016) The professional side of co-production. Acta Universitatis Tamperensis 2163, Tampere

Van Thiel S (2016) A principal-agent perspective. In: Van de Walle S, Groenewald S (eds) Theory and practice of public sector reform. Routledge, Oxford, pp 44–60

Varabyova Y, Müller JM (2016) The efficiency of health care production in OECD countries: a systematic review and meta-analysis of cross-country comparisons. Health Policy 120 (3):252–263

Virtanen P, Kaivo-oja J (2015) Public services and emergent systemic societal challenges. Int J Public Leadersh 11(2):77–91

Virtanen P, Sinokki M (2014) Hyvinvointia työstä [available only in Fiinish, well-being from work, in Finnish]. Tietosanoma, Helsinki

Virtanen P, Stenvall J (2014) The evolution of public services from co-production to co-creation and beyond – an unfinished trajectory for the New Public Management? Int J Leadersh Public Serv 10(2):91–107

Virtanen P, Kaivo-oja J, Ishino Y, Stenvall J, Jalonen H (2016a) Ubiquitous revolution, customer needs and business intelligence. Empirical evidence from Japanese healthcare sector. Int J Web Eng Technol 11(3):259–283

Virtanen P, Laitinen I, Stenvall J (2016b) Street-level bureaucrats as strategy shapers in social and health service delivery: empirical evidence from six countries. Int Soc Work 16(3):1–14. https://doi.org/10.1177/0020872816660602

Vrangbaek K (2009) The political process of restructuring Nordic health systems. In: Magnussen J et al (eds) Nordic health care systems: recent reforms and current policy challenges. McGraw-Hill, New York, pp 53–77

Vrangbaek K, Christiansen T (2005) Health policy in Denmark: leaving the decentralized welfare path? J Health Polit Policy Law 30(1–2):29–52

Vuorenkoski L (2008) The next health care act. Health Policy Monit, October 2008. Available at www.hpm.org/en/Downloads/Half-Yearly_Reports.html

Weissert WG, Weissert CS (2012) Governing health. The politics of health policy. The Johns Hopkins University Press, Baltimore

Young OR (2008) Choosing governance systems: a plea for comparative research. In: Moran M et al (eds) The Oxford handbook of public policy. Oxford University Press, Oxford, pp 844–857

Chapter 3
Intelligence in Public Policy

Abstract This section of the book is especially based on the latest literature on public policy analysis. It discusses broadly the current challenges in organising and running public policies and health policy in particular. We argue that there is a lot of talk about complexity in society, but there is eventually little evidence on what actually constitutes this complexity and how public policies deal with the complexity domain. Moreover, it seems that the problem of existing policy-planning mechanisms and public policy-evaluation paradigms is that they do not fit in with, in particular, the current societal challenges and nexus problems (embedded and constructed somewhere in between existing policy areas). This, in turn, means that there is an urgent need to constitute new kinds of evaluation systems incorporated with the idea of intelligent public policy making. This calls for new methods and methodologies, new institutional settings for evaluation systems and new accountability understanding. This part of the book deals with what the promotion of intelligence presupposes from the perspectives of public policy, decision-making, implementation and evaluation. The starting point in our reasoning is especially knowledge management and decision-making procedures at the level of health policy. In this chapter, we discuss issues like forecasting and the urgent need to develop specific ex ante evaluation methods and procedures, and it underlines putting an emphasis on forecasting societal and health policy-related problems instead of ex post trials. As a result, we argue that a new governance model is evolving within the complexity framework: the New Public Integration. Moreover, this chapter analyses the emergence of new information bases for health policy and the role of big data and the Internet of (Intelligent) Things in particular.

3.1 Health and Public Policy: The Contents and the Actors

It is useful to start this chapter by asking how to understand the mechanisms of intelligent health policy. Is it possible to understand policy processes or are they—as Cohen et al. (1972) have noted—incoherent and perhaps impossible to explain?

The concept of intelligent health policy is not the kind of topic on which you could find a lot of books and articles. There are no discussions on intelligent health policy making, the definition of intelligent policy or the intelligent policy process. Actually, in general, if the question is what public policy actually is, there is no exhaustive answer available. This is because there are different kinds of public policies. They fall in different policy domains, and they can be grouped by issue (say, in the field of health policy, entitlement to access services), by target audience (say, children, the workforce, the aged), by the level of policy change (i.e. comprehensive or incremental) or by period of time (say, health policy after the economic recession of 2008/2009).

We approach public policy from the perspective of policy analysis. It describes the investigations that produce accurate and useful information for decision-makers. The importance of sound public policy analysis in achieving various goals related to the growth and development of a nation and its citizens cannot be overemphasised.

There are a lot of discussions in literature on how useful policy analysis and public policy approaches are in the context of health policy. We agree with Embrett and Randall (2014) who have noted that using a policy analysis tends to help in identifying why healthy public policies are typically not being adopted. On the basis of this perspective, it is almost impossible to make an analysis without an understanding of the mechanisms of making intelligent health policy.

The essential value issue of public policy was to what extent the public sector should take responsibility for people's health. These issues are still important. In addition to this, it is important to pay more attention to the flexibility and resilience of welfare-state policy. In this chapter, we start with the discussion on public policy. After this discussion, we will present the model that has been developed for public policy in a changing and complex environment.

In general, it is possible to argue that the challenge is how to create collective intelligence in public policy. In public policy, we are not interested in an individual person's influence in policy making only. The challenge is how to formulate whole systems. In this sense, we have to consider, for instance, how individual practices, like experiments, affect the entirety of policy making. We should be aware that intelligence is not only a thing that should be considered in public policy. It should be moral, future-committed and pluralistic, for instance. Public policy depends on values, history and the situations within which the public is operating (Dror 2001). Intelligence is linked with different kinds of contextual aspects like the targets of policy making.

There is a lot of discussion in scientific literature on what the contents of successful public health policy are. This is especially related to the discussion on how we understand the concept of health. The new paradigm of understanding health as a comprehensive phenomenon has affected the definitions of health policy (Acheson 1988; Law 2010; Beard and Bloom 2015). Some researchers have started to talk about integrative public health policy. Various approaches also (sometimes implicitly) recommend the use of integrated public health policies, such as the 'whole-of-government', 'whole-of-society' and 'governance-for-health' approaches (Davies et al. 2014; Rosen 2015; Brownson et al. 2017).

From this perspective, it is possible to think that intelligent health policy is based on a comprehensive approach that integrates different kinds of factors that affect health. The process integrates an enormous number of actors with different professional backgrounds into policy making and implementation. Collectively, intelligent health policy is produced by multi-scientific approaches. The aim is to enhance the well-being of citizens. When this is the case, one categorisation is to look at the contents of public policy. They can be either substantive (i.e. aiming to improve the healthcare of a certain target group) or procedural (which refers to how government or public administration does things once the policy objectives are laid down). Intelligent health policy means the ability to adapt policy making and implementation in complex environments as well. The next question is who makes intelligent health policy.

Traditionally, at the core of health policy lie national governments, with their specialised health ministries, departments or agencies and, in the case of donor nations, health programmes of their respective bilateral development cooperation agencies. Policy making for public health will be carried out by a range of organisations within the society—government departments (including but not limited to health), other public bodies, commercial enterprises and voluntary organisations—and this policy making operates at different levels: international, national and local (Law 2010).

There is more and more discussion on global health policy as well. Especially the reform-era agenda appeared to be in descent around the mid–late 1990s or so as a range of new ideas about health policy, health system structure and service delivery have made their way into the global policy agenda and that of national governments. These ideas faced various difficulties with the reform era and new thinking about and research into how to best organise health systems and improve their performance in the face of growing demand and costs, advancing technology, ageing populations and concerns about quality (Gauld 2009).

The global system is a group of actors whose primary intent is to improve health, along with the rules and norms governing their interaction. Faced with a set of health conditions, a country articulates a response through its national health system. At the global level, the key concept in understanding the pattern of health conditions is the international transfer of health risks, that is, the way in which the movement of people, products, resources and lifestyles across borders can contribute to the spread of disease (Frenk and Moon 2013).

It is also obvious that the medical profession, as an elite group, has a particular place in health policy at both national and international levels. It has traditionally been the most powerful provider group with often unrivalled access to policy makers. There is a range of reasons for this, including a monopoly on medical knowledge and the crucial role of medical practitioners within health systems, which have given doctors a position that is not to be questioned in health policy (Gauld 2009; Purtilo and Doherty 2016).

The reallocation of human capital and financial resources towards health promotion is possible by introducing and strengthening the evidence-based health promotion approach in policy making. The role of the government (and the government agenda and the respective performance monitoring systems), ministries, government agencies and the soon-established autonomous regions (responsible for organising and producing health services from 2017 onwards) is of importance in this process. At the service system level, primary healthcare is at the peak of change, since its role is about to transform from disease treatment into well-being provider. One of the key challenges is the current service delivery for the heavy users of health services.

Moreover, as Weissert and Weissert (2012) suggest, other problems related to public policy ambiguity lurk behind the corner. One of these is the relationship between policy makers and the public. Public policy formulation does not happen in a vacuum. Policy makers listen to their constituents, their colleagues, their parties and lobbyists and—what is very important to note—increasingly also rely on polls and focus groups (which are often very active in social media) for policy guidance. Health policy is really an interesting policy domain in this respect, since the public is very susceptible to the symbolism of politics, and politicians and, retrospectively, policy makers in the government are often very dexterous at manipulating value-laden issues related to health to seek public support. This also happens, for sure, in all public policies. In our research, we found while analysing government unity in a comparative study that government institutions are very capable at storytelling and communicating with the public to achieve legitimacy for their policy proposals (Virtanen et al. 2016c; see also Jacobsson and Sundström 2015).

In this chapter, we concentrate on what kinds of aspects are important in analysing intelligent health policy. We concentrate on how to make intelligent policy at national and organisational levels. However, we are aware that the national level is linked with global trends like the development of information technology. The contents of policy might vary from country to country depending on their history, values, resources, etc. Still, there are similar kinds of processes and practices in health policy which make healthcare more or less intelligent.

3.2 Easton's Public Policy System Revisited

In this book, we think of public policy as a system. Easton (1965) was one of the first to introduce system thinking in the public policy domain. He also emphasised that political systems should adapt to technological and environmental changes. According to Easton, the political system consists of all those activities or interactions that relate more or less directly to the authoritative allocation of values for the whole society. Interactions that do not partake of this characteristic are excluded from the political system and are viewed as external variables in the environment (Fig. 3.1).

Easton's model is a typical input–output model. The key thing is to think of public policy as a cycle. When the input–output exchange is viewed as a process that continues over time, it appears as an unbroken cycle in which each phase influences the succeeding phase. From our perspective, Eason's model helps in analysing the basic issues that are relevant in making intelligent public health policy. First, intelligent public policy depends on getting and collecting inputs. There are many kinds of inputs in public policy. Some of them are directly related with democracy. Data and information are inputs that affect policy making as well. Information that tells about the cost-effectiveness of services in health problem solving might be a relevant input in policy making.

In the real world of healthcare, there are a lot of actors who produce inputs for public health policy. One of the inputs is what kinds of political choices get support from

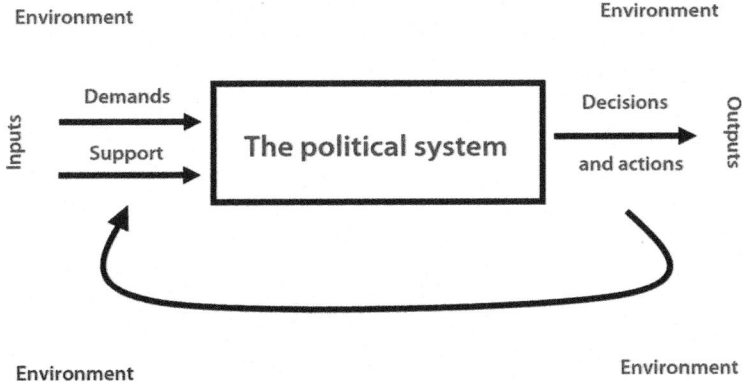

Fig. 3.1 Public policy as a system (Easton 1965)

citizens in elections. The system—the people who work in administration or the technological solutions—might produce inputs. Even the business sector—healthcare companies or the pharmaceutical industry—might have a role in producing inputs for the political system when they try to influence by lobbying.

In this context, the intelligence of public policy depends on the quality of evidence. The inputs should more or less tell what is happening around the systems. The second critical issue is that the inputs should give a sufficiently versatile picture of what is happening in the environment. This might mean that the diversity of evidence is important as inputs in creating intelligent public policy. Third, the inputs determine the content of relevant intelligence in public health policy. Citizens' needs and values have an effect on what kind of public health policy is meaningful for people.

The system has three roles in public policy.

- The first of them is response. It means that variation in the structures and processes within a system may usefully be interpreted as constructive or as positive alternative efforts by the members of the system to regulate or cope with the stress flowing from environmental as well as internal sources.
- The second role is formulation. It means that analyses and politics determine how an agenda item is translated into an authoritative decision: a law, rule or regulation, administrative order or resolution.
- The third role is implementation. The authorised policy must be administered and enforced by an agency of the government. The agency must take instructions as stated in the policy but will probably be called upon to provide missing pieces and to make judgements as to the intent, goals, timetables, programme design and reporting methods. The agency's mission may be well defined or poorly understood, but the field of action will have shifted.

It is self-evident that the quality of the response, formulation and implementation has an effect on intelligent health policy. The capacity of response is directly linked with evidence-based health policy. It is, for instance, able to understand why changes happen. In practice, this might be very complex. Most pertinent for health promotion, the deep-seated opinions and beliefs that have an effect on response may be highly emotional and even based on moral consciousness (McQeen 2010).

Policy formulation is above all problem solving. It includes the formulation of means as well. This is related to the question of how intelligent policy is implemented in practice. If the means are formulated wrongly, it is possible that the actors will not be able to use their professional knowledge purposefully, or the means will be effective in solving the wrong problem.

Feedback is an essential part of public policy. Actually, in Easton's model, the capacity of a system to persist in the face of stress is a function of the presence and nature of the information and other influences that return to its actors and decision-makers. The concept of a 'feedback loop' by Easton includes the identification of not only the information that returns to the system but all the actions that result from the effort to take advantage of this information. The authorities use information feedback to determine successive outputs, which, in turn, affect subsequent inputs and so on. The feedback system works well in intelligent health policy. It can be, for instance, an evaluation system that produces ongoing feedback on the implementation of policy making.

Easton's model takes up the key processes that affect health policy intelligence. The problem is that a public policy system is much more complex in reality than Eason expected. Public policy is not always based on a hierarchical, top-down approach. It is possible that there are several systems that try to integrate inputs and outputs by formulating means. The discussion of governance has emphasised that networks are necessary in effective public policy (Klijn and Koppenjan 2016; Osborne et al. 2013).

3.3   Public Policy Cycle

As Embrett and Randall (2014) have noted, a successful health policy advocacy requires a thorough understanding of the policy process. The policy cycle helps to more strictly describe the public policy practices that are relevant for intelligent health policy. In practice, the policy cycle is a simplified model of the public policy process.

Despite its limitations, the policy cycle approach has been deployed in public policy making as the most widely applied framework to organise and systemise research on public policy. The policy cycle focusses attention on the generic features of the policy process rather than on the specific actors or institutions or particular substantial problems and respective programmes (Jann and Wegrich 2007).

There is some overlap between Eason's model and the traditional policy cycle approach. Policy making presupposes the recognition of a policy problem. The second step would be that the recognised problem is actually put on the agenda for serious consideration of public action (agenda-setting). During policy development (policy formulation and decision-making), the expressed problems, proposals and demands are transformed into government programmes. Policy implementation is broadly defined as 'what happens between the establishment of an apparent intention on the part of

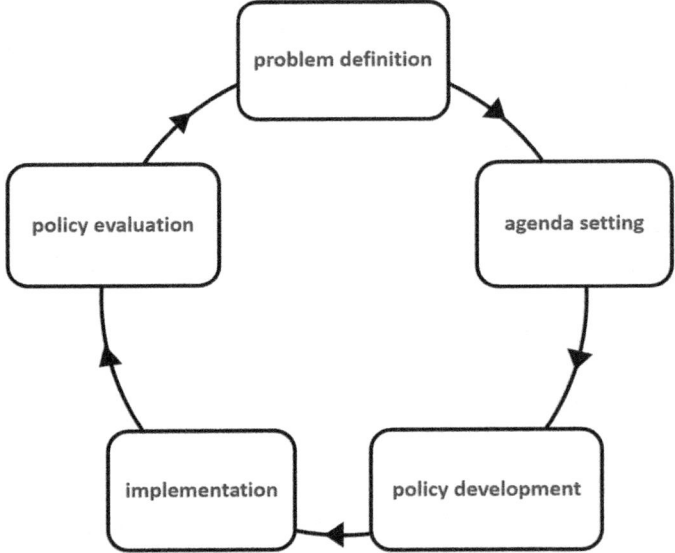

Fig. 3.2 The policy cycle

government to do something, or to stop doing something, and the ultimate impact in the world of action'. During the evaluation stage of the policy cycle, these intended outcomes of policies move to the centre of attention (Jann and Wegrich 2007).

Figure 3.2 describes the stages of the public policy cycle.

There is a lot of discussion in public policy literature on the issue of how the stages of the policy cycle differ from each other. The agenda-setting covers both agenda-setting and policy formulation and adoption. Policy is made, or changed, when three independent streams of activity intersect: problems, policies and politics (see Berlan et al. 2014). The problem stream fits cleanly within agenda-setting, but both the policy and the politics streams can be perceived as fitting within both agenda-setting and some conceptualisation of policy formulation and adoption. The policy stream, perhaps the most relevant to this stage, is the development of competing proposals by experts.

In the context of intelligent health policy, the critical question is how to make decisions in policy making. In practice, decision-making typically focusses on the *policy formulation* stage, including problem definition, agenda-setting and policy development. Public policy is made up of consciously created entities that are the result of decision-making and choice. Policy analysts should bring alternatives together with their recommendations to the attention of political decision-makers. However, it is not very clear at the practical level where and how decision-making and policy analysis are happening as a part of public policy. At the conceptual level, the issue of 'where to go' can be considered agenda-setting, whereas 'how to get there' includes formulation or policy programming. In practice, the agenda-setting/formulation distinction is a difficult one, with strong interactions between the two very likely (Hill 2014).

According to Mintzberg et al. (1976, see also Kuoppakangas 2015), the problem definition phase has two sub-phases. The first of these involves sensing that there is a problem and recognising the need to solve it: an action may be triggered when the problem has grown to the point where it cannot be ignored. The nature of the problem is defined during the second sub-phase, and the possible cause-and-effect relationship in the situation is assessed. Information gathering is needed at this point to clarify the problem.

If the challenge is to improve decision-making, one of the most obvious ways to do so is to provide decision-makers with an understanding of the specialised knowledge or expertise that can assist them in making wise choices among the alternatives. In this context, intelligent problem definition, agenda-setting and policy development increase the rationality of public policy. Intelligence and expertise serve as both instrumental and enlightening functions in the policy formulation phase.

The area between agenda-setting and policy implementation is rather neglected in literature on health policy as well. However, it is crucial to policy design and in determining whether the policy will achieve its intended purposes (Berlan et al. 2014). The key question is how to formulate policy development. According to Hill (2014), public policy programming includes the following aspects:

- More precise definitions of policy objectives
- Operational elements, including the instruments to be used to make policy effective—a topic discussed further below
- Political–administrative arrangements, involving the specification of the authorities whose duty is to implement the policy—the notion that such authorities need money and other resources to do that follows self-evidently from that point
- Procedural elements, namely, the rules to be used in the implementation of the policy

It is also an intelligent question per se how to formulate policy programming. Evidence-based policy needs, for instance, a comprehensive understanding of the content and system of healthcare. Successful policy programming requires knowledge on the drivers that have an effect on health policy implementation.

There are a lot of studies available that have shown the complexity of implementation (Murray 1971; Pressman and Wildavsky 1984; Virtanen and Stenvall 2014). Implementing a health policy is thus definitely a complex process. Policy implementation itself is complex because policies are subject to multiple reinterpretations throughout implementation. In the case of comprehensive health policy, specific challenges might arise from the involvement and coordination of several policy sectors, each with their own interests, institutions and ideas. This implicates that implementation involves complex interaction between the actors.

Due to the complexity of the public sector, actors cannot design and implement public policy by themselves, and they need to collaborate with third and private sector actors in making public policy. It is also possible that so-called street-level bureaucrats—like doctors—make decisive decisions on health policy. They interpret political aims and make decisions on the basis of the feedback they get from customers (Lipsky 1980; Virtanen et al. 2016a, b, c; Tuurnas et al. 2015). In this context, the key question of public policy and governance is how the system manages to integrate different kinds of practices and actors into the processes—like policy formulation, response process and getting feedback—to increase intelligence.

3.4 A Pragmatic Approach to Public Policy?

It is almost impossible to understand discussions on public policy without the understanding of public policy approaches. They all demonstrate different kinds of sides of policy making. The following three approaches are the most common in public policy discussion: the institutional approach, interpretation-based approach and process-based approach. The institutional approach has been important in the discussions on new governance (Pierre 2011). It emphasises the structural aspects of public policy.

Institutionalism is the perspective of how different kinds of actors—like government, stakeholders, etc.—are shaping the contents of public policy. The other important question is what are institutional practices that affect the relationship between the actors and what does this mean for public policy. As Birkland (2016) noted, one way to conceive politics is to see it as a process helping societies to figure out how to organise and regulate themselves; that is, how to govern themselves. What makes this political is its location in the public sphere where the decisions are made to address issues that affect people in the community.

The essential concern of the behavioural and interpretation-based approach is the issues with which people actually interpret public policy as the result of interactions with a powerful force (cf. Gerston 2015). The interpretation approach includes several kinds of schools with different assumptions based on philosophy and epistemology. The behavioural school might take up the importance of an individual in the interpretation. In the discursive approach, policy and the public are understood to take shape through socially interpreted understanding, and their meanings and the discourses that circulate them are not of the actors' own choosing or making (Fischer 2003).

Third, policy making can be considered a continuous process. Policy making is not a discrete event but a continuous process, often depicted as a cycle. This may be described as starting with a description of the problem for which a policy is desired, followed by a cycle of policy development and specification, implementation, assessment of impact, learning from experience and then contributing that learning to further policy development.

In our book, we analyse intelligent health policy in a very pragmatic manner. We are not going to go through pragmatic philosophy, which has been established since 1870 by authors like Pierce, James and Dewey. It is still important to note that there are long traditions in pragmatism about discussing public policy issues. Dewey, for instance, wrote on topics relevant in public policy.

In our approach, pragmatism means that we think that the intelligence of health policy—like public policy in general—is related to concrete practices and processes which include policy making. For this reason, we go through the practices of political systems, for instance. The other side of pragmatism is that what works as health policy depends on the context. Complexity and developing technologies are especially important for intelligent health policy.

Our pragmatic approach means that we assume that practices affect the interpretation of public policy. We are also interested in public policy processes and institutionalism because they affect intelligence. Welfare-state change is, for instance, a work in progress, leading to patchwork mixes of old and new policies. Generally speaking, the contents of health policy were quite stable and predictable. For instance, people's expectations and needs were unchanged. In this kind of context, the main issue is how to create and produce better quality and more effective services. Health policy is a mix of unchanging institutionalism and adaptivity.

Intelligent health policy is dependent on policy making practices. In this context, institutionalised practices affect public policy.

In some respects, institutionalism raises questions about the extent to which human actions are structurally determined. The social world within which organisations are created draws attention both to the impact of the external environment and to the way people bring in their own needs and affiliations into organisations, which then shape the social systems that develop there. In this way, modern institutional theory embodies 'cognitive and normative frames' which 'construct "mental maps"' and 'determine practices and behaviours' (Hill 2014, pp. 70–71).

In practice, institutionalism defines the context and framework for the ways in which policy issues are understood (Hall 1993). Particular kinds of intelligence—like in the medical framework—might be an institutionalised frame in policy. Another possibility is that some of the practices included in policy cycles (like feedback loops or policy framing) are based on institutionalised intelligence practices. For instance, the purpose of feedback systems might be institutionalised in a form that increases evidence for informing policy making.

The main point is that institutionalism produces the context that shapes intelligence in public policy, including health policy. Acemoglu et al. (2012) put forward the idea that how institutions work in practice has an effect on the success of a nation. Successful countries have stable institutions that make public policy more cleverly and reliably without corruption or opinion-based policy making. According to Acemoglu et al. (2012), institutions affect comprehensive policy making as well. This includes the idea that institutions enable innovation and lead to continuing growth. Extractive institutions can only deliver growth when the economy is catching up with the technological frontier, but, when innovations are needed to push to the front, they will fail.

Generally speaking, institutional arrangements are important, but they do not allow you to predict policy outcomes. By establishing the rules of the game, institutional arrangements enable you to predict the ways in which policy conflicts will be played out (Immergut 1992). There might be institutionally based tensions included in policy making. The essential reasons for this are the differences in understanding and framing relevant issues. Some institutions might emphasise in their arguments due to their institutionalised tasks and roles in society that sports and health habits should be the key elements in the welfare-state policy. Other institutions could have a more medically oriented frame for health. In the midst of these kinds of policy conflicts, it is often quite difficult to predict what the outcomes of power games in making public policy will be.

In health policy, the essential position of the medical profession can be considered as one form of institutionalism. Actually, it is almost impossible to understand the content of health policy without understanding the position of the healthcare profession. As Scott argued, 'the professions in modern society have assumed leading roles in the creation and tending of institutions' (2013). This is related with intelligence because, as Larson (1977) noted, professionalisation institutionalises a link between expertise and collective mobility. Institutions— like social and healthcare ministries—quite often have a strong representation of institutionalised medical professions involved in health policy.

For the record, institutionalism is not unchanging and never has been. The concept of institutional entrepreneurship describes a situation in which some actors are able to make changes in existing institutional arrangements. New kinds of intelligence can be a driving force for institutional entrepreneurship as well. The new knowledge might question the institutional arrangements.

The governance approach can also be a source of transformation for existing institutional arrangements in health policy. This was one of the outcomes in Scott's study of shifts in professional governance in healthcare in the San Francisco Bay Area (2013; see also Muzio et al. 2013). Their longitudinal study tracked changes in each of the three pillars over five decades and revealed pressure from non-professional organisations (i.e. government, insurance companies and health maintenance organisations) that effectively dismantled the long-standing dominance of professional control in the field. This meticulous study effectively demonstrates the erosion of professional institutions in the US healthcare system and their replacement by a much more fragmented amalgam of government and corporate controls.

The other side of the coin is that institutionalism may be a threat to intelligent health policy as well. In some cases, institutionalism even negatively affects intelligence. There are a lot of professional-based silos between organisations and in policy making in these kinds of contexts. This means that it is almost impossible to implement a comprehensive health policy in which different kinds of actors work together in solving policy problems (Ranade and Hudson 2003; Miller and Tucker 2014). Smiths's (2013) research has shown that institutions limit the extent to which evidence-based approaches can inform decision-makers in health policy. It demonstrates how policy silos and hierarchies work as filters to research-based ideas, encouraging those ideas that support existing institutionalised ideas (or policy paradigms), while blocking or significantly transforming more challenging ideas. Yet, a lack of institutional memory within policy making enables recycled ideas to appear innovative, creating an impression of meaningful, ongoing dialogue between intelligence and policy.

Due to institutionalism, the public sector quite often has well-established, complex, institutional arrangements, including standard operating procedures, cultures and value systems. In other words, complex bureaucratic practices that are institutionalised into the system constitute hindrances to making intelligent public policy. In the next section, we focus on approaches that help to overcome problems of adaptivity in making intelligent health policy.

3.5   Adaptive Health Policy

Health policy has provided a fertile source of inspiration for research on adaptive capacity in a complex environment. It is not a big surprise that the lack of adaptive capacity has been used to explain failures in health policies (Tenbensel 2016). One of the reasons might be the existing institutional arrangements that decrease adaptive capacity. Another reason is that health policies do not include activities that increase intelligence.

In this book, we argue that intelligent health policies need at least four policy directions to increase the capacity of policy making:

1. New principles of policy making that emphasise flexibility and self-organising
2. Agility practices in policy making
3. Learning in policy making
4. Evidence-informed policy making

The essential principles of adaptive intelligence policy are flexibility and self-organisation. There should also be a capacity to manage emerging problems (Tenbensel 2016). Flexibility and self-organisation give more space to individual institutions in public policy. In outcome-based policy, actors can use their intelligence to find the means to get outcomes, for instance.

Self-organising might be a process that creates a more integrated health policy based on intelligence. This was an essential theme in Lindblom's classical book on the *Intelligence of Democracy* (Lindblom 1965). 'Partisan mutual adjustment' is the concept that describes how coordination is achieved in the absence of a central coordinator. Partisan mutual adjustment is the process by which independent decision-makers coordinate their behaviour. It involves adaptive adjustments 'in which a decision-maker simply adapts to decisions around him' and manipulated adjustments 'in which he seeks to enlist a response desired from the other decision-maker' (Lindblom 1965, p. 33; Hill 2014). Each of these forms of adjustment is further divided into a variety of more specific behaviours, including negotiation and bargaining. Lindblom notes that although there is no necessary connection between partisan mutual adjustment and political change by small steps, the two are usually closely linked in practice.

Policy learning refers to alternations of actors' understandings and beliefs or frames of reference in the light of new information and experiences. For this reason, the facilitation of policy learning is a central feature in adaptive public policy.

There are different kinds of conceptual frameworks that have tried to catch the content of learning as a part of policy making. Hall (1993) has emphasised the aspect of social learning. This approach helps to understand the collective intelligence in contemporary health policy. According to Hall 'much political interaction has constituted a process of social learning expressed through policy' (1993). The key agents pushing forward the learning process are the experts in a given field of policy, either working for the state or advising it from privileged positions at the interface between the bureaucracy and the intellectual enclaves. Social learning can be defined as a deliberate attempt to adjust the goals or techniques of policy in response to past experience and new information. Learning is indicated when policy changes as the result of such a process.

Hall also makes a note that the challenge of learning is a complex phenomenon. Faced with conflicting opinions from experts, politicians will have to decide whom to regard as authoritative, especially in matters of technical complexity, and the political community engages in a contest for authority over the issues at hand.

In the context of our book, it is possible to ask which kinds of intelligence frames shape social learning in health policy. This is related to the question of institutionalism and the transformation of existing institutional arrangements made by institutional entrepreneurship. Another challenge is that adaptive intelligence policy quite often needs changes in the mindset, not only in practices. This makes social learning even more demanding. Quite often the social learning of a mindset takes place due to political crises and failures (cf. Virtanen and Stenvall 2014).

Increasing adaptivity is a strategy choice for policy making. Developed the agility approach for organising business units and public policy and orchestrating public administration in a novel way. According to them, governments need to think more strategically and holistically. They need to achieve greater resource allocation flexibility, and they need greater cooperation among their ministries and agencies, with a wider array of stakeholders. In short, they need greater strategic agility. Kosonen and Droz identified three enabling vectors of strategic agility: strategic sensitivity, resource fluidity and collective commitment. They need to be developed together in an integrated manner. First, governments must develop the ability to gain insight into evolving situations within a complex environment—a combination of attentiveness, foresight, real-time analysis and sense-making and pattern recognition. Second, to benefit from strategic sensitivity, governments must be capable of mobilising and redeploying resources to take action in a timely manner: this is resource fluidity. Third, to achieve strategic agility in action, collective commitment and unified leadership are crucially important.

The adaptiveness of policy making is related to evidence-based policy. As we have noted, the intelligence of public policy increases if the system has the ability to utilise evidence in policy making. This is related to the feedback loop and the position of evaluation as well.

Adaptiveness is an ongoing and dynamic process in policy making. It depends on contextual factors as well. Different kinds of research can play an important role in identifying factors that foster adaptability in different contexts, so that policy makers can promote adaptability. In the context of intelligent health policy, the development of technology is especially a factor that has the potential to increase adaptive capacity.

3.6 Complex Public Policy?

Conventionally speaking, public administration policy instruments are usually divided into legal (regulatory), economic and information steering of the society (Bemelmans-Videc et al. 1998). At the practical level, it is a question of how society is governed through legislation by directing economic resources and by collecting and analysing different types of knowledge. To give a concrete example: ministries channel economic resources to local- and regional-level authorities in public administration on the basis of performance-related estimations of the goals attained with regard to inputs, outputs, results and impacts of service delivery. Based on this knowledge, in turn, conclusions on the effectiveness of operations are drawn, the conclusions are reflected back to the level of legislation and they trickle back to the rules on the distribution of economic resources.

This is how the performance-related policy instruments have functioned in policy planning up till today. However, in order to be intelligent, public policies and public health policies in particular have to be rethought and reconceived, taking into account the changing role of society. In this rethinking process, the digitalisation of society and the emerging systemic governance challenges play a pivotal role as we underlined earlier in this chapter.

We share the view of Colander and Kupers (2014), who underlined the changing role of public policy in contemporary society. According to them, public policy discussion has pretty much concentrated so far on two polar options: a juxtaposition between market orientation and government control has evolved, and now this dual setting needs rethinking because of the complexity of society. That being said, we hold the view that neither the market-dominated, laissez-faire paradigm nor government activism and control can offer solutions to this complexity issue. As we have noticed, complexity offers new perspectives towards public policies.

The central components in this regard are the notion of complex society, the roles of government and the market and the meta-policies the government adopts in order to influence policy making. We believe that public health policy, then, is about trying to achieve some goal or goals in society in terms of health. Our point is, regardless of the rather conventional interpretation of the public policy concept, the context of public policies, health included, has changed dramatically. These above-mentioned components of new public policy making are discussed as follows.

The central narrative of complex society—and complexity science as a scientific framework—involves capturing public health policy, public health institutions and organisations as well as publicly financed and influenced service ecosystems as a complex and open system. Consequently, this evolving system is definitely beyond the control of government and political decision-makers. This view holds that government is only one component of the endogenously evolving control mechanisms of current public health policy. Other important actors in the field of public health policy are the market, the civil society and the service user (both potential and real; on this, see Virtanen et al. 2016a, b). In this new setting, decision-makers encounter a new challenge: if the society cannot be governed in the way it used to be—by means of goal-setting and controlling if the goals are achieved—then what is the role of public policy and public administration?

This leads to a conclusion that is noteworthy to underline here: policy making in complex society is a continuous process, and the social system of policies is constantly in the process of reorganising and transforming itself with the aim of influencing policy-related matters, not setting the rules to make control possible. This is not an easy mission for modern policy makers since they ought to have basic knowledge about the complexity science's toolbox in order to understand the accumulation of knowledge. This toolbox consists of, for instance, fractal analysis, game theory, nonlinear dynamic models, agent-based models and various other social science-related approaches such as the network analysis; on these, see Colander and Kupers (2014, pp. 57–59). Moreover, performance measurement and performance management practices also change as the result of the complexity of public policy making, which we discuss later in this book. Performance monitoring systems and included metrics evolve towards the direction that emphasises social mechanisms in public policy goal-setting, the role of effectiveness attributes and the public value added by public policy making.

In Fig. 3.3, we have sketched a model to our argument to highlight the changing role of public policies in complex society. In the middle of figure, there is a conventional (at least in the sense of how NPM and NPG management doctrines conceived public policy making) diagram indicating the result chain in between the objectives, inputs, outputs and outcomes of public health policy end up in varieties of effectiveness considerations and evaluations. This procedural chaining of objectives with inputs and outputs reflects the idea of a 'simple world', which unfortunately does not exist anymore due to globalisation, new path dependencies of policies, overlapping policy objectives of single public policies and overall societal uncertainties (caused by, in particular, the new systemic governance challenges).

The pressure for a new kind of public policy conceptualisation comes from two directions. The first is from the need to rethink the public sector organisations' modus operandi by introducing the role of innovations and innovativeness, affecting multiple policy changes and new coordination mechanisms needed in the new health service ecosystems. This, in turn, calls for a new adaptive change capacity and new impetus for public sector leadership. The other pressure comes from societal changes and from the perspective of complexity. Figure 3.3 makes explicit the fact that a new kind of complexity-based health policy positioning is evolving. This is simply because of the changes in the health-related issues in society based on the rapid change of society (the emergence of new health problems, the emergence of individual- and community-based health-related consciousness, the changing role of well-being in society including new conceptualisations of the concept and so on).

The role of government is of special interest here, and it deserves further clarification. According to Colander and Kupers (2014), for instance, government develops and influences objectives and strategies for different levels of society. They are articulated at the public health policy level but also towards the civil society and the public in general. Colander and Kupers (2014, pp. 23–25) call these government meta-policies,

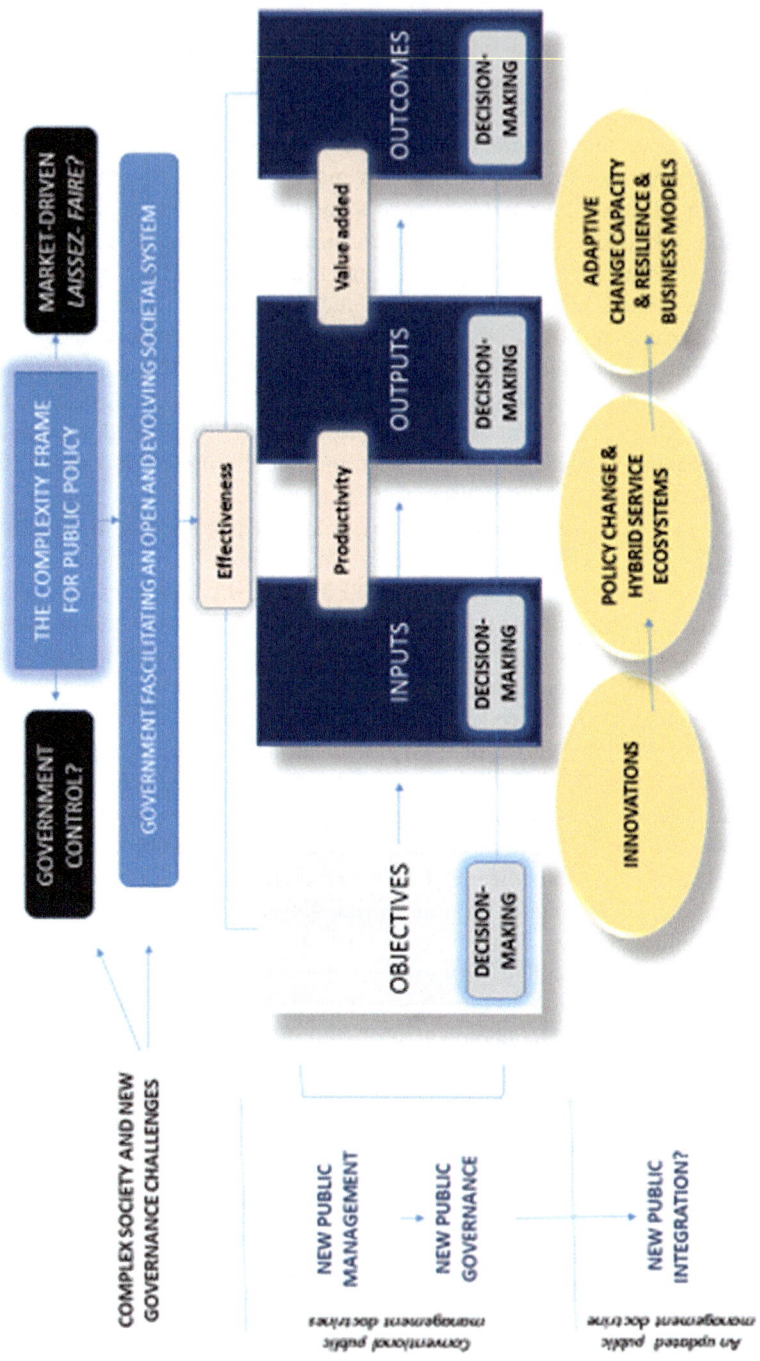

Fig. 3.3   The changing role of public policy

which imply the government's strength to design an ecosystem in which policy has embedded control is limited. From the perspective of the health policy field, these meta-policies can be strongly supportive of bottom-up activities and health-related behaviour. The well-known chronic care model—aimed at improved self-diagnosis competencies and healthy lifestyle options for individuals—is an example of these.

Japan offers an interesting example of a government meta-policy incorporated with the issue of health. Japan is an interesting country because of the health level of the population as well as their life expectancy at birth, which is the highest in the world. According to Ikeda et al. (2011), the improvement in the population's health became evident after the mid-1960s through the government implementation of primary and secondary preventive community public health measures as well as through an increased use of advanced medical technologies through a universal insurance scheme.

Moreover, health-related lifestyle choices were put forward by the government—such is the case, for instance, with the importance of personal hygiene. As a result, disparities in health across regions and socioeconomic groups in Japan have narrowed in this homogenous and egalitarian society, and, over time, the average population's health has increased. With regard to market orientation, Japan is a good example as well. Approximately 60% of Japanese die from cancer, heart disease or stroke (Shiba and Shimokawa 2008). Improving and maintaining people's lifestyles before becoming sick can extend their healthy life. This is understood both by the government and, to a growing extent, by the market. In Japan, the demand for IoT-driven healthcare systems has been increasing during the last decades, and the health-related is market booming currently. The market of IoT-based systems for preventive medicine has an especially huge potential. In the field of healthcare, ubiquitous technologies and their principles have been applied to improve access to medical care, increase the quality of care and reduce the cost of care. In this process, private companies have played an important role. IoT-driven or ubiquitous healthcare systems are constituted from a network of sensor devices that connect to the Internet to capture and share human vital data through a secure service layer that connects to a central server.

As a result, the IoT is very significant in Japanese healthcare for at least three reasons (Pang et al. 2015). It is important in clinical care. This includes the idea that the physiological status of hospitalised patients can be constantly monitored using IoT-driven and non-invasive sensor devices. Second, it is useful in *remote monitoring*. When patients suffering from chronic diseases have neither easy access to hospitals nor present acute symptoms, wireless solutions connected through the IoT can constantly monitor fluctuations in observable data related to the chronic disease. Finally, it has a very important role in early prevention. Healthy and active people can also benefit from IoT-driven monitoring of their daily activities as the IoT-driven system can detect some signs of change in everyday activity and report it (Virtanen et al. 2016a, b, c).

The Japanese example is also a good illustration in terms of the complexity frame. It underlines the role of the market in creating the contents of health policy from the bottom-up and not from the top-down perspective. A well-functioning market is a consequence of previous, successful and future government meta-policy in relation to health issues. The main target of the complex public policy in the field of health is not healthcare but health of the service users. The objectives look alike, but they are totally different at a closer look.

Complexity thinking in terms of health policy means acknowledging that neither the government nor the market can really fully understand the evolution of policy itself. From the decision-makers' points of view, the stage is, however, set in a totally novel way: the systems of health policy cannot be controlled but can be influenced in many ways. A definite prerequisite of the complex policy is that it derives its origins both from the government's new role as well as from the well-functioning market. Another important aspect is the role of bottom-up activism and 'the wisdom of the people', so to say. Bottom-up activism and co-creation (between service providers and service users) of publicly financed health services can make a difference in terms of sustainable public spending, improved productivity and enhanced and better targeted effectiveness. This is precisely the fact why we policymakers should be very interested in what the service users have to say about the development of services. [See Colander and Kupers for their interesting analysis of the US healthcare reform from this perspective (2014, pp. 248–253).]

It is reasonable to ask, what are the components of the new public sector management doctrine in this new situation? We believe trust is crucial and perhaps the only fundamental factor in leading and managing the new complexities and changing roles of public, private and nongovernmental institutions. The *New Public Integration* derives its origins from trust—the trust between policy makers, public policies, public organisations, service users and citizens. The New Public Integration—as a management framework—incorporates the ideas of cooperation, coordination, networking and joint agenda-setting with all relevant stakeholders. Then, the government's role is not any more to govern or control but to make sure that the various and multiple institutions and agencies aim in the same direction.

Two essential issues need clarification with regard to the New Public Integration: (a) the role of policy instruments and (b) the unity of government and the role of policy coordination.

Complex society brings about the need for the dynamic deployment of policy instruments. We share the view of Lascoumes and LeGales (2007), who argue that the value and worth of policy instruments equal their dynamic nature—i.e. by how they can be of help in pinpointing emerging societal problems, which call for action at the level of public policies. According to them, the elasticity and deployability of policy instruments enhance the resilience of public policies and public organisations, which becomes evident in how decision-makers allocate and reallocate public finances in crises and hazardous shocks. In a word, this means that policy instruments interlink with foresight methods and processes. Steering by information is probably the most elastic policy instrument in this sense, bearing in mind the lengthy processes of law drafting and legislation as well as the budgetary processes with the state administration.

As this is the case, then the nature of information, which steering is based on, becomes relevant: how the information for decision-making is collated, analysed, interpreted and reported. To summarise, the possibility to use policy instruments raises two important aspects. These aspects concern the appropriateness of public policy instruments and the appropriateness of performance review-based policy instruments. The first one of these is the question of how different policy instruments identify relevant societal phenomena (which are dealt with through public policies), whereas the second one focusses on how performance management procedures manage to measure the effects of public policies.

It is reasonable to ask if the unity of government and the coordination of public policies are possible solutions for the management of systemic governance challenges in the field of health. They can be but not necessarily. For example, Virtanen et al. (2016c) made a comparative study about the effectiveness of public decision-making and government-level administration systems in six countries (Finland, Sweden, Norway, Estonia, the Netherlands and New Zealand). The topics of the research were elementary in terms of managing government and public policies in the times of multidimensional societal complexity. Their study made explicit that in political decision-making, Sweden, Holland and New Zealand form a cluster with regard to collegiality in government decision-making and the prime minister's status (de facto and de jure). Regarding collegiality, Virtanen et al. (2016c) suggest that it is a matter of political decision-making tradition.

With regard to the functioning and reform of the government's administrative system, their study noted that in each of the focus countries, in principle, ministries operate very independently, with Sweden as a clear exception with its dual system of administration. In the evaluation of policy coordination across administrative branches and administrative accountability, the Netherlands and Sweden emerge as clusters of broad-based policy coordination and strong accountability. Both countries have a strong tradition and well-functioning practices in applying interministerial coordination mechanisms, which clearly support the unity of government from the point of view of policy management. A further commonality between Sweden, the Netherlands and New Zealand is the fact that they have a good capacity for the implementation of governmental reforms, and governmental development is underpinned by a development vision that spans across terms of government.

The lesson learned from Virtanen et al. (2016c) study is that there is no single structural mechanism that ensures the coordination of public policies in the field of health. What seems to be more important are the ways how people at decision-making positions work and cooperate with each other, regardless of the public policy structures and organisational boundaries. The central government administrative structures do not have any intrinsic value as factors of unified government. It all depends on the way in which key actors of public policy and governance wish to cooperate with one another.

What is important from the perspective of health policy now is the clear vision for governmental policy goals, reaching beyond the sequence of parliamentary elections and the determination of overall responsibility for health goals to support continuity in healthcare reforms. One should remember that there are no ideological bottlenecks for this: neither political representation nor distribution of power appears to be an important determinant of health policy (Machenbach and McKee 2015). This means that public spending on health is rather similar regardless of the political system. One explanation for this is that the health sector is strongly science- and technology-driven and therefore somewhat autonomous to political debates and the changing political climate. Health policy and service systems appear to become even more complex.

3.7   Synthesis

In this chapter, we have concentrated on the concept and practices of intelligent health policy. We have argued that the starting point of intelligence is how to frame health policy. Weissert and Weissert (2012, pp. 283–284) have bluntly argued that it would be naïve to think that the purpose of healthcare or other public policy is always obvious or rational. Issues on policy agenda are—intentionally or unintentionally—often left vague so that stakeholders with different perspectives may intervene and get their views represented. This eventually leads to the ambiguity of public policy. Ambiguity is also strengthened due to the fact that policy makers usually define policies with no understanding about the outcomes of the given policy. No wonder then that public policies evolve over time, and they definitely are not written in stone.

As a consequence, public policy is an emergent, dynamic potpourri of vague and indefinite laws, all sorts of often late and changing regulations, government officials' and other stakeholders' interpretations of the policy objectives and delivery mechanisms, sometimes bizarre and controversial court decisions and, finally, the level of compliance by service providers, fiscal intermediaries and patients themselves. Our experience is that these 'ambiguity news' do not end at the boundaries of health policy. In our previous research, we have found similar policy formulation and delivery mechanisms also in the field of employment and social policy (Virtanen and Uusikylä 2004).

Complexity creates the context and even the criteria for intelligent health policy. We have emphasised that intelligent health policy is typically based on integrated and contemporary health policy. We have presented a model that contains the changing role of public policy.

The essential conclusion is that intelligent health policy includes the policy processes and practices—like decision-making, policy designing, implementation and evaluation—which are typical in policy making. The key issue is how the system of policy making works as a whole from the perspective of intelligence. Different kinds of policy making stages are more integrated with each other due to complex and fast-moving environments.

The dilemma of institutionalism and adaptiveness in intelligent health policy is evident. Both of them are necessary in policy making. Institutionalism can, for instance, shape the use of intelligence in public policy. Adaptiveness is necessary in fast-moving environments. It is also possible that institutionalism can decrease adaptiveness and intelligence in public policy.

According to our argumentation, the development of technology tests intelligent health policy. Technology can make health policy more intelligent. The other aspect of policy making is that intelligence in health policy increases when using new technological solutions.

Overall, all policy instruments need to be mobilised in order to make sustainable and health promotion-based changes in people's way of life, well-being and health based on both experience and diagnosis. Health policies ought to be more coherent (between policy areas, taking into account the emergence of nexus policy problems), evidence-based and intelligent. From a public healthcare services point of view, this development means the transformation of traditional public services towards service systems at the local and regional levels.

Therefore, it is important to note that systemic governance challenges, emerging austerity agendas (related to public sector finance crises), the technology revolution, the development of more personalised service models in healthcare and overall service integration are driving the new governances of services beyond interorganisational coordination into more closely coupled service systems in which service users (as co-creators) play an active role. In this chapter, we called this transformation as the emergence of trust-based New Public Integration.

References

Acemoglu D, Robinson JA, Verdier T (2012) Can't we all be more like scandinavians? Asymmetric growth and institutions in an interdependent world (No. w18441). National Bureau of Economic Research

Acheson ED (1988) Public health in England. Report of the committee of enquiry into the future development of the public health function. HMSO, London

Beard HP, Bloom DE (2015) Towards a comprehensive public health response to population ageing. Lancet 385(9968):658–661

Bemelmans-Videc M, Rist RC, Vedung E (eds) (1998) Carrots, sticks, and sermons. Policy instruments and their evaluation. Transaction, New Brunswick

Berlan D, Buse K, Shiffman J, Tanaka S (2014) The bit in the middle: a synthesis of global health literature on policy formulation and adoption. Health Policy Plan 29(suppl_3):iii23–iii34

Birkland TA (2016) An introduction to the policy process. Theories, concepts and models of public policy making. Routledge, New York

Brownson RC, Baker EA, Deshpande AD, Gillespie KN (2017) Evidence-based public health. Oxford University Press, Oxford

Cohen MD, March JG, Olsen JP (1972) A garbage can model of organizational choice. Adm Sci Q 17(1):1–25

Colander D, Kupers R (2014) Complexity and the art of public policy. Solving society's problems from the bottom up. Princetown University Press, Princetown

Davies SC, Winpenny E, Ball S, Fowler T, Rubin J, Nolte E (2014) For debate: a new wave in public health improvement. Lancet 384(9957):1889–1895

Dror Y (2001) The capacity to govern. Frank Cass, London

Easton D (1965) A system analysis of political life. Wiley, New York

Embrett MG, Randall GE (2014) Social determinants of health and health equity policy research: exploring the use, misuse, and nonuse of policy analysis theory. Soc Sci Med 108:147–155

Fischer F (2003) Reframing public policy: discursive politics and deliberative practices. Oxford University Press, Oxford

Frenk J, Moon S (2013) Governance challenges in global health. N Engl J Med 368(10):936–942

Gauld R (2009) The new health policy. McGraw-Hill Education, London

Gerston L (2015) Public policy making: process and principles. Routledge, London

Hall P (1993) Policy paradigms, social learning, and the state: the case of economic policymaking in Britain. Comp Polit 25(3):275–296

Hill M (2014) Policy process: a reader. Routledge, New York

Ikeda N, Saito E, Inoue M, Ikeda S, Satoh T, Wada K, Stickley A, Katanoda K, Mizoue T, Noda M, Iso H, Fujino Y, Sobue T, Tsugane S, Naghavi M, Ezatti M, Shibuya K (2011) What has made the population of Japan healthy? Lancet 378(9796):1094–1105

Immergut EM (1992) Health politics: interests and institutions in Western Europe. Cambridge University Press, Cambridge

Jacobsson B, Sundström J (2015) Governing the state. In: Pierre J (ed) The Oxford handbook of Swedish politics. Oxford University Press, Oxford, pp 347–361

Jann W, Wegrich K (2007) Theories of the policy cycle. In: Fischer F, Miller G and M (eds) Handbook of public policy analysis: theory, politics and methods. CRC, Boca Raton, FL, pp 43–62

Klijn EH, Koppenjan J (2016) Governance networks in the public sector. Routledge, London

Kuoppakangas P (2015) Decision-making and choice in the adoption of a municipal enterprise form in public sector healthcare organisations – Reasoning, goals, legitimacy and core dilemmas. Turku School of Economics in the University of Turku, Doctoral dissertation A-9: 2015, Juvenes Print, Turku

Larson MS (1977) The rise of professionalism. University of California Press, Berkeley

Lascoumes P, LeGales P (2007) Introduction: understanding public policy through its instruments—from the nature of instruments to the sociology of public policy instrumentation. Governance 20(1):1–21

Law C (2010) Policy and evidence based public health. In: Looran A, Kelly M (eds) Evidence based policy public health. Oxford University Press, Oxford, pp 16–26

Lindblom C (1965) The intelligence of democracy: decision making through mutual adjustment. The Free Press, New York

Lipsky M (1980) Street-level bureaucracy. Dilemmas of individual in public service. Russell Sage Foundation, New York

Machenbach JP, McKee M (2015) Government, politics and health policy: a quantitative analysis of 30 European countries. Health Policy 119(10):1298–1308

McQeen DV (2010) Ethics and evidence in health promotion. In: Looran A, Kelly M (eds) Evidence based policy public health. Oxford University Press, Oxford, pp 27–42

Miller AR, Tucker C (2014) Health information exchange, system size and information silos. J Health Econ 33:28–42

Mintzberg H, Raisinghani D, Theoret A (1976) The structure of "unstructured" decision processes. Adm Sci Q 21:246–275

Murray E (1971) Politics as symbolic action. Markham, Chicago, IL

Muzio D, Brock DM, Suddaby R (2013) Professions and institutional change: towards an institutionalist sociology of the professions. J Manag Stud 50(5):699–721

Osborne S, Radnon Z, Nasi G (2013) A new theory for public service management? Towards a (public) service-dominant approach. Am Rev Public Adm 43(2):135–158

Pang Z, Zheng L, Tian J, Kao-Walter S, Dubrova E, Chen Q (2015) Design of a terminal solution for integration of in-home health care devices and services towards the internet-of-things. Enterp Inf Syst 9(1):86–116

Pierre J (2011) The politics of urban governance. Palgrave Macmillan, Basingstoke

Pressman JL, Wildavsky AB (1984) Implementation: how great expectations in Washington are dashed in Oakland: or, why it's amazing that federal programs work at all, this being a saga of the Economic Development Administration as told by two sympathetic observers who seek to build morals on a foundation of ruined hopes. University of California Press, Los Angeles

Purtilo RB, Doherty RF (2016) Ethical dimensions in the health professions. Elsevier Health Sciences, Missouri

Ranade W, Hudson B (2003) Conceptual issues in inter-agency collaboration. Local Gov Stud 29 (3):32–50

Rosen G (2015) A history of public health. JHU Press, Baltimore

Scott WR (2013) Institutions and organizations: ideas, interests, and identities. Sage, Los Angeles, CA

Shiba N, Shimokawa H (2008) Chronic heart failure in Japan: implications of the CHART studies. Vasc Health Risk Manag 4(1):103–113

Smith K (2013) Beyond evidence based policy in public health: the interplay of ideas. Palgrave Macmillan, New York

Tenbensel T (2016) Complexity and health policy. In: Geyer R, Cairney P (eds) Complexity and public policy. Edward Elgar, Cheltenham, pp 369–383

Tuurnas S, Stenvall J, Rannisto PH (2015) The impact of co-production on frontline accountability: the case of conciliation service. Int Rev Adm Sci 82:131–149. https://doi.org/10.1177/0020852314566010, first published on July 2, 2015

Virtanen P, Stenvall J (2014) The evolution of public services from co-production to co-creation and beyond – an unfinished trajectory for the New Public Management? Int J Leadersh Public Serv 10(2):91–107

Virtanen P, Uusikylä P (2004) Exploring the missing links between cause and effect. A conceptual framework for understanding micro-macro conversions in programme evaluation. Evaluation 1 (10):77–91

Virtanen P, Kaivo-oja J, Ishino Y, Stenvall J, Jalonen H (2016a) Ubiquitous revolution, customer needs and business intelligence. Empirical evidence from Japanese healthcare sector. Int J Web Eng Technol 11(3):259–283

Virtanen P, Laitinen I, Stenvall J (2016b) Street-level bureaucrats as strategy shapers in social and health service delivery: empirical evidence from six countries. Int Soc Work 16(3):1–14. https://doi.org/10.1177/0020872816660602

Virtanen P, Uusikylä P, Jalava J, Tiihonen S, Laitinen L, Noro K (2016c) Valtioneuvoston yhtenäisyys – kansainvälinen vertaileva tutkimus [available in only in Fiinish, The unity of government – an international comparative study]. Valtioneuvoston kanslia, Helsinki. Accessed at www.tietokauttoon.fi

Weissert WG, Weissert CS (2012) Governing health. The politics of health policy. The Johns Hopkins University Press, Baltimore

Chapter 4
Knowledge Management and the New Configurations of Health Markets

Abstract Throughout this book, we make a strong case for complex society. Complex society is an entity which becomes conceivable by deploying the concepts and methods of complexity theory. In this chapter, we argue that both complex society and complexity theory affect how health policy is formulated and planned, as well as how knowledge management functions are implemented in the field of service ecosystems constituted by public, private and non-governmental healthcare organisations. Organisational knowledge management has attracted considerable attention in recent years in the fields of public policy, public management and health policy in particular. Nonetheless, there are few widely shared views according to which the term itself is defined, much less a consensus on how best to apply it in healthcare service delivery. In this chapter, the role of organisational knowledge is explored (by making a distinction, for instance, between the use and exchange value of information). This chapter discusses how to manage knowledge internally and externally in order to achieve organisational success in healthcare services. We propose that intelligent knowledge leadership has to address how health organisations and service systems overcome their fundamental knowledge problems, and these problems have to be approached from the service-user point of view. Until this problem—and the constitution of two-dimensional horizontal accountability addressing the collaboration of service providers and the value produced for the service users addressed in the upcoming chapters in this book— is explored and defined, organisations run the risk of addressing the symptoms rather than the causes. Since we live in an age of a complex society and complex public policies, uncertainty refers to a lack of information.

4.1 The Nexus Between Complex Society, Complexity Science and Complex Knowledge

The overall purpose of this chapter is to define the new landscape of knowledge management in the field of health—to explore how evolving complexity and service ecosystems change the demand and supply of knowledge in planning policies and delivering services. The ongoing digitalisation of society affects knowledge management thinking, mechanisms and practices. Our arguments are based on the assumption that knowledge is a critical organisational resource

© Springer International Publishing AG 2018
P. Virtanen, J. Stenvall, *Intelligent Health Policy*,
https://doi.org/10.1007/978-3-319-69596-9_4

irrespective of economic sector or type of organisation. It is the essence of leadership—both at the policy and service system levels. We think that it is difficult, if not impossible, to maximise the value of this resource without an adequate understanding of how to influence and share knowledge throughout the web of public policies and service-providing organisations.

Organisational knowledge is relative, contextual and based on relations within organisational systems. This means that organisational knowledge is not absolute in the sense that it is based on multiple variations of information and data—each of them bringing about different interpretations of an organisation's functions, performance, merit and legitimacy. Contextual refers here to the fact that organisational knowledge should be constituted, defined and also contested within organisational frameworks, which means serious trouble for those who think that organisational knowledge is generic and thus transferable directly from one context to another. Relationships matter in the formulation of organisational knowledge because knowledge is created and interpreted in relationships between organisational actors.

In terms of management theory, the above-mentioned commitment to relative, contextual and relation-based organisational knowledge is not a novel or unique insight. One example of this is provided by Mary Parker Follett, a management prophet of the 1920s, who advocated the role of organisational relationships and applied general systems theory in making sense of the organisational life. Her ideas about the dynamic nature of organisational processes are well-suited to the world of organisational knowledge in complex society and complex organisations (e.g. Graham 1996).

Our book looks upon public policies from the framework of complexity science. This means that public policy making in the field of health should be seen as complex, not linear, processes. It also means—to elaborate the definitions put forward by Johnson (2016: 150–151)—a shift from a simple policy system to complicated policy and beyond to a complex policy domain. The differences between a linear and complex way of policy making are profound—they concern the nature of policy making, the context of policy making and initial conditions that affect policy process—to mention a couple of definite differences in the thinking modes of these policy-approach varieties.

The complexity model, which views government and public institutions as self-organising entities which implement emerging and complex policies countered by entropic tendencies towards chaotic policy disorder, is based on complex human and agency-driven relationships with different and often unspoken agendas, paving the way for non-rationalistic policy delivery acknowledging the futility of pro forma, pre-justified and pre-planned rational generic policy implementation (e.g. Givel 2016).

This complexity framework affects the role of knowledge in public policy making. The task of knowledge management is to provide data and information from the real-world universe of public policies—to makes sure that the decision-makers are provided with necessary information for their decisions. The role of knowledge is of particular importance here—i.e. there is the question how truthful information is or, alternatively, what kind of alternative truths exist and how they are fed into the decision-making process. This is not say that alternative truths are lies per se, but they are alternative in the sense that they provide different points of view, angles or emphasis to the societal phenomena they ought to describe.

The essence of knowledge management in healthcare is social learning. Without it, knowledge management practices are not very useful. Our view on social learning comes very close to that of Paquet (1999: 13); for him, the learning economy within public policies is the source of wealth creation, and it is rooted in the social and collective mobilisation of knowledge. That means that organisational learning harnesses the collective intelligence of the policy planners and decision-makers as a source of continuous improvement. That being said, the field of health constitutes a learning community, which is both adaptive and foresight-driven. This is possible only if learning occurs in the form of interaction by relevant stakeholders. Openness and access to information are the keywords and concepts in this algorithm. Social learning is policy- and organisation-based and derives its origins from human interaction.

Commitment on complexity brings about profound and pervasive challenges to traditional knowledge management practices in health policy and healthcare services. It also affects policy making. This is because complexity theory's point of departure is reductionism—an attempt to break down an object of public policy into its subordinate components (e.g. Sanderson 2006). From the point of view of complexity theory, this kind of reductionism is not only fatally flawed because complex policy systems are always bigger and multifaceted than the sum of its parts, but it also provides a limited understanding of reality in the domain of public policy making.

In practice, this dilemma entails that health policy is looked upon only within the conventional frames and boundaries and not in relation to other policy fields—or vis-á-vis emerging nexus or wicked problems. Another problem relates to the fact that public policies are usually path-dependent, meaning that previous policy decisions affect current and future policy making. Policy making is also affected in the field of health in many ways because of complexity, especially in terms of how quick a policy is. Peck and Theodore (2015: 224–225) have advocated for faster public policies—i.e. acknowledging the increasing reflexivity and porosity of policy making, adding further emphasis on cross-boundary debates and dialogues, allowing free access to information about service best practices and foreshortening of planning and development cycles.

Some complexity scholars, e.g. Little (2016) and Flyvbjerg (2001), have underlined that knowledge formulation in complex society calls for a unique connection in the analysis of general complexity (of health policy matters) with an account of real politics, which in fact means the (re-)emergence of the Aristotelian concept of *phronesis*. It means to attempt to enhance socially relevant forms of knowledge, conceived as 'practical wisdom', on how to address and act on social problems in a particular public policy or organisational context. This leads us to think about the knowledge base of the decision-makers in the field of health and to problematise the contents of knowledge upon which the health policy decisions are actually made.

We should therefore ask more precisely: how does complexity theory help us in public health policy making in a truly complex and somewhat complicated world, where politics seem to be affected by all sorts of prejudices, misunderstandings, pure manipulation or alternatively 'alternative truths'? In short, the complexity approach helps to alleviate policy planning problems, since it makes visible the different time frames and scales in planning policies (and also pinpoints various policy options and scenario possibilities). Sanderson (2009) makes explicit (and it is easy to agree with him) that this kind of positioning in public policy constitutes a move from simplified rationalistic, closed-system anchored and evidence-based policy making towards more intelligent policy making that contains a review of ideas that underpin policy planners' and decision-makers' thinking about the evidence-based policies and the emergence of knowledge about complex adaptive policy systems. The complexity approach means bringing bad news for 'hard-nosed' enthusiasts of evidence-based policy and randomised controlled trials, since the capture of societal phenomena does not occur in straightforward methods and approaches that are not aligned with complex and agency-crowded policy ecosystems.

The field of health has provided a fertile source of analysis from the complexity theory point of view since the late 1990s (e.g. Kernick 2004; Tenbensel 2016). One good example of adopting the complexity approach to the planning of health interventions is offered by Gray (2016), who deploys complexity methods to planning for a pandemic. In terms of health policy, complexity thinking has proved to be useful both at the macro level of analysis (health or health-related policies as part of the policy system) and at the micro level of analysis [patients' behaviour in using health services, choosing between different service providers, assessing the quality of health services provided to them, boundaries between healthcare service staff and service users (e.g. Virtanen et al. 2016b)]. In Hunter's (2003) terminology, macro- and micro-level implications refer to the 'upstream' health policy (policy formulation, policy planning and budgeting, evaluation of policies, etc.), whereas the 'downstream' health policy concerns the policy delivery of health objectives (such as the actions taken by healthcare organisations, resource allocations in-between healthcare service providers, regulation of health policies, deployment of healthcare-related legislation and so on).

Complex society does not only affect the way in which public health policies and healthcare organisations formulate their knowledge for decision-making, it also affects the adaptive capacity of policy makers and public organisations. Therefore, we see an essential link between knowledge management and the role of the adaptive capacity of public policies and public organisations. We maintain (following Nohrstedt 2016; Staber and Sydow 2002; Argyris 2010) that adaptive capacity is a dynamic organisational and individual process of continuous learning and adjustment that permits ambiguity, complexity and unlearning. In Pacquet's (1999: 187) words, 'organizational learning is, therefore, not only adaptive learning, i.e. about copying, it is also generative learning, i.e. about creating, adjusting goals, norms, and assumptions as required'. Therefore the message is: do not copy, but take into account as much as you can and develop further.

We would like to add the *change* aspect to this definition of adaptive capacity, which emphasises the role of organisational knowledge and foresight. In terms of enhancing adaptive change capacity in current, and particularly future, healthcare organisations, three aspects are paramount—(a) diversity (inclusion of all relevant stakeholders in the strategy and delivery process, including also patients), (b) opportunity for interaction (access to forums for face-to-face dialogue) and (c) the deployment of methods selection (capacity and insight to weigh opportunities and to eliminate ineffective strategies and processes).

These prerequisites are not self-evident in the field of health, which is a field of action stuffed with different professions and organisational barriers and which sometimes lacks strategic and leadership capacity due to changing political agendas, pressure from civil society and an overall lack of resources to meet the demand of health services per se. One important barrier to the application of complexity theory in the field of health is fixed ideas about the number of possible solutions to certain severe health problems. For instance, Gray (2016: 396–397) argues that there are a number of vested interests that would like us to believe that there are only simple solutions available to health problems—particularly in the pharmaceutical industry. We believe that strong health professions can be added to this list.

4.2   How Rational Is Public Policy Decision-Making?

The steering of public policies and the governance of public finances are key elements in public decision-making. Academic and semi-academic textbooks usually make a distinction between policy analysis, policy planning, policy delivery and policy evaluation. In this book, we cut the corners a bit and argue that these aspects are subprocesses in something we call 'public policy steering'. However, it is very important to understand that these subprocesses are interlinked, and it is actually public policy decision-making that binds together these subordinate elements of public policy steering.

Decision-making—in different sections of public policy steering—is based on the information provided by public policy delivery and public funds spent during the delivery. This relates to what has been achieved during the policy delivery and how these effects and outcomes relate to the objectives set prior to the policy.

Academic textbooks often make another kind of distinction. Public policy planning and decision-making are looked at separately from public policy delivery. Figure 4.1 indicates a simple setting based on Browne and Wildavsky (1984), who analyse public policy decision-making vis-á-vis policy delivery. Browne and Wildavsky (1984) suggest that both public policy decision-making and policy delivery can be either bad or good. This, of course, greatly simplifies reality, but it nevertheless opens up four possible categories for managing public policies. Decision-making is good if decisions are based on reliable and valid information and if decisions are made at the right place at the right time. Alternatively,

Decision making

Fig. 4.1 The relation between public decision-making and policy delivery (Adopted from Browne and Wildavsky 1984)

decision-making can be poor if the information provided to decision-makers is of no use—time-wise or topic-wise—or if the decision-makers are unable or unwilling to make the necessary decisions.

According to Browne and Wildavsky (1984), public policy implementation can be either good or bad. Policy implementation is normally considered to be of good quality if the implementation of the public policy achieves its set goals, if its implementation achieves something else important in the domain of the policy (and the goals of the policy are updated accordingly during the delivery process) and if the policy delivery successfully meets the set timetable and manages to meet the objectives with the allocated resources allocated during the planning phase. Alternatively, the policy delivery is bad if the delivery mechanism of the policy does not meet the policy objectives, if the timetable objectives are not met or if the delivery consumes more public resources than planned.

Figure 4.1 makes explicit the ideal type of public policy decision-making and public policy implementation. If public policy related decision-making and policy implementation are both 'good', then running public policies occurs without problems—at least, they are not identified and verified. However, we suggest that policy makers should always be conscious of the implications of a complex society. If policy problems are not detected, it does not mean that they don't exist. A control problem arises when reasonable and consensus-based policy decisions are not converted into action through policy delivery mechanisms. This may be caused by multiple reasons, such as lack of capacity in programme and project leadership, inadequate human and economic resources, rapid changes in the operating environment (e.g. refugee waves over Europe during 2015–2016), a lack of commitment by stakeholders and so on. Another possible explanation is that the public policy goals and objectives are too ambitious and there are no possible policy instruments to be mobilised for them.

Policy problems can also be caused by bad decision-making. The government may be 'paralysed' because of decision-making capacity or by the huge amount of issues of its agenda. In this case, good policy implementation does not help if decisions are lacking or if they are not reasonable. Political issues can also be very political in the sense that decisions are very hard to make. In the field of help, a plethora of examples from this prevail. For example, consider the problems with smoking vis-á-vis taking into account the business interests of the tobacco industry. Perhaps the most problematic juxtaposition occurs when public policy decision-making is good but the implementation mechanism functions badly. This constellation leads without exception to the wasting of human and economic resources, which is always a problem from the accountability point of view.

Overall, we would like to remind our readers that understanding public policy implementation requires an understanding of theories on how decisions are made in public policy and public organisations. We think that decision-making theories have been a very important field of scientific treatise as far as the evolution of organisational theory is concerned. To simplify a bit, decision-making theories have brought about an interesting ingredient to the general understanding about organisations in fact because in practice nothing happens in organisations—not in healthcare organisations or anywhere else—if somebody does something. This 'doing something' requires decision-making since 'doing' follows decisions if we think about this matter conceptually.

To avoid a lengthy academic discussion about the different types of decision-making theories, we would like to conceptually divide decision-making theories into two main categories: (a) *rational decision-making models* (based on the idea that policy options are well-articulated and the decisions are grounded on scientific or quasi-scientific evidence) and (b) *models that are based on bounded rationality* (which, for instance, deals with questions of decision-makers' overall capacity and the limits of reliable evidence in decision-making).

To echo Dror (1964, 1968), complete rationality in decision-making refers to a situation in which political aims, societal values and public policy goals are addressed in a consensual manner. If this is the case, the domain of public policy making is about choosing the most appropriate means to achieve the goals of the public policy. Dror (1964, 1968) also emphasised the meaning of feelings in the process of organisational decision-making. According to Dror, subconscious aspects of human mind are always present in decision-making, and it not only affects how decisions are made as an interactive process but also affects contents of the decisions. He also stressed the fact that context of decision-making varies a lot. Take, for instance, the role of different crises in decision-making, which implies that decisions have to be made very fast and without thorough information about the issue to be decided on.

The idea of complete rationality in decision-making raised considerable criticism from the policy and social science point of view from 1950 onwards. This criticism was based on the idea that decision-making is inherently irrational.

Bounded rationality (as the critics labelled this approach) is built on the idea that the rationality of decision-making was contested by the fact that knowledge resources for decision-making are always limited and that there are too many decisions to be made vis-á-vis the reliable and valid information available (e.g. Simon 1955, 1972, 1978; March 1978, 1987, 1994).

However, the peak in criticism against the rational decision-making model was reached in the writings of Braybrooke and Lindblom in the beginning of the 1960s (e.g. Braybrooke and Lindblom 1963). According to them, the most obvious limitation of rationality came from the fact that the cognitive and processual capacity of humans to deal with a plethora of issues in the decision-making agenda is limited. Moreover, they criticised the limitations of the information itself. According to them, decision-making situations are so plentiful that there simply is not enough evidence for each and every decision to be made. Braybrooke and Lindblom (1963) therefore underlined that decision-making is always incremental—i.e. it takes places step by step, as a process continuum. As this was the case, Braybrooke and Lindblom advocated the idea that decision-making is always path-dependent one way or another and decision-making usually was determined by the usefulness of the available policy measures and tools. Their viewpoint is of course rather contradictory because it means that policy tools determine public policy goals and objectives.

The irrationalities of public policy decision-making joined up with the limits of decision-making rationality—with the belief that knowledge and rational wisdom are supreme powers during the moment decisions are made. Put forward by March (1987, 1994) and Cohen et al. (1972, 2012) in particular, the garbage can model of decision-making implies a lot semantically about the practical limits of rational decision-making. According to this conceptual model, decisions are more or less always made in a chaotic setting, where decision-makers are in a hurry and have to react very quickly. This resembles a kind of organised anarchy in the sense that organisational conditions make decisions difficult to make because the cause and the presumed effect of the given decision are either hard to foresee or is overall very unclear. The garbage can model then refers to the metaphor where decision-makers bring into decision-making 'moments' or 'forums' not only the appropriate information and knowledge but also their personal preferences, incompetence and possibilities to choose from various options and values. In the following section, we will discuss in more detail the role and the possibilities of public decision-making in an era that has been recently labelled an era of alternative truths or post-truth policies.

4.3 Public Policies and Alternative Truths Have Been Siblings for Ages

We are sorry to throw a wet blanket on the face of those who (still) believe that public policies—and health policies in particular—are solely based on knowledge-based architectures, data-driven decision-making or high-class data collation, analysis and reporting. This is due to the many uncertainties that prevail in the field of health in addition to the fact that the world has changed dramatically during the last decades. The truth is out there, which in this case means that the role of knowledge—and knowledge management practices in formulating health policy and in the delivery of healthcare services for that matter—is highly contested today.

Just think about the public discussion about climate change. It seems that despite a plethora of scientific evidence, there still are political leaders who consider the idea of climate change as a political fraud and manipulation. (As an example, just search 'climate change evidence' in Google Scholar and see how many 'hits' you get? On Monday 2.1.2017, the number was 116,000!)

The government of President Donald Trump in the USA and the British referendum approving the withdrawal from the European Union ('Brexit') have led to a public discussion of alternative truths. Consequently, 'alternative truth' has a malevolent connotation. It refers to the manipulation of facts, the deployment of opinion-building, pure lying and twisting the arguments as well as using counter-arguments in public debates, which are not rational or evidence-based. According to our view in this book, alternative truth is a necessary concept since it makes explicit what knowledge management scholars have known for at least 40 years.

Policy makers make decisions based on different facts and knowledge and not based on absolute truth provided to them in the policy analysis phase of policy planning and delivery. Coined with Cohen, March and Olsen, this decision-making mechanism in public policy has been called a garbage can model underlining the limited role of knowledge (and science for that matter) in decision-making. Cohen et al. became famous by maintaining that organisations are in essence organisational anarchies which are naturally characterised by problematic preferences, unclear technologies and fluid participation (e.g. Cohen et al. 1972, 2012). Thus, the idea of alternative truths is not a novel thing in public policy making—rather it is a fact and a tested theory which have been there for almost half a century.

Our view on alternative truths in health policy builds upon the idea put forward by Wildavsky (1979), who advocated the view that policy analysis rests upon a variety of different forms of knowledge. We sympathise with this view and we develop Wildavsky's idea further by arguing that healthcare service users constitute a unique agency in the current (and especially in future) health policy making and healthcare service delivery.

Patients, service users or consumers—regardless of what we call people who use healthcare services—are important knowledge formulators and providers since we foresee the future trend of healthcare increasingly becoming a knowledge-based service industry. This is due to the ongoing medical–technical progress in medicine, innovations, emergent technologies and nanotechnology in particular, as well as the personalisation of healthcare processes and the plethora of e-health services already available today. (See also Ewert and Evers 2012: 64–65.)

In the next section, we focus on knowledge management from the perspective of changing healthcare market dynamics and the pervasive nature of technology. Our analysis builds upon and further develops our current research (see Wallin et al. 2017) on the future role of knowledge management mechanisms in the health sector, as overarching digitalisation is shaping policy making, service delivery strategies, organisational business models, service markets and ecosystems in the most profound ways. In our analysis, we strongly believe that the digitalisation of services and policy planning and decision-making is a fundamental driver of health policy (Yeh et al. 2006).

Additionally, we think it is absolutely necessary to rethink the theoretical foundations of organisational knowledge management. In fact, this is necessary because organisations themselves change dramatically. Conceptually speaking, as single organisations transform into more nuanced service platforms and service ecosystems, knowledge management must also be theorised accordingly. From this point of view, our theoretical foundation is the recent integration of traditional knowledge management theory with the notion of dynamic capabilities, emphasising fractal structures and socialisation with customers for knowledge creation (Nonaka et al. 2016).

4.4   The Changing Landscape of Knowledge in the Field of Health

Next, we will discuss—based on our current research on the topic (see Wallin et al. 2017)—the three fundamental changes affecting the field of health due to digitalisation and challenging the role of knowledge deployed in policy analysis and policy making as well as service delivery: the redefinition of markets, the reallocation of resources and the reinterpretation of business logic.

Firstly, there is *the redefinition of the health market that is underway, and it profoundly affects the role healthcare professionals and knowledge management practices in healthcare services.* Health has traditionally been perceived from the perspective of healthcare, implying that the focus has been on how care professionals can support citizens once their state of health has deteriorated. Until now we have not been accustomed to the idea that a top-down regulated health system, the compliance with the advice of medical doctors and the rather isolated patterns of person-to-person interaction (classical doctor–patient constellation) can be contested or criticised from outside the healthcare professionals' box. Healthcare professionals are stepping down from the temples of medical wisdom and paternalistic mindset when deciding on the treatment instead of the patients, which gives patients more freedom—and responsibility—for mobilising health resources at their disposal in co-production and decision-making in the field of health.

Traditional views on healthcare service delivery have largely formed our implicit notion of the health market, which has been preoccupied with how to get the best possible result out of the work provided by the healthcare professionals—the more efficient and productive, the better. The problem has been that what has been won in the race for high-level productivity, the same has been probably been lost from the perspective of healthcare interventions and their effectiveness.

There have been attempts to also address the issue of health in a preventive way through various forms—e.g. through campaigns against obesity, encouraging people to exercise more in gyms and take up sports as a hobby, limitations on sugar consumption at schools and restrictions on the sale of tobacco and alcohol in many countries. These attempts have been rightly addressed but their effects rather poor until this new constellation constituted by healthcare professionals and service users are co-producing services together. We think that the most profound change now taking place in preventive health is the opportunity for the individual to take more responsibility for his or her own health—thanks to digitalisation. This is also transforming the field of health from being predominately focused on healthcare to becoming increasingly preoccupied by well-being. Moreover, at the same time, there is a shift from a producer perspective to a customer perspective.

We are just in the very beginning of this transition, but we can see that the field of health is undergoing a major shift due to the opportunities offered by big data, cloud computing, artificial intelligence, robotics, mobility, social media and the digitalisation of services and industries. As we have been advocating in this book, digitalisation changes both the supply and demand for health services. For example, we foresee that smart machines and the Internet of Things in the future can do things that previously seemed unique to people, and service automation will evolve from the realm of robotic process automation towards the realm of cognitive automation. The world of health policy will most definitely not be the same anymore. For public, private and third-sector organisations involved in the field of health, this implies considerable threats, but also major business opportunities.

This transformation will most definitely mean—particularly from the perspective of healthcare ecosystems at the local and regional levels of governance—that concepts such as co-production, co-management and co-governance will emerge as future top leadership concepts in the field of health. Co-production refers to an arrangement where health services are provided by professionals and service users, with both actively participating in the service delivery. Co-management then is about an arrangement in which public, private and third-sector organisations work together in cooperation to deliver the best possible service for the service users. Co-governance reflects the idea and arrangement of public, private and third-sector institutions and organisations working together during the various phases of public health policy analysis, planning and evaluating the outcomes of the adopted policies (Pestoff 2012: 18–19).

The effects of the redefining of the healthcare market are already visible today. Well-being is now the framework for supporting a rapidly growing market for diets and healthy food as well as healthcare digital devices and sensors. The new 'well-being market' is now the target for technology companies offering products like the

Apple Watch and Fitbit for health-conscious customers. Through these new technologies, there is suddenly much more information available about the state of a person's health.

To summarise, the marketisation of healthcare is actually about promoting healthcare as a 'consumer good'—to deploy the terminology of Ewert and Evers (2012: 65)—which accelerates competition between service providers and service users' choice within the future healthcare system. Consequently, this affects how the health market is evolving and expanding, and this happens rapidly. This in turn radically changes the role of patients. They become customers, implying consumer behaviour which aims at making the right choices in the emergent health service space and among competing service providers. All of this is a transformation process that raises the importance of knowledge and knowledge management. It concerns not only health policy planners and decision-makers but also healthcare service providers and service users as 'customers'.

Secondly, there is *the overall economisation of the healthcare and the reallocation of resources designated to health policy and healthcare services,* which increases the demand of knowledge to a level never before experienced. This view holds that the economic aspects of healthcare have been underlined and addressed in vain in the previous and ongoing fiscal constraints of public policies and political decision-making throughout the OECD countries. But this is only one aspect of the economisation of healthcare. There is also another aspect, one related to the reallocation of healthcare resources and—to be more precise—to the rethinking of the idea of value creation in the field of health, taking into account a new conceptual understanding of individual and collective well-being previously discussed in Chap. 2.

The increased theoretical discussion and practical focus on well-being makes explicit the role of the citizen as a co-producer of value. Value creation is not unique in business studies and business operations and not even in 'performance-tuned' healthcare management (e.g. Nordgren 2009). As another example, Porter (2010) states that

> ...achieving high value for patients must become the overarching goal of health care delivery, with value defined as the health outcomes achieved per dollar spent. This goal is what matters for patients and unites the interests of all actors in the system. If value improves, patients, payers, providers, and suppliers can all benefit while the economic sustainability of the healthcare system increases...

Our approach to value creation in healthcare is based on a relational framework for value co-creation. This means that value is the perceived utility derived from the use of the value proposition. Accordingly, 'value creation' does not happen in isolation; it is created when the value beneficiary accepts the value propositions offered by the value provider and when the value creation is based on an upgraded version of subjective well-being.

Our treatise (discussed in detail in Wallin et al. 2017) of value in healthcare thus indicates that value is co-created in exchange processes in which different partners interact with others without an explicit division between value providers and value beneficiaries. Co-created value does not apply only on the level of the individual transaction or service but to the more profound question of how markets and ecosystems are co-created, constructed, managed and governed. Subsequently healthcare service providers from different sectors—public, private and non-governmental—need to consider how the increased importance of citizen and service-user engagement in the future can be channelled to advance the quality, access and efficiency of services, but also to provide ways to constantly develop and improve the whole service system.

We foresee a tremendous transformation in the role of service user in healthcare in the future. This transformation is about a shift from a passive recipient of health services towards a more active co-producer of healthcare interventions, both subjective and collective. In fact, we definitely think that there is massive potential in increasing activities of the citizens and service users, for instance, in preventive health and well-being activities which offer new possibilities to improve the overall efficiency and quality of health systems.

Bearing in mind that digitalisation enables service users to increasingly take charge of the various services and technologies contributing to their well-being, service users can also more and more become the orchestrator of their own well-being ecosystem. Without exaggeration, we could therefore say that service users will soon be the key resources in the whole healthcare service ecosystem. This also casts huge demands on the knowledge management practices of healthcare service organisations. The question is: how is this new value creation and the new role of the service user taken into account when service providers in the field of health plan deliver their services?

Thirdly, *the reallocation of healthcare resources is underway, which will eventually create the need to rethink the business logic in the field of health.* As we maintained in Chap. 2, the concept of health is a rather elusive, elastic and evolving concept, and it is moving towards a more comprehensive concept of well-being. Well-being underlines subjective aspects of health and brings into the picture the active citizen as a service user.

Conceptualised from a service science point of view (e.g. Vargo and Lusch 2015), well-being implies a customer-centric perspective, which is different from the producer-centric view of healthcare. This proposition suggests that there is a need for a more comprehensive understanding of how value and knowledge is co-created with and for the service user. This means that resources and assets that must be mobilised for the benefit and use of the service user do not originate from one single healthcare organisation at a single point in time, but there is a need for the simultaneous efforts of multiple service providers to offer an integrated flow of well-being-enhancing inputs to the life of the service user. This is the essence of the service and ICT integration when we try to look at the matter from the perspective of the service user. Integrated service constitutes a service path for the service user, and this relates to how knowledge and resource flows are measured, allocated and evaluated (e.g. Cameron et al. 2014; Fisher and Elnitsky 2012; Lyngsø et al. 2014; Virtanen et al. 2017a, b). We assume that the configuration of the value-creating system becomes customer-centric, dynamic and systemic. The need to find better ways to match the resources with the needs of the individual customer makes orchestration a central activity in the field of health. At the same time, it also underlines the needs for complimentary roles and capabilities to be mobilised in the orchestration process.

To summarise, the business logic landscape of healthcare is on the move. Knowledge management mechanisms with regard to health policy and related to healthcare service systems are thus challenged from multiple angles. In addition to the new kinds of knowledge needs from the decision-makers' and healthcare managers' point of view, we would like to emphasise the data, information and knowledge needs of the service users. In order to be active and participating service users, knowledge definitely becomes an asset—knowledge about service options, service costs, service access and service prices, just to mention a few examples. This means that the domain of healthcare knowledge management will be enlarged to the next agency level, comprised of service users and citizens. This process goes very well in hand with the transformation shift from vertical to horizontal accountability.

4.5 Sense-Making in Health Policy and Healthcare Organisations

We have tried to convince our readers that information and knowledge are not always the basic premises of public policy making in the health domain. Moreover, we have tried to outline—albeit briefly—the change in the logic of the health market. Next we discuss the role of knowledge creation at the level of healthcare organisations. Organisational 'knowing about things' is, by definition, about data, information and knowledge. In this algorithm, data is raw material about what organisations gather, information is about how they have managed to combine data from different sources and knowledge is about how they are able to make sense of this information.

Knowledge management and combining pieces of information in sequence (which makes sense from the point of leadership) is about knowledge integration. Knowledge integration and sense-making are essential parts of management systems and require what Stenvall and Virtanen (2015) and Virtanen and Vakkuri (2015) have described as organisational intelligence. The key ingredients of organisational intelligence derive their origin from a customer-driven organisational culture, knowledge-based decision-making, visionary leadership throughout the organisation and an understanding of accountability focused on the service users.

Based on our understanding, organisational sense-making in intelligent healthcare organisations—and of course, at the level of health policy—should be anticipatory, reflexive, inclusive and responsive.

Anticipatory sense-making refers to diagnostic and prospective competence and the capacity of the healthcare managers, health policy planners and decision-makers. Health is a good example of a policy field where difficulties exist to develop substantive diagnoses and correspondingly good prospects or figurations for the future. This is due to many reasons, mainly related to difficulties in judging the health impacts of certain human behaviour and the lack of competencies to foresee future trends on how people behave in relation to choices for a presumed healthy life. Moreover, there seems to be a lack of knowledge and understanding on how to realise the potential of technology and digitalisation in general in relation to desired societal development and health-related policy goals.

Reflexive sense-making involves deploying healthcare expertise and capacity with a different kind of expertise (e.g. sociological, ecological, management science, cultural, technological) to better identify and discuss prerequisites for research, innovation and service delivery activities, bearing in mind the emergent role of service users. Service ecosystems flourish only if communication and cooperation exist. A greater degree of organisational sense-making reflexivity is vital in order to provide directionality in the delivery of healthcare services as well as in innovation processes aimed at renewing service models and designs.

Inclusive sense-making is synonymous with interactive dialogue. This view holds that sense-making is a joint venture—at its best, healthcare professionals, managers, local-level stakeholders and service users working together. The informative, explanatory monologue by healthcare professionals has been replaced by social dialogue. After a period of seeking to develop various types of dialogue mechanisms, such as service-user or stakeholder juries, lay public conferences, consensus conferences and focus groups to 'enable society to speak about how to deliver healthcare services', attention is now increasingly being directed towards the healthcare organisations and their environments themselves. What is addressed here is the fact that new communication and interaction skills needed to open up healthcare service processes and service design options recognise the limits of one's own knowledge and competence and the ability to ask for help in dealing with the potentially landscape-changing effects of these processes.

Responsive sense-making entails the development of horizontal or distributed governance schemes and forums that encourage collaboration with partners (health policy-related, social partners, political decision-makers, lobby groups, and non-governmental organisations) that are involved in policy making in the field of health or in healthcare service delivery. We are convinced that there is a need to open up different perspectives relating to dilemmas and irreducible uncertainty with health policy-related issues. This must take place through broad-based involvement, not only on the part of healthcare professionals from different professions but also by bringing on board policy actors, including political decision-makers, representatives of service users, media, the health industry, relevant non-governmental and interest organisations and society at large.

We have previously researched the role of knowledge and knowledge management in the field of health in the framework of digitalised society (e.g. Kaivo-oja et al. 2015, 2016). Our main conclusion from our previous work has been that besides knowledge integration in the organisational context, sense-making from collated or accumulated knowledge also calls for new theoretical and conceptual thinking. In this book, we maintain the view that traditional and classical models of organisational knowledge creation are in a state of transformation due to the transformation of healthcare organisations towards more service ecosystems consisting of multiple healthcare organisations rather than single organisational entities. This results in the need for organisations to make sense of their operating environment and their contribution in a web of organisations working and cooperating together as well as competing with each other.

Consequently, the need to rethink the idea of organisational knowledge management also concerns Nonaka's and Takeuchi's (1995) popular theory of knowledge creation, the so-called SECI model (socialisation, externalisation, combination, internalisation), which introduced concepts such as tacit and explicit knowledge (see Nonaka 1991, 1994; Nonaka et al. 2014). In our previous research (Kaivo-oja et al. 2016), we criticised the SECI model because it does not cover organisational systems thinking and the role of certain key challenges of digitalised society, such as social media, ubiquitous interfaces, socialisation with robots, the open innovation paradigm, cultural openness and curiosity, crowdsourcing techniques, enabling wireless networks, big data, machine-to-machine communication, digitalisation skills, improved customer insight and best practices in cybersecurity. (For further criticism of Nonaka's and Takeuchi's SECI model, see Becerra-Fernandez and Sabherwal 2001.)

In this book, we have advocated the idea that single organisations are transforming into service ecosystems that exist in the so-called service space. Our theoretical and conceptual model of organisations come very close to the ideas about how Nonaka et al. (2014) developed and upgraded their SECI model of organisational knowledge creation. Nonaka et al. (2014) have updated their model, based on criticism, by introducing a conceptual entity called the dynamic fractal organisation. According to them, dynamic fractal organisations build and utilise a triad relationship of knowledge that integrates and synthesises *tacit* and *explicit* knowledge across organisational boundaries and creates a third type of knowledge, *phronesis*. The triad relationship is an upward spiral process of converting tacit and explicit knowledge and propels sustainable knowledge transformation across the diverse boundaries within and between organisations and their environment.

The basic idea of the fractal organisation is actually a web of organisations that consists of interlinked organisations whose boundaries are blurry or even non-existent—at least compared to how we used to think about organisational boundaries. Fractal organisations form configurations and reconfigurations depending on the angle from which you view them. This causes enormous challenges, not only for knowledge management but also for leadership and management. Take, for example, the leading competencies. Fractal organisation leaders think that it would be useless to run a competence development programme within one public healthcare organisation. Instead they think that it would highly useful and appropriate to have a competence development plan for the personnel concerning the whole service ecosystem, regardless of the traditional organisational boundaries.

4.6 Digitalisation, Health and Organisational Knowledge

Societal complexity and organisational knowledge—how data is collated, analysed and processed from the perspective of organisational decision-making—are closely intertwined. Let us theorise this connection next.

Our starting point relates to the fact that business diagnostics and analytics increase organisational adaptiveness. By diagnostics and analytics, we mean—echoing Davenport and Harris (2007: 7–8)—the extensive use of data, statistical and quantitative analysis, explanatory and predictive models, qualitative narratives and overall fact-based management for driving public policy-related and organisational decisions and actions. For decades, there has been growing interest in enhancing organisational analytics and business intelligence to maximise organisational adaptiveness in competition. This has happened in a variety of industries, such as consumer products, financial services, hospitality and entertainment, industrial products, pharmaceuticals, retail, telecommunications, transport, ecommerce and health (Davenport and Harris 2007).

From our previous research (Kaivo-oja et al. 2015, 2016), we have learned that public policy-related complexity and organisational complexity cannot be reduced by increasing data and information because complexity arises from the intricacy and connectivity of various elements and entities. Analytics and diagnostics are the key elements in this—instead of adding information, analytics and diagnostic procedures should be strengthened. This is because current 'knowledge problems' in the field of health are increasingly complex and nuanced. The problems faced by healthcare organisations include many potential and interrelated variables, solutions, options and methods.

Complex problems are tricky to solve because they can be addressed in multiple ways. And the complexity of the society involved is not absolute. Therefore, we have proposed in Kaivo-oja et al. (2015, 2016) two approaches to manage complex knowledge problems: one that focusses on the organisation's knowledge capabilities and the other that addresses the decomposition of complexity. Both approaches create the essence of future knowledge management and sense-making practices in the field of healthcare, and both of these approaches can be supported by digitalisation.

By definition, the contents of organisational knowledge capabilities are based on routines that maintain, promote and update the organisation members' ability to locate and analyse data that is important one way or another for organisational success. Organisational knowledge capacities thus concern both formal and informal processes with data collation and analysis. Knowledge capacities have both individual and collective connotations since they can be approached from both perspectives—which are, in essence, profoundly interlinked, as Nonaka and Takeuchi (1995) have stressed already in the 1990s.

Nonaka et al. (2016) have recently emphasised that the dynamic capabilities, framework and the organisational knowledge creation theory represent complementary approaches. They argue that that dynamic capabilities stem from team-level interactions among individuals rather than from individual cognitive capacities. We agree with Nonaka et al. (2016) that there is an important role to be played by the 'meso-level' and that top management alone has great difficulties to seize sensed opportunities and transform organisational capabilities through asset orchestration. However, in the health sector, the unit of analysis is no longer the single enterprise but rather the ecosystem consisting of a variety of organisational types. This suggests that the notions of top and bottom need to be replaced by centralised and decentralised. This enables us to avoid organisation-specific categorisations and base the analysis and recommendations on activities that are co-produced, and increasingly so with the participation of many actors, including customers.

The decomposition of complexity, then, rests on the restructuring, reconfiguration and redefining of complex healthcare service problems to resemble something more understandable. The 'direction' of conceptual analysis is important here, as we emphasised earlier in this chapter. Complex problems are better understood and solved when analysed from a wider societal perspective. This means that reductionism is not of much help in these kinds of organisational analyses and diagnostics. On the contrary, if a reductionist mindset is predominant in organisational sense-making, then many of the wicked and nexus health problems remain subliminal and unconscious.

Coming back to digitalisation, we would like to advocate the view that digitalisation—fully deployed and mobilised—is going to revolutionise organisational knowledge management practices and routines. This is because digitalisation creates a new dimension for organisational sense-making by adding knowledge resources and by bringing about a new understanding of what constitutes societal complexity and how it can be managed and governed.

Firstly, digitalisation enriches and diversifies an organisation's knowledge resources by offering more options to collate various data and diagnostics. The richer and more diversified the knowledge resources of the healthcare organisation are, the greater complexity the organisation can handle. Digitalisation provides the organisation with a possibility to harness collective intelligence and the wisdom of crowds within and crossing organisational boundaries and integrating various stakeholders (service planners, organisers, and users) in knowledge-creating processes. Secondly, digitalisation provides new means for decomposing complexity by breaking things up into simpler parts and for linking complex problems to a wider reference world, consisted of intertwined networks of societal factors creating and sustaining various complex problems and complex phenomena. This means that complex problems related to health interventions can be tackled better in service delivery when they are analysed in a way that takes into account the nature of *complexity* in the complex problems.

Digitalisation thus improves and strengthens not only an organisation's absorptive capacity but also its adaptive capacity. Absorptiveness relates to an organisation's ability to adopt, value and apply new knowledge and new knowledge management methods and practices. Adaptiveness refers to an organisation's capacity to change, which emphasises the role of a visionary and mature leadership in directing the organisation in a turbulent operating environment and business landscape. The greater the absorptive capacity is, the more likely it is that the organisation can make complexity accessible.

Just think about social media, for example, which supports the enactment of the environment and brings about a new bridge between the organisation and its stakeholder institutions and organisations. This is achieved by providing a context in which ongoing dialogue and narratives can be preserved, retained, shared and collectively used. This is why we consider social media as an organisational boundary mediator that provides reciprocal interaction with its environment. (For our theoretical arguments, see Kaivo-oja et al. 2016.)

In this light, social media acts as the organisation's 'senses', enabling interactive openness and access. Social media thus enables and mobilises the context for an individual's interpretations to become evident through narratives that convey the sense they have made of events and societal phenomena. Social media is—when theorised from the organisation's point of view—a forum that converts individual knowledge into collective (and common) knowledge, which is important from the point of what is known about complex societal problems. Collective and common knowledge is required because no actor (individual or collective) alone has the capacity to solve epistemic and systemic problems that manifest themselves as ambiguity.

In our thinking, social media represents an analytical lens to equivocality, manifested in society's complexity (see Kaivo-oja et al. 2016). Equivocality arises from multiple and partly contradictory points of view. Complexity related to equivocality cannot be resolved literally and conceptually, but only if reflected by different stakeholders and agency representatives. Equivocality involves political and ethical–moral tensions and contains mutually exclusive views, which call for dialogue and joint discussion and sense-making forums. Therefore, instead of 'solving' problems together and accepting the principle of equivocality, we think that the first step to a problem's solution is knowing how to encounter and approach them together in a dialogue. When encountering equivocal knowledge problems, it is essential to accept the fact that one event can be interpreted in different ways and from different starting points. Therefore, collective trust is important because without mutual trust, a joint approach to complex equivocal problems remains impossible.

4.7   Synthesis

Decision-making theories have evolved alongside of organisation theory. For at least the past 50 years, scholars working with decision-making theory have more or less shared the view that public policy decision-making is not very rational—on the contrary, far from it. Emotions, alternative truths, multiple sources of information, decision-makers' intellectual capacity, values and assumptions about life all reflect how decision-makers behave in decision-making situations. In terms of health, one additional issue is the new landscape for health organisations and markets. This transformation affects the role of healthcare organisations and professions and creates a new setting where single healthcare organisations are replaced by healthcare ecosystems, consisting of various healthcare service providers, woven together by a new impetus for cooperation and competition.

In this chapter, we have developed the idea that public policy-based and organisational knowledge management occurs in a complexity framework. Complexity and uncertainty underline the role of data, information and knowledge. In the field of health, two issues are at stake here. First, due to evolving technology and digitalisation (and sensor technology and big data applications in particular), patients and citizens have more and more information about their health—they actually have more information than the public healthcare organisations.

Digitalisation enables citizens to take a more active role in developing and maintaining their health using various sensing devices, mobile apps and web services. As citizens' motivation to maintain and improve health grows, significant cost savings also become possible. An individual's everyday behaviour and actions are traceable by using various data sources, and future behaviour can be modelled and learned using predictive analytics methodologies and mathematical modelling. Second, the amount of data is not equivalent to power anymore—the power is vested in data analysis and synthesis and the owner of the health data.

Overall, the combination of lifestyle-related behavioural data and digital footprint data with clinical data and genomics provides vast possibilities for highly personalised and tailored care and for disease prevention. Behavioural data, when combined with population-level health statistics, is utilisable in profiling the health attitudes and everyday behaviour of both individuals and groups of people. Digitalisation impacts healthcare at all levels—public health policy, service systems, citizens and patients/service users. Personalisation is at the heart of the current global transformation of healthcare ideology. The vision of health measures that are predictive, preventive, personalised and participatory ('P4') is not a new one, however. For instance, the systemic integration of biology, health and medicine is now beginning to provide patients, consumers, and healthcare professionals with personalised information about individuals' unique health and disease status at the molecular, cellular and organ levels. This information will make disease care radically more cost-effective by personalising care to each person's unique biology and by treating the causes rather than the symptoms of disease.

From an organisational perspective, uncertainties caused by societal complexities can be reduced by decent problem formulation and effective information acquisition as well as the improvement of the service culture. Organisations ought to understand how patients behave and what kind of preferences they have in using the healthcare services. From an organisational perspective, problem formulation refers to the proper identification of the problem to be addressed in service delivery—to avoid the risk of solving the wrong problems. Information acquisition means the process of collecting and filtering new information. Upgraded service culture refers to better understanding of the service user (patient) service needs, both from retrospective service usage and upcoming service use intentions and preferences. These processes are intertwined, meaning that problems cannot be formulated without acquiring information and that the acquisition of information is useless without the problem being formulated. We suggest that digitalisation helps in all of these processes. This means that there is an urgent need to rethink conceptually the mechanisms for knowledge management in healthcare service organisations operating in the emerging service space.

From the healthcare profession's point of view, digitalisation is definitely an asset. It increases the connectivity within and across organisations, lowering the thresholds for sharing knowledge. Digitalisation is thus a prerequisite for a true learning community. Data protection mechanisms and confidentiality issues need to be rethought as an essential topic in this data circulation process. The role of organisational knowledge management is to provide new architectures that will integrate decentralised value creation and learning with centralised capability building. This asks for a fractal system and organisational architecture, where the use of the capability map as a tool for the design of knowledge management architecture is primary.

We feel that the mainstream theories of knowledge management need to be reassessed because of the introduction of machine learning as a parallel stream to the traditional human leaning process. Traditional human learning and communication have been cornerstones in knowledge management theories since the introduction of the famous SECI model (Nonaka 1991; Nonaka and Takeuchi 1995). We are certain that healthcare organisations' success in the future will depend on how citizens are deeply engaged in the value-creating and information-gathering process—to be able to constantly upgrade the dynamic capabilities of the enterprise and its partners in health and well-being ecosystems.

Knowledge management practices and theories—as well as intelligent health policy making and intelligent healthcare service delivery—are particularly important in the field of healthcare because the field of health will see one of its most disruptive periods in the forthcoming years and decades. We hold the view that putting more financial resources into the health systems does not necessarily enhance health at the population level. The healthcare systems in the Western democracies face problems today that relate to the implementation of health policies and healthcare service delivery.

This means that healthcare systems and their management practices and knowledge management procedures ought to provide contested information about how to perform more efficiently and how to perform better in terms of citizen-driven well-being models aiming at a systemic change in the field of health. Achieving this asks for a more profound understanding of the potential of knowledge management in this new information-driven, citizen-centric world of health as well as a new understanding of the concept of well-being.

References

Argyris C (2010) Organizational traps. Leadership, culture, organizational design. Oxford University Press, Oxford

Becerra-Fernandez I, Sabherwal R (2001) Organizational knowledge management: a contingency perspective. J Manag Inf Syst 18(1):23–55

Braybrooke D, Lindblom CE (1963) A strategy of decision: policy evaluation as a social process. The Free Press, New York

Browne A, Wildavsky A (1984) Implementation as exploration. In: Pressman JL, Wildavsky A (eds) Implementation. University of California, Berkeley, pp 232–256

Cameron A, Bostock L, Lart R (2014) Service user and career's perspectives of joint and integrated working between health and social care. J Integr Care 22(2):62–70

Cohen MD, March JG, Olsen JP (1972) A garbage can model of organizational choice. Adm Sci Q 17(1):1–25

Cohen MD, March JG, Olsen JP (2012) A "garbage can model" at forty: a solution that still attracts problems. In: Lomi A, Harrison JR (eds) The garbage can model of organizational choice: looking forward at forty (Research in the sociology of organizations, vol 36). Emerald Group Publishing, London, pp 19–30

Davenport TH, Harris JG (2007) Competing on analytics. The new science of winning. Harvard Business School Press, Boston, MA

Dror Y (1964) Muddling through: science or inertia? Public Adm Rev 24(3):153–157

Dror Y (1968) Public policy making re-examined. Chandler Publishing, Scranton

Ewert B, Evers A (2012) Contested meanings and challenges for user organizations. In: Pestoff V, Brandsen T, Vershuere B (eds) New public governance, the third sector and co-production. Routledge, London, pp 61–78

Fisher MP, Elnitsky C (2012) Health and social services integration: a review of concepts and models. Soc Work Public Health 27(5):441–468

Flyvbjerg B (2001) Making social science matter. Cambridge University Press, Cambridge

Givel M (2016) What the big deal?: complexity versus traditional US policy approaches. In: Geyer R, Cairney P (eds) Complexity and public policy. Edward Elgar, Cheltenham, pp 65–77

Graham P (ed) (1996) Mary Parker Follett – prophet of management. A celebration of writings from the 1920s. Harvard Business School Press, Boston, MA

Gray B (2016) A case study of complexity and health policy: planning for a pandemic. In: Geyer R, Cairney P (eds) Complexity and public policy. Edward Elgar, Cheltenham, pp 385–398

Hunter D (2003) Public health policy. Polity Press, Oxford

Johnson L (2016) Complexity modelling and application to policy research. In: Geyer R, Cairney P (eds) Complexity and public policy. Edward Elgar, Cheltenham, pp 150–170

Kaivo-oja J, Virtanen P, Jalonen H, Stenvall J (2015) The effects of the internet of things and big data to organizations and their knowledge management practices. In: Luden L et al (eds) Knowledge management in organizations, vol 224. Springer, Heidelberg, pp 495–513

Kaivo-oja J, Virtanen P, Stenvall J, Jalonen H, Wallin J (2016) Future prospects for knowledge management in the field of health. KMO 2016. In: Proceedings of the 11th international knowledge management in organizations, Article no. 40. https://doi.org/10.1145/2925995.2926006, ACM, New York. http://dl.acm.org/icps.cfm

Kernick D (2004) Complexity and healthcare organization: a view from the street. Radcliffe Medical Publishing, London

Little A (2016) Complexity and real politics. In: Geyer R, Cairney P (eds) Complexity and public policy. Edward Elgar, Cheltenham, pp 32–47

Lyngsø AM, Godtfredsen NS, Høst D, Frølich A (2014) Instruments to assess integrated care: a systematic review. Int J Integr Care 14(3):1–15

March JG (1978) Bounded rationality, ambiguity and the engineering of choice. Bell J Econ 9(2):587–608

March JG (1987) Ambiquity and accounting: the elusive link between information and decision making. Acc Organ Soc 12(2):153–168

March JG (1994) A primer on decision making. How decisions happen. The Free Press, New York

Nohrstedt D (2016) Complexity theory and collaborative crisis governance in Sweden. In: Geyer R, Cairney P (eds) Complexity and public policy. Edward Elgar, Cheltenham, pp 332–347

Nonaka I (1991) The knowledge creating company. Harv Bus Rev 69:96–104

Nonaka I (1994) A dynamic theory of organizational knowledge creation. Organ Sci 5(1):14–37

Nonaka I, Takeuchi H (1995) The knowledge-creating company. How Japanese companies create the dynamics of innovation. Oxford University Press, Oxford

Nonaka I, Kodama M, Hirose A, Kohlbacher F (2014) Dynamic fractal organizations for promoting knowledge-based transformation – a new paradigm for organizational theory. Eur Manag J 32 (1):137–146

Nonaka I, Hirose A, Takeda Y (2016) Meso-foundations of dynamic capabilities: team-level synthesis and distributed leadership as the source of dynamic creativity. Glob Strateg J 6 (3):168–182

Nordgren L (2009) Value creation in health care services – developing service productivity: experiences from Sweden. Int J Public Sect Manag 22(2):114–127

Paquet G (1999) Governance through social learning. University of Ottawa Press, Ottawa

Peck J, Theodore N (2015) Fast policy. Experimental statecraft at the thresholds of neocapitalism. University of Minnesota Press, Minneapolis

Pestoff V (2012) Co-production and third sector social services in Europe: some crucial conceptual issues. In: Pestoff V, Brandsen T, Vershuere B (eds) New public governance, the third sector and co-production. Routledge, London, pp 13–34

Porter ME (2010) What is value in health care? N Engl J Med 2010(363):2477–2481. https://doi.org/10.1056/NEJMp1011024

Sanderson I (2006) "Complexity", "practical rationality" and evidence-based policy making. Policy Polit 34(1):115–132

Sanderson I (2009) Intelligent policy making for a complex world: pragmatism, evidence and learning. Polit Stud 57(4):699–719

Simon HA (1955) A behavioral model of rational choice. Q J Econ 69(1):99–118

Simon HA (1972) Administrative behavior. Cambridge University Press, Cambridge

Simon HA (1978) Rationality as process and as product of thought. Am Econ Rev 68(2):1–16

Staber U, Sydow B (2002) Organizational adaptive capacity: a structuration perspective. J Manag Inq 11(4):408–424

Stenvall J, Virtanen P (2015) Intelligent public organizations? Public Organ Rev, published on-line 2.12.2015. https://doi.org/10.1007/s11115-015-0331-1

Tenbensel T (2016) Complexity and health policy. In: Geyer R, Cairney P (eds) Complexity and public policy. Edward Elgar, Cheltenham, pp 369–383

Vargo SL, Lusch RF (2015) Institutions and axioms: an extension and update of service-dominant logic. J Acad Mark Sci 44(1):5–23

Virtanen P, Vakkuri J (2015) Searching for organizational intelligence in the evolution of public sector performance management. NISPAcee J Public Adm Policy 8(2):89–99

Virtanen P, Laitinen I, Stenvall J (2016b) Street-level bureaucrats as strategy shapers in social and health service delivery: empirical evidence from six countries. Int Soc Work 16(3):1–14. https://doi.org/10.1177/0020872816660602

Virtanen P, Stenvall J, Kinder T, Hatem O (2017a) Do accountabilities change when public organisations transform to service systems? Financ Account Manag (In press)

Virtanen P, Smedberg J, Nykänen P, Stenvall J (2017b) Palvelu- ja asiakastietojärjestelmien integraation vaikutukset sosiaali- ja terveyspalveluissa [Effects of service and customer information systems integration in social welfare and healthcare]. Valtioneuvoston tutkimus- ja selvitystoiminnan julkaisusarja 2/2017, Helsinki

Wallin J, Virtanen P, Kaivo-oja J, Jalonen H, Stenvall J (2017) Future prospects for knowledge management in the digitalized health. Unpublished article manuscript

Wildavsky A (1979) Speaking truth to the power. The art and craft of policy analysis. Transaction, New Brunswick

Yeh YJ, Lai SQ, Ho CT (2006) Knowledge management enablers. Ind Manag Data Syst 106 (6):793–810

Chapter 5
Intelligent Healthcare Organisations and Patient-Dominant Logic in the New Service Space

Abstract This chapter examines the characteristics of intelligent healthcare orga- nisations. We propose that an intelligent organisation is able to operate interactively at the boundaries between different organisations and institutions. This view holds that an intelligent organisation shares its expertise and cross-social and healthcare professional silos, learns from mistakes, has unlearning capabilities and acts adap- tively in relation to changes in the operating environment. This means that the existing and classical organisation theories do not suffice anymore. This chapter discusses the need for a new interpretation of organisational theories from the perspective of intelligence with special emphasis on research discussion concerning the crossing of organisational interfaces. We also discuss the role of isomorphic mechanisms in the field of healthcare: this view holds that healthcare organisations are becoming more and more homogeneous. In addition, we incorporate the concept of 'service space' into the development of intelligence in the field of healthcare organisations, developed and theorised by the authors in our earlier publications. To briefly formulate this concept, we understand a 'service space' as a space of relations and networks of service providers, embedded as integral parts in service (eco)systems, among agencies (personal, organisational) acting through communication (flows), utilising the possibilities of ubiquitous technologies and providing customer-driven services by deploying service-dominant logic. This chapter puts the healthcare organisations at the heart of the emerging service systems. This perspective includes the idea that intelligent organisations and ser- vice systems strengthen their legitimacy only if they take seriously the role of service users, patients and citizens in various forms of co-creation and co-production of services. The concrete topics of this chapter include the rise and fall of classical organisation theories, the evolution of 'service space' and the new challenges for public management leadership theories and service-dominant logic—putting service users at the heart of service planning and implementation. These topics highlight the transformation from co-production to co-creation and beyond, patient-centred service models and processes as well as the role of orga- nisation's development activities in enhancing organisational intelligence.

5.1   From the Iron Cage of Bureaucracy to the Isomorphic Change of Organisations

The topic of this chapter reminds us that we have a one-track mind. We more or less see everything in our lives through the prism of organisations and human collectives. We are convinced that organisations and human collectives per se are too important to be left solely to management experts, and healthcare organisations are far too important to be left solely to health managers. In the world of co-production, co-management and co-governance (e.g. Pestoff 2012) of healthcare organisations, organisations and human collectives matter to every one of us, regardless of our position or hierarchical status.

According to Starbuck (2003: 156), the word *organisation* derives from an ancient Indo-European root that spawned the words 'organ' and 'work'. The original Roman verb 'organizera' initially meant 'to furnish with organs so as to create a complete human being'. Later on, the Romans gave the term the larger meaning of 'to endow with a coordinated structure'. Organisations have been around for ages. Pugh (2007: xi) wisely reminds us that we live in an 'organisational world' that surrounds us everywhere and in every phase of our lives. When we are children, we begin with schools, youth clubs and football teams and eventually progress, for instance, to colleges and other related institutions. As consumers, customers, citizens and employees, we are continually served and positioned by large formal organisations such as ICT companies, media conglomerates, banks, insurance companies, multiple chain stores, oil companies, company-based work environments and healthcare organisations.

Organisational theory is, to put it shortly and simply, a collection of general propositions about organisations (Starbuck 2003). The contents and dimensions of organisational theory—or the plethora of organisational theories—are vital in grasping and understanding intelligent health policy and public policy as a whole. Reed places organisation studies' proximate historical roots in the socio-political writings of nineteenth-century thinkers, such as Marx, Dürkheim and Saint-Simon, who attempted to anticipate and interpret the nascent structural and ideological transformations wrought by industrial capitalism.

According to Reed, the growth of an 'organisational society' was synonymous with '. . .the inexorable advance of reason, liberation and justice and the eventual eradication of ignorance, coercion, and poverty'. This view holds that organisations were rationally designed to solve permanently the conflict between collective needs and individual wants that had bedeviled social and societal progress since the days of Ancient Greece. According to Starbuck (2003: 144), contemporary organisation theory owes its existence to social and technological changes that occurred during the last half of the nineteenth century and first half of the twentieth century. This view holds that organisational theory—or theories—started to evolve in the aftermath of the Industrial Revolution.

On an everyday level, public, private and non-governmental organisations are often seen as unchanging, scornful of citizens, incapable of reform and even as downright functional backwaters. However, these seeming stiffness and stability are an illusion, as organisations are changing constantly.

Take the public sector, for example. Pollitt and Bouckaert (2011) have stated that administrative reforms in OECD countries have been systematic and comprehensive ever since the 1990s. According to them, this public sector change has been pervasive and has not left any public sector organisations untouched. Bouckaert and Halligan (2008), in turn, have reflected on the reasons for these continuing reforms and have sought an answer in the change of the economic and political conditions of public administration. In their view, the background to the changes in administration lies in the complex world of complicated problems, which also requires new modes of operating.

Public organisations are not the same as they used to be. And the theories and concepts about organisations are not what they used to be, say, at the beginning of the twentieth century. For example, Max Weber, one of the classical thinkers in the field of sociology, considered bureaucracy to be a blessing, not a curse. According to Weber (1947), the purely bureaucratic type of administrative organisation was, from a purely technical point of view, capable of attaining the highest degree of efficiency and was in this sense formally the most rational known means of carrying out imperative control over human beings as employees. Weber thought that the primary source of the superiority of bureaucratic administration lay in the role of technical knowledge, based on modern technology and business methods, which had become completely indispensable.

At the heart of Weber's theory was the organisation's authority and division of labour. His treatise on the organisation's division of labour took him very close to the thinking of another contemporary thinker, Émile Durkheim, who also emphasised the role of set roles as fundamental elements of formal and informal organisations (e.g. Fournier 2013). To put it in simple terms, Weber thought that organisations functioned well only if everybody knew what their task in the organisation was. Professionalism—an important aspect still today in the field of healthcare—was also an important gesture in Weber's genealogy of thoughts: conventional professional training more or less guaranteed the appropriate way to implement organisations tasks.

The world has changed tremendously since the beginning of the twentieth century. Globalisation, topped with the development of ICT technologies and the pervasive role of innovation, has actually made the globe smaller. As the world has changed, the waves of change have also reached the organisational shores. No wonder then that the ways organisations are labelled and called have also altered over time—today, organisations are considered to be complex, 'postmodern and 'world-making' (Chia 2003), hybrid (Billis 2010), pirate (Durand and Vergne 2013) and fractal (Nonaka et al. 2016), to give a couple of examples of today's 'organisational vocabulary'.

We would like to underline that the twentieth century has in a way proved the prophecy laid down by Max Weber—and simultaneously it has manifested the need to rethink the great organisational classics of the early decades of the twentieth century, such as Frederick Taylor, Elton Mayo and Mary Parker Follett. In short, the time has passed the once-revolutionary thinking of the classics.

From the healthcare organisations' point of view, the question of organisational diversity and homogeneity is a very interesting topic. DiMaggio and Powell (2012) make a substantial point by reminding us that much of modern organisational theory has so far posited a diverse and differentiated world of organisations and thus sought to explain variations among organisations in structure, processes, behaviour and overall functions. Instead, DiMaggio and Powell urge that it is equally important to explain the homogeneity of organisations and not just the variations. We follow DiMaggio and Powell (2012) and maintain that the organisational field of modern healthcare contains an inexorable push and shift towards homogenisation, not variation.

Following DiMaggio and Powell (2012), there are three mechanisms which endorse overall isomorphic change and homogenisation process in the organisational fields of healthcare. These mechanisms are coercive isomorphism, mimetic isomorphism and normative isomorphism, all of which strengthen the homogenisation of healthcare.

Coercive isomorphism results from, for instance, both formal and informal pressures exerted on healthcare organisations by other organisations and institutions active within the same sphere of the operating environment. Budget deficits and financial constraints are examples of this kind of pressure. Another example related to coercive isomorphism is legislation put forward by the government. Legislation stipulates that organisations act accordingly, which might enhance isomorphic development—i.e. the organisations per se will eventually come to resemble each other: healthcare centres look alike since the legislation concerning the issues related to social welfare and health is the same for every single organisation.

Mimetic isomorphism derives from societal uncertainty and also because of the current 'naming and shaping' philosophy of ranking organisations. This occurs today with the help of standardised protocols, quality assurance systems and benchmarking. Modelling is thus a response to the prevailing uncertainty. The rapid proliferation of quality circles, balanced scorecard-related management models, prevailing leadership doctrines and quality-of-work-life thematics in certain healthcare organisations is, at least to a certain extent, an attempt to model success achieved in other healthcare organisations.

This relates to the situation that DiMaggio and Powell (2012: 182) describe as a setting in which organisations tend to model themselves after similar organisations in their field which they perceive to be legitimate or successful. In Bourdieuan terms, this means that mimetic isomorphism is actually a mechanism that eventually results in healthcare organisations competing with each other in a given field of service space. They compete with each other in terms of various forms of capital—those being related to financial resources, prestige, image, good feedback from patients and service users and so forth. This setting derives from the logic of societal fields—according to Bourdieu (1984; Bourdieu and Wacquant 1992)—which means that to think in terms of field is to think relationally: a field is a network, or in another way shaped configuration, of objective relations between healthcare organisations operating in the field. The structure of organisations is based on their present and potential situation in the field. This relates heavily on the distribution of capital valuable in the given field of action.

Normative isomorphism stems primarily from professionalisation, which from the point of healthcare has been a fundamental issue. Professionalism affects how the work is carried out in healthcare organisations, how the organisational knowledge is accumulated and disseminated at the horizontal and vertical boundaries of healthcare organisations and how smoothly patient- and service-user-related processes function (Currie and White 2012; Praetorius and Becker 2016; Saks 2013). Two aspects of professionalisation are at stake in this isomorphic mechanism (DiMaggio and Powell 2012: 182–183): the importance of formal education and the growth and elaboration of professional networks that span across organisations. Both of these have multiple effects in organisations, and they affect how personnel is recruited, what kind of people are filtered in organisations as a result of recruitment and how members of the personnel advance in the organisation hierarchically (in terms of career paths, for instance).

To summarise, we maintain in this book that public healthcare organisations are in a transformation process for two reasons. The first one of these is the isomorphism tendency—due to the coercive, mimetic and normative reasons that DiMaggio and Powell (2012) have suggested. Changes in operating environments of healthcare organisations and overall systemic governance challenges are in this respect very noteworthy. These changes and challenges include budgetary constraints and fiscal pressures as well as the changes in the technology environment of healthcare as a policy. This has affected how healthcare organisations are conceived today. We argue that there has been a transformation phase during which single public service organisations change dramatically. Today, public healthcare organisations operate more or less as network partners in the service space and no longer as 'single' and 'separate' organisations. Together with other service space actors and institutions, they constitute a systemic ensemble.

The second reason for the transformation of the public healthcare organisation relates to the service point of view. We think this point of view is of crucial importance as far as the legitimacy and reputation of healthcare organisations are concerned. Next we will discuss the role of the service point of view and the meaning of service science as the fundamental recipient in the development of healthcare services.

5.2 Enter Service Science and Service-Dominant Logic

The dominant elements of existing public management theory are multilevel and multi-organisational governance, the role of organisational networks, collaboration between organisational actors and the transformation of public services towards a less hierarchical arrangement, organisational intelligence, service implementation structures, public service-dominant logic applications and finally—to a minor extent—public service ecosystems. Overall, we think it is appropriate to ask: what is the role of public services anyway in the structures of public administration?

The proliferation of previous (New Public Management of the 1990s) and existing (New Public Governance since 15 years ago) management doctrines in public administration has brought about two major problems. Firstly, they focused on intra-organisational processes at a time when the reality of public service delivery is inter-organisational and thus based on networks within the space between organisations. Secondly, they draw upon management theory derived from the experience of the manufacturing sector, which ignores the reality of public services, taking into account issues such as service culture, service systems, service production and delivery and so forth. Given this, we consider the claim that the above-mentioned public management theories have thoroughly 'permeated' the public service sector to be an improper claim—and perhaps a mistaken one as well.

It is clear, however, that the dominant public management theories have called for savings in public expenditure, better productivity, improved quality, more efficient government operations, better market-oriented services for service users and better implementation of public policies (Hood 1991; Osborne 2010; Osborne et al. 2013). This has called for a new approach to integrate service more intensively, both in the existing management theories of public leadership and in the structures of public administration. The idea has been to place public services more clearly into the overall picture (Virtanen and Stenvall 2014), to associate public services with the idea of service management (Normann 1995) and to deploy the service-dominant logic approach to public services (Grönroos 2011; Maglio and Spohrer 2013; Maglio and Breidbach 2014; Vargo and Lusch 2008).

If they are so important in the domain of the current healthcare service paradigm, then what really is service science and how does it relate to service-dominant logic? Let us start to discuss with these concepts.

Service science refers to the study of complex service systems (Maglio and Spohrer 2013; Maglio and Breidbach 2014). In the area of business studies and marketing theory, the role of customers, the essence of marketing, the accountability aspects towards service users and the development of service culture have emerged as vital research topics. Moreover, the value of service innovations and service leadership has been under extensive scrutiny during the last decades (see Shostack 1977; Vargo and Lusch 2004, 2008; Brodie et al. 2006; Djellal et al. 2013; Grönroos 2011; Spohrer and Maglio 2008; Spohrer et al. 2007).

Service science has not developed in an intellectual vacuum or as a clearly defined field of scientific activity. It was Normann (1995) who eventually gained an academic reputation in the domain of service science by making sense of its paradigmatic emergence and by providing a distinction between three stages or generations of service science. According to him, the first generation of service science concentrated primarily on the situation of single public services and service sectors during the 1970s and 1980s. At this stage, service science scholars emphasised the fact that the main idea or objective was to understand the laws governing certain services. This meant that services were organised principally around the identification of customer needs, but largely with activities implemented in production-oriented or co-production approaches. The notion of first-generation service science referred to the fact that each service organisation constituted an independent unit as an organisational actor. In this framework—and discussed from the public service and public healthcare point of view—services provided production-oriented service delivery in a top-down manner, with the legislative framework defining the mandate and clientele of services.

In Normann's (1995) vocabulary, the second generation of service science, which started to gain influence, aimed at the creation of a comprehensive organising approach, arranging services in order to solve each individual customer's or service user's problems. As such, second-generation service science views service models, prototypes and architecture as solutions to customers' problems. This view holds that service products and services themselves were more or less interlinked and incorporated. Similarly, second-generation services also emphasised operational service integration, which became a central operating concept in the field of social and health services around the 1990s (see, e.g. Kodner 2009; Lyngsø et al. 2014). This emphasis directed the focus of healthcare services to the transformation and mobility information and information systems as well as skills and know-how necessary to integrate functionally separate services into larger organisational networks. In this setting, operating across organisational boundaries and boundary crossing between organisations acts as a catalyst for learning (e.g. Shultz 2001).

The third stage of service science, then, broadened the scope of analysis even wider than the second generation ever did. Service science of the third generation builds upon the view that services function within the framework of systemic thinking, deploying the ideas of MST (on this, see Checkland 1981; Prahalad and Ramaswamy 2004; Virtanen and Stenvall 2014). From this MST perspective, services and service ecosystems appear as constantly developing interactive processes, where reformation and learning derives from information, experience and in-process learning, including the realisation of services as well as the planning of service processes. In third-generation service development, it is possible then to apply the methods of learning by experience and learning by doing (e.g. Argyris 1993, 2010; Kolb 1984). The third-generation services also introduced, more or less, the concept of service co-creation and influenced the culture of horizontal accountability in public services (e.g. Schillemans 2011). From the healthcare services point of view in the Nordic countries, then, this brought about the 'upgraded' role of the service users and patients in service development and in terms of freedom of choice.

Service-dominant logic, then, makes explicit an approach that integrates services and products/goods as a service process. In the field of healthcare, patient-dominant logic would be an appropriate definition—highlighting both dimensions of service: the service itself as well as the 'service product' provided by the personnel in healthcare organisations (guidance provided by front office nurses, doctor's activities such as medicine prescriptions and so on). The notion of service process, in turn, converts the idea of producing products for the masses into a service logic that embodies service culture, service orientation and the adding of true value for customers (and, as said, in the field of healthcare—patients or service users).

Consequently, this new role of the service user (patient), combined with new participation modes and co-creation techniques, has meant that public services are held more accountable by service users and patients than was previously the case (Schillemans 2011; Virtanen et al. 2016c). This view holds that accountability is a flow incorporated and embedded within service systems and facilities—that is, flows between agents the content of which includes not only knowledge on the outputs of public healthcare services but also on values, empathy and so forth, thus creating a multilayered understanding of accountability.

What is important here is in fact how service users and patients participate in developing the services. The co-production ideology of the above-mentioned second service generation referred to services defined and developed together with the customer (Bovard 2007; Tuurnas 2016). This was the leading principle of the service development, even though the development was still set more or less from the top-down perspective. This means that healthcare professionals were in charge of service development, which certainly brought about service development, but in a somewhat paternalistic mode.

The concept of co-creation of the third generation, on the other hand, refers to the planning of these services together with their customers in the spirit of an open innovation paradigm (e.g. Vargo and Lusch 2004; Virtanen and Kaivo-oja 2015). This meant a new era for service development as a whole, since in this framework, service users are equal development actors along with the healthcare professionals. In a co-creation mode of development, the role of technology as a whole, added to patient-level data and big data related to the service user, is critical (e.g. Kaivo-oja et al. 2015, 2016).

Until today, however, only a few examples exist of how service-dominant logic is set as the operating principle in public services and public healthcare. This is somewhat odd, bearing in mind the existing theoretical and conceptual discussions about service users as customers also in the domain of public services. Osborne et al. (2013), for instance, have stressed that the reality of public service delivery today is that it draws upon management theory derived from the experience of the manufacturing sector, which ignores the reality of public services as 'services'. Not surprisingly, then, Osborne et al. (2013) therefore conclude that the adoption of service-dominant logic could make an innovative contribution to the existing and evolving public management theories.

We very much share the point made by Osborne et al. (2013), who stress the importance of services in public administration. This is due to the fact that the integration of public services into a framework of public management theories would highlight the delegation of decision-making, a new kind of quality thinking, intensification of service production, privatisation of public services and, above all, the importance of measuring the profitability of service production. This is not an easy task since public administration is by nature a network organisation where management issues are much more complicated and multidimensional than in traditional branches of (private sector) administration. Underlying this thinking is a vision of the complexity of society, which brings with it totally new types of management problems. In practice, the change will cause a shift in attention from individual public service organisations towards wider service ecosystems.

In crystallised form, the management ideology of the service-dominant logic is about a radical change in the way of thinking about the role of a service user in the joint service ecosystem formed by all service providers. At the practical level, this has meant that the rhetoric of service organisers and producers is changing little by little from service-user-*centred* thinking to service-user-*driven* thinking, which emphasises the ever more active role of service users in reforming and developing services (e.g. Tuurnas 2016). Thus at the practical level, this has meant that social workers and healthcare professionals would identify service needs better than before and, above all at a sufficiently early stage, proactively.

As a management ideology, service-dominant management therefore means genuine efforts to take the needs of service users seriously. Service-dominant management modes, however, have thus far received little attention in public administration research, and management practices have not been paid much attention to in the framework of thinking that emphasises citizenship (Osborne et al. 2013; Virtanen and Stenvall 2014).

Overall, much remains to be done in terms of integrating service-dominant logic into the production and delivery of public healthcare services. To this end, we have constructed a model (Fig. 5.1) that builds upon the ideas presented not only by Vargo and Lusch (2004, 2008) but also the contributions by Cook et al. (2002), Shostack (1977) and our own (Virtanen and Stenvall 2014). Figure 5.1 presents a

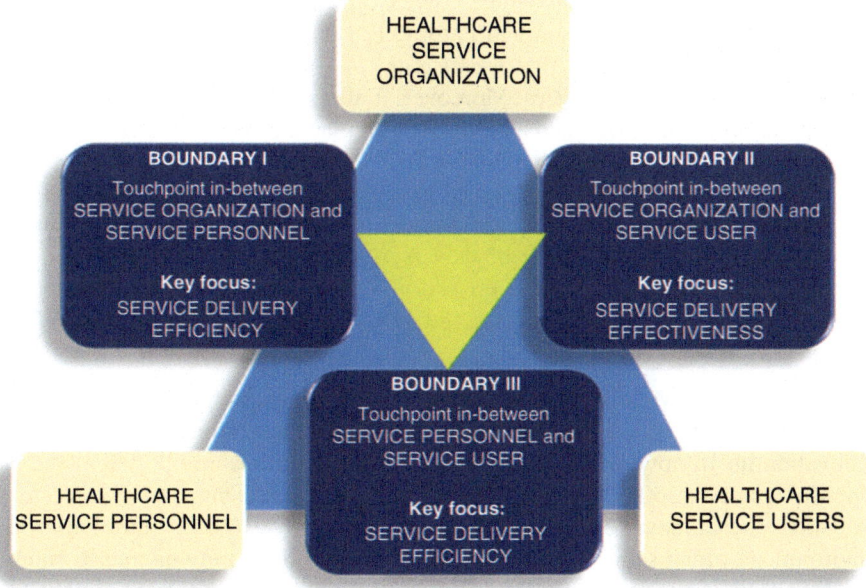

Fig. 5.1 A three-dimensional trajectory of public healthcare services (developed from Virtanen and Stenvall 2014)

triangle with three key dimensions—service organisation, service personnel and service user. The 'key' to the triangle is the three boundaries that exist in the spaces between these three dimensions. We call these boundaries 'touchpoints' (inspired by Shostack 1977) while, of course, being aware of the much narrower definition Shostack originally used. These boundaries exist between service organisation and service personnel (*service delivery*), between service organisation and service users (*service effectiveness*) and finally between service users and service personnel (*service interface*).

The purpose of the model in Fig. 5.1 is to understand the nature of the service delivery process—it is a process that derives its components from:

(a) *Service organisation* itself, the system, service personnel and service users. The functions of a service organisation are numerous of course, but leadership aspects, management procedures, planning and forecasting and organisational processes as well as strategic human resource management are clearly of the utmost importance here. In the existing research literature, the role of strategic agility has been consistently forwarded as a potentially useful mechanism to help redesign service production at the organisational level (e.g. Larsen et al. 2007; Doz and Kosonen 2010).

(b) *Service personnel* implement the delivery of healthcare services in practice. Depending on the particular sector involved, notions of professionalism often constitute an important factor in the carrying out of such service tasks. Organisational changes and reforms in the public sector have also had an effect on the work of the service personnel—this includes changes in work roles, organisational learning procedures, work orientations, job descriptions and so forth. For instance, Jansson and Parding (2011) concluded that organisational changes and changes in the organisation of work affect intra-organisational relations between employees. Moreover, it also seems that the strengthening of service-user orientation and an emphasis on placing 'the customer at the centre of attention' precipitates a remodelling of service organisations.

(c) *Service users* are the clients in terms of public services—the recipients of these services, including electronic services, which are rapidly expanding. From the service-dominant logic point of view, service-user feedback and participation opportunities (e.g. co-production and co-creation models) provide important mechanisms in terms of fulfilling the needs of service users (e.g. Alam 2006; Matthing et al. 2006).

The role of service development and service innovation introduces capacity issues (technology, know-how, financial resources) into the picture. The nature of innovation itself, however, is changing. According to Chesbrough (2006; see also Chesbrough et al. 2008), the only possibility for advancement today is through the so-called open innovation approach—that is to say, in today's information-rich environment, organisations can no longer afford to rely entirely on their own ideas to advance their business, nor can they restrict their innovations to a single path to market. In the public sector, and relating to public services in particular, this calls for a totally new level of openness and transparency with regard to development plans, the information relating to these initiatives (e.g. open data), development processes and participation in these processes.

The role of innovation in particular should also be emphasised here. To be innovative, much is required of the healthcare service organisation and the personnel as well as of the patients. Djellal et al. (2013) are correct to conclude that innovation in the public sector has been neglected in the mainstream of innovation studies. Djellal et al. explored four different theoretical perspectives used in studies of service innovation within the public sector (assimilation, demarcation, inversion and integration/synthesis) and found that innovation in the public sector domain remains a highly diverse entity. This implies that there is still much more to do in the area of research with regard to this field of innovation. The body of evidence available from within the disciplines of marketing and business studies suggests that a key role in the innovation process does not stem from organisational or personnel points of view but rather from the service-user side (e.g. Alam and Perry 2002; Michel et al. 2008; Bogers et al. 2010)

To conclude, improving the service mentality and service culture in the public sector domain associated with public service delivery is dependent on a number of issues. This brings to the fore the issues of change management and change leadership in healthcare organisations. The research literature from public sector change programmes offers some practical evidence on this theme, but the evidence is far from consistent (e.g. Fernandez and Pitts 2007; Fernandez and Rainey 2006). It is quite clear however that change management procedures across the public sector differ significantly from those in the private sector. Organisational learning in the public healthcare could definitely make use of the experiences already gained in the private sector, although the special nature of public sector organisations and leadership (including its political aspects—the role of service users as consumers and as citizens) should obviously be central to this discussion. The point is then to echo what March (1991) has advocated—to learn and to unlearn, to exploit experiences from different spheres and to try to make the best use of them.

5.3 Service Space, Patient-Dominant Logic and Technology

Earlier in this chapter, we stressed the fact that an essential condition of the service-dominant logic approach is placing the service user as a co-producer and co-designer of the service production in the services being delivered by a consortium of organisational and non-organisational agents. Next we would like to continue with a concept clarification. The concept of 'service space' deserves a clarification since it is not a codified term yet—at least in an academic sense.

To formulate this concept in brief, we treat and understand a 'service space' as a space of relations and networks of public, private and non-governmental service providers, embedded as integral parts in service (eco)systems, among agencies (personal, organisational) acting through communication (flows). This concept builds on the notion of public networks, which are—to echo what Molin and Masella (2016) have recently underlined—increasingly implemented at different government levels and across policy areas to increase coordination of services, decision-making and service delivery. It is important to note that service providers operating in the service space utilise the possibilities of ubiquitous technologies and deliver service-user-driven services by deploying service-dominant logic as well as various co-creation and service design mechanisms (e.g. Virtanen and Kaivo-oja 2015). This scope of the definition broadens the conventional service space thinking and opens up a framework that goes further than just addressing the connection between service organisations, service products and service engineering (e.g. Spohrer and Freund 2013).

In addition, our treatise of service space takes into account the role of power, competition, gatekeeping and governance in the field of healthcare as well as the private companies' manufacturing healthcare technology—elements that have been somewhat neglected in the service industry research literature so far. This broad definition is inherently multidisciplinary and calls for understanding from policy, administrative and service sciences and also from social sciences and from Pierre Bourdieu's field theory in particular (e.g. Hilgers and Mangez 2015; Bourdieu 2000).

The concept of service space immanently shifts the focus from overall organisational features towards specific organisational arrangements. These arrangements refer to leadership issues in particular and to ubiquitous technologies that affect healthcare organisations—to healthcare services and their organisational processes, to leadership models and especially to mechanisms for organisational change.

Two issues are especially at stake here. First, an emergent and very distinctive space of services dominates the production of goods and services today—and tomorrow. Secondly, the service space described and explained earlier consists of embedded and integrated service providers (public, private and hybrid versions), and it is strongly influenced by immanent societal governance challenges such as the Internet of Things, big data, cloud computing, smart technologies, robotics, artificial intelligence and disruptive innovations. Finally, we must maintain that the service space is not easy to govern since it is (or wants to be) independent and autonomous in a novel way—in particular in the vertical sense of accountability and favouring and addressing the importance of service users, i.e. horizontal accountability (see, e.g. Virtanen and Kaivo-oja 2015; Kaivo-oja et al. 2015).

An interesting question is how technology affects healthcare organisations in the emergent service space. In one of our recent research projects—reporting empirical research from Japan—we found out that the field of healthcare is evolving rapidly because of technology and this has an effect on the dynamics of the service space (Virtanen et al. 2016a).

The role of healthcare-related technologies—with the idea of further incorporating these technologies as IoT systems in the field of health service providers (technology providers as well as service providers, both from public and private organisations)—definitely establishes a landmark in healthcare service delivery. Moreover, as our Japanese case study suggested (Virtanen et al. 2016a), ubiquitous technologies accelerate social and societal change by putting more emphasis on the customers' and patients' voice in healthcare. Healthcare organisations definitely move towards a more service-dominant logic, and this concerns both organisations providing health technologies and organisations providing healthcare services. Thus, in conclusion, customer-centric or customer-oriented approaches become stronger due to ubiquitous technologies.

The complexity of customer preferences with regard to health-related technologies is immanent. This relates to cultural differences between various countries and with regard to different social and health policy contents. To continue with our research project from Japan (Virtanen et al. 2016a), it is clear that what matters to the Japanese with regard to health, and how the people deploy health-related technologies, does not necessarily matter to Germans, Americans or Finns, not to speak of Bangladeshis. The complexity of the need preferences also echoes difficulties and complexities in understanding the link between health policies (as a cause) and health impacts (as an effect).

Research evidence reminds us that governance mechanisms (i.e. with regard to the healthcare 'service space' as how services are delivered, on what principles, how the services are made accessible, how patients are treated in the service process and so on) are an important factor in converting health policies into health-related impacts. The Japanese case also illustrates how other 'intervening' variables exist between health policies, service governance mechanisms and health impacts. According to Ikeda et al. (2011), for instance, two factors explain a lot about the health status of the Japanese: the Japanese lifestyle (and high importance of personal hygiene) and the health consciousness among Japanese people. By saying this, we indicate the 'missing' link between government policy and health impacts.

The complexity and dynamics of the service space are pivotal challenges for organisational adaptiveness. This is because they challenge organisational business models among organisations in healthcare service delivery as well as technology providers in various ways. We feel that the changes in patient needs and the possibilities of ubiquitous technologies can develop in nonlinear and unpredictable ways. In networks, for instance, different kinds of actors—like service agencies and service users—might take the role that directs the process of knowledge creation or transformation. In complex and dynamic social relationships, this means that even human agents are not necessarily interconnected and autonomous, and they respond to each other—producing unpredictability (e.g. Stacey 2010).

Based on our previously published case study (Virtanen et al. 2016a), we argue that organisational resilience is an essential key point in understanding organisational change. Resilience in the organisational context refers to a healthcare organisation's capacity to anticipate disruptions, adapt to disruptive events and create lasting value in a turbulent environment. Organisational resilience is thus the ability of an organisation to overcome an internal or external shock and to return to a stable state. From the individual's perspective, this change challenges organisational unlearning processes and reshapes existing learning capacities and competencies (Argyris 2010; Virtanen and Kaivo-oja 2015).

On a more practical level, we think healthcare organisations need to develop their 'basic' activities, procedures and mechanisms to meet the challenge of patient-dominant logic, added to a growing tendency for freedom of choice (of services) by the patients. This is necessary to gain legitimacy and a lucrative brand in the service space. In Fig. 5.2, we have illustrated the patient-driven organisational process, which emphasises the role of the service users.

Figure 5.2 suggests that patient-dominant logic first requires better communication and marketing to enhance the organisation's brand and reputation. Second, healthcare organisations need to upgrade their digitalised services and e-tools to provide patients and service users with more channels to get better access to services. Digitalised services function only if they are accessible, functional, easy to use and fast in the sense of service delivery. Information and communication technologies and patient-based information should be consolidated and converted into the process of managerial decision-making. Patient-level information systems derive from organisation processes, based on the needs of the patients. The patient-level information follows the patient—not the other way around. Third, patient services prior, during and after treatment are touchpoints where the patient meets service face to face, 'live' so to say. These phases of the patient process bring into the picture call-centre facilities, physically visible services, the front offices of the healthcare organisations (including the atmosphere of the service surroundings) as well as the location and accessibility of services provided for the patient. During the treatment, the patient experiences the actual service provided by the doctor, nurse or other medical/care personnel. During this phase,

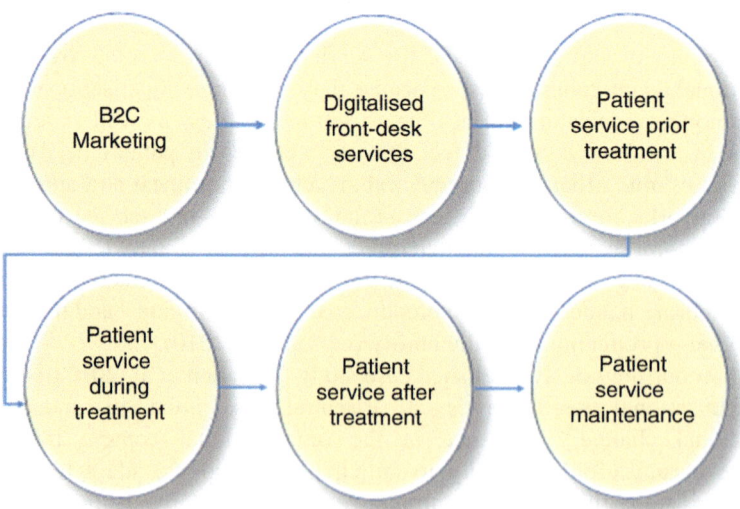

Fig. 5.2 Patient-dominant service process

the patient gets hold of actual health *service* and gets an understanding of the organisation's service *culture*. Patient service after the treatment procedures consists of billing, customer-feedback facilities, providing the patient with follow-up measures and practicalities as well as patient guidance for further treatment. Finally there is the patient service maintenance which incorporates follow-up monitoring, communication with the patient as well as targeted continuing marketing with the patient served earlier.

To summarise, healthcare services face dramatic changes in the upcoming years. Growing patient awareness and the rapid emergence and proliferation of health-related technologies call for new approaches in delivering services to patients. Service science and service-dominant logic in particular offer new approaches to improve the healthcare service repertoire and to gain strengthened legitimacy for health as a public policy as well. In this new framework, patients are not paternalistic targets for interventions of treatment; they are active and conscious living subjects participating in the process of how healthcare services are planned, delivered and evaluated. We believe this also gives a new dimension and new content to the policy agenda in which health policies are shaped, consulted and agreed upon.

5.4   Street-Level Intelligence

One very interesting question is how health policies and strategies get their shape and form in the service space. Who are the key actors in this process? In our previous research, we have strongly suggested that in order to answer this question, we should not look at only policy makers and patients. Our suggestion is that we should analyse how street-level bureaucrats—front-line workers (including doctors, nurses, social workers, psychologists and especially their bosses)—function and their role in this strategy formulation (Virtanen et al. 2016b).

According to Lipsky (1980), street-level bureaucrats (SLBs) are powerful actors who have the possibility to influence public policy implementation and public service delivery (see also Evans and Harris 2004; Walker and Gilson 2004). According to Lipsky (1980: 161), SLBs are professionals who make decisions about other people, and they typically are teachers, social workers, nurses, doctors, police officers and public bus drivers. This means that they encounter service users in their work. Another distinctive feature related to SLBs is that they have many kinds of responsibilities. They work, for instance, in the fields of social and healthcare as supervisors, planners or developers of services, controllers, negotiators and cooperation agents (or network gatekeepers).

We found out in our research (Virtanen et al. 2016b) that the concept of the SLB, as developed by Lipsky (1980), needs to be embedded in a more sophisticated discussion highlighting the tensions inherent in the role and one which is dependent upon organisational context and personal interests. For instance, the assumption that SLBs develop explicit strategies to maintain themselves as resources and powerful actors in the system misses the relevant discussion on discretion, coping under the pressure of change, resisting change, adopting a paternalistic attitude towards service users and even engaging in policy sabotage. Consequently, we concluded that two issues are at stake here. First, there is the role of middle managers in implementing public sector reforms; and second, there is the need to understand the SLB's role as strategy shapers in the field of social and health policies.

Let us start with the notion with regard to middle managers. It is appropriate to ask what it actually means to say that SLBs and especially middle managers in service delivery play an active role in the construction of the healthcare services as part of the service space (e.g. Wright 2006). Why are middle managers important among all possible street-level bureaucrats in Lipsky's (1980) sense? To answer this question, we have to bear in mind what research evidence tells us in terms of the implementation of public sector reforms. For example, Fernandez and Pitts (2007), Fernandez and Rainey (2006) and Rashman et al. (2009) and Fernandez et al. (2010) claim that middle managers have an essential role in organisational changes in the public sector. To put it briefly and somewhat simply, organisational changes are either successful or unsuccessful, depending on the way middle managers operate and lead the front-line staff. Therefore the idea in trying to understand middle managers in healthcare is of interest because they are key actors in transforming healthcare services facing the challenges of the service space caused by the rapid technology revolution. To this end, we interviewed 100 informants for our study in 2012. These were middle managers responsible for managing service delivery in the social and healthcare sectors from six countries (in the Greater London area and Glasgow in the UK, the state of Vermont in the USA, Toronto and Vancouver in Canada, Den Bosch in the Netherlands, Barcelona in Spain and Melbourne in Australia).

Next, we approach the role of SLBs by deploying Lipsky's (1980) conceptualisations and ask specifically what kind of strategies the SLBs put in place between patients and services on the one hand and top management and political decision-makers on the other hand. In our analysis, we found the typology related to SLB strategies put forward by Tuurnas (2016) and Tuurnas et al. (2015) very useful, since it helped us to focus on healthcare services operating in the service space.

The first strategy conveys the idea that SLBs are not passive actors in the strategy formulation process. Instead, they play an active role as policy makers at the front-line level of healthcare. We think that Lipsky (1980) offers an interesting point to explore how SLBs demonstrate their capabilities as policy shapers turning the traditional picture of strategy-making (which is formulated and implemented top-down) upside down. We found out that despite the fact that there are formal rules and vertical control over their work, SLBs apply the rules and create their own ethical codes in order to tackle their work tasks in healthcare organisations. SLBs act within the boundary between the two 'worlds'—the public service system and the user domain of services—translating policy goals into concrete and perceived actions. This relation is reciprocal in essence, meaning that the SLBs also transfer information on the effectiveness and productivity of the service interventions (from the boundary between the system and service users) vertically from 'street level' to the upper levels of decision-making. As such, it is from here that the idea of SLBs as policy makers comes.

The second strategy deployed by SLBs in the field of healthcare relates to actual working practices. This means that SLBs take an active role in defining the content of their day-to-day work. A significant amount of research evidence already exists on SLB actions in relation to working methods, values and practices, as well as on the discretion, freedom and self-interest of front-line workers in public services and particularly in healthcare organisations (e.g. Evans and Harris 2004; Ellis et al. 1999). SLB's ability to increase their level of discretion in respect of their working practices is a key tool in their day-to-day existence. Discretion here concerns the extent to which a doctor, a nurse and a social worker have, in a specific context, the freedom to innovate and focus on the factors that give rise to that freedom in that context. Looking more closely at the debate over this notion of discretion, it is clear that significant differences exist between what we may term the 'continuation' and 'curtailment' positions, differences which focus on beliefs about an organisation's desire for and ability to secure control and on the workers' ability to resist control and seek discretion (Evans and Harris 2004; Hupe and Buffat 2014).

Finally, SLB's third strategy refers to professionalism. This relates to the fact that SLBs try to increase their professional groups' autonomy as a part of the service system. This perspective highlights the role of professionalism and the notion that SLBs face constant difficulties in maintaining control in different organisational structures, especially in large organisational settings in healthcare administration and services. These include the need to consider signals from political decision-makers, multiple organisational arrangements and changes, enhancements in staff capacity and managerial supervision. It is important to note that these days—when performance standards and indicators are centrally set and where service users have actionable rights and do not just receive state 'charity'—the level of discretion open to SLBs is apparently much smaller.

To summarise, SLBs try to make public service systems and healthcare services in particular more flexible through strategies related to policy making, working methods and professionalism. An interesting conclusion is that while Lipsky (1980) emphasised the tensions between policy makers and the interests of street-level bureaucrats, we did not discover such conflicts when the broad picture is taken into account. It seems that SLBs and the middle managers supervising them are critical agents in developing services at the local and regional levels of governance. It seems that SLBs try to solve conflicts or bridge gaps between policy making and practical work in the boundaries between the SLBs and service users. This conclusion is valid in all of the six countries we studied, which gives us reason to think positively about the generalisability of our findings. It definitely seems that SLBs do not necessarily work according to the service system's principles, but rather they develop their own strategies to work with service users. The interesting question that remains is how SLBs really fulfil their tasks in respect of front-line service—serving the service users at the 'service touchpoints'—and how organisational cultures change when working habits and attitudes change. In a way, the SLB's role is that of a broker between policy makers and service users, and this role makes the position of the

SLBs very important and valuable. SLBs work in tandem with service users and the community, which makes them the key players from the perspective of the comprehensive service system. Interaction between SLBs and service users is crucial in terms of developing co-creation models holistically with service users and patients.

Finally, we would like to stress that the interlinkages between SLBs and service users is crucial in understanding the dynamics of horizontal accountability. Since patient-dominant logic healthcare services are co-created and produced with patients and service users, the service manager's relationships involve not only employed staff and networked contributors. Their relationship also includes focusing on the contributions of service users in systems delivering the users' personalised service needs. The services-as-a-system perspective therefore introduces closer relationships over design and delivery between managers, providing professionals and users and creating new forms of accountability.

Adopting a service systems perspective allows us to view accountability as a *processual* flow within the healthcare service system: flows between agents the content of which we argue includes knowledge, value, empathy and accountability. Attention then moves from governance *structures* to accountability *processual flows*, for which we have suggested a new analytical framework in our earlier research (Virtanen et al. 2016c).

This framework holds the view that—while centring co-producing patients in healthcare services—service delivery is the responsibility of a consortium of public, private and non-governmental healthcare organisations (including networks), which invites a new perspective on local service design and delivery. This service systems perspective on healthcare organisations simply means that from the point of view of the patient and service user, organisational boundaries and structures lessen in importance relative to the service system. Consequently, this change will have a tremendous effect on accountability. In short, it means that the role of patient is radically altered once patients participate in the development of healthcare services, which implies that the patients also have a very good reason to acknowledge their 'upgraded' role in the service delivery mechanism.

5.5 Intelligent Innovations

So far, we have discussed the concept of intelligent organisation from the structure, service, leadership and strategy formation point of view. Until now, we have deliberately left out the development aspect. In this section, we focus on the dynamics of the intelligent development mechanism within the service system operating in the service space. To this end, we will now provide a short analysis from our previous research that took place at the University of Tampere during 2014–2016.

At the local level of governance, municipalities have great operating autonomy in Finland by constitution. Haveri (2008) has suggested that this autonomy is one of the most extensive in all of Europe. Municipalities have the power—based on legislation—to provide services at the local level of governance. During the last few years, there has been an evolving tendency by the state to enhance cooperation within and between municipalities. According to Haveri (2008), this has been due to the state's objective to reduce the number of municipalities and to reorganise the local level of governance by creating larger administrative units. Our research concerned eight Finnish municipalities. We asked in our research how municipalities develop their local service space in an intelligent way and what factors constitute intelligence in reforming service systems at the local level of governance (see Kurkela et al. 2016). In this research project, we were interested to learn how experimental activities could increase the intelligence of municipal organisations and to understand how municipal organisations can change their practices and their way of thinking and overcome possible obstacles to experimental activities in municipalities.

Conceptually speaking, by the intelligent management model, we refer to efforts to reform public administration and public services—in part owing to the scarcity of resources associated with economic crises and in part as a result of society's complexity and the consequential emergence of new social problems—by highlighting a more intelligent management method and a more patient-driven mode of operating in the field of healthcare. This starting point holds the view that public interventions are seen as a means of value creation and that citizens are open-mindedly included in the service reform through co-production and co-creation (e.g. Tuurnas 2016). Also underlying this development is the change associated with the new systemic governance challenges of public administration. Challenges are brought about, for instance, by robotics, artificial intelligence, the Internet of (Intelligent) Things, machine learning, big data, nanotechnology and, most of all, the intensified digitalisation of society (e.g. Brynjolfsson and McAfee 2014; Schneier 2015). Overall, these systemic changes represent a much broader theme than a mere economic issue because it is a result of changes in the quality and quantity of human beings, the stock of human knowledge (particularly as applied to human command over nature) and the institutional framework that defines that deliberative incentive structure of a society (North 2005).

It is important to note that organisational intelligence in development activities is not an ultimate goal in itself. As a concept, organisational intelligence has no intrinsic value. Instead, organisational intelligence incorporates—in the framework of continuous learning and development—innovations in public or hybrid organisations, constituting a local service ecosystem. In using the concept of public service innovation, we follow Osborne and Kelly, who define public service innovation as the introduction of new elements into a public service—which can take place in the form of new knowledge, new organisation, process and service and which represents discontinuity with the past. In the terms of our empirical data, the innovations took place in different healthcare services and represented a variety of types of innovation—product and service innovations, process innovations, organisational innovations, local governance innovations and conceptual innovations.

Our research indicated that an innovative development culture at the local level of governance and service space refers to risk-taking in development ideas, partners and funding opportunities. However, from a development point of view, the pioneers of innovations at the municipal level renew their operations regardless of the prevailing economic situation. A culture of development thus evolves over time, and development integrated into municipal functions is an integral part of the renewal of operations from a service-user perspective. Long-term commitment in the renewal of operation models is a distinctive feature of pioneering municipalities. It takes decision-makers (political and local government officers), interest groups, clients and personnel into consideration. Courage and organisational resilience are important factors in experimentation and development activities. In Fig. 5.3, we have summarised the enabling factors for the intelligent modus operandi at the local (municipal) level of governance (Kurkela et al. 2016).

The commitment of key people in a municipal organisation is definitely the most important prerequisite in improving experimentation and developing practices. In a municipality, a culture of development also requires overall project management skills. Trusting employees is also crucial. Consistent leadership and management and a sort of employee-led development seem to have an effect on how the municipal organisation's intelligent operation models and leadership develop. Moreover, knowledge and customer-oriented approaches in development work are distinctive features of an intelligent operation model at the local levels of governance. Our data indicated that a customer-oriented or service-user-oriented

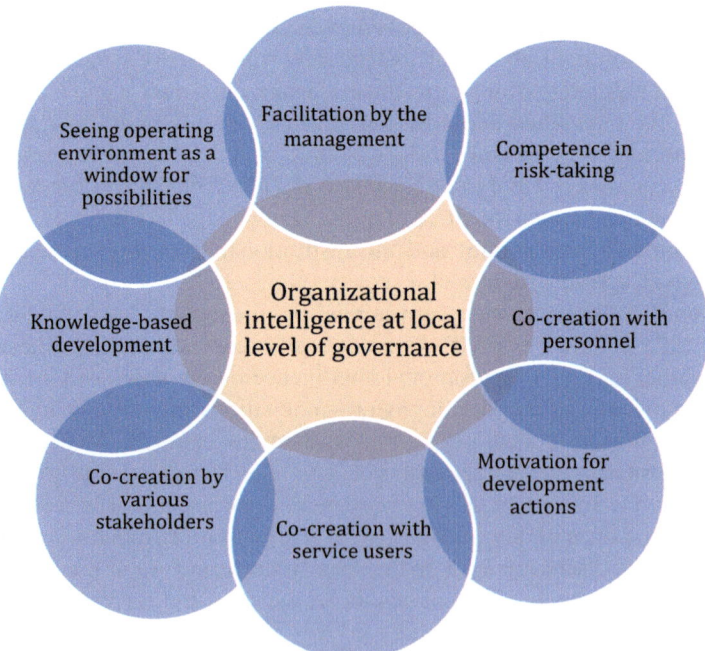

Fig. 5.3 Factors enhancing organisational intelligence in local-level service delivery (adapted from Kurkela et al. 2016)

approach is a valuable principle and is at the centre of the discussions concerning development at the local level of governance. However, the world is far from being mature in this respect, and there is much to do in terms of co-creation with service users at the municipal level. Service users are still more like development targets than partners. The participation of interest groups continues to be sporadic, and there is still a place and opportunity for improvement in the cooperation with them.

Factors such as leadership, motivating personnel, recognising changes in the municipal organisation and the ability to manage and lead changes have a considerable influence on how operations are thought of and implemented accordingly. Change management based on positive psychology greatly contributes to creative development and change. It entails inspiring employees in a way where changes are regarded as possibilities and the role of the employees is viewed as substantial in the implementation of changes. The empirical data pretty much underlines the employees' development potential. The employees' role is crucial when strategic policies and new practices are implemented at the level of organisational practice. The personnel's role as a source of information also needs to be strengthened.

Although our empirical findings showed that there definitely are critical factors that can hinder experimentation and development of services, our data suggests that development does in fact happen—although slower—to a certain level despite obstacles. It is noteworthy that an organisation's intelligent and flexible practices demand closer scrutiny and that leadership is a key phenomenon in this process. Development-oriented leadership entails future orientation, ability to change, dynamic leadership, openness, creativity, organisational culture and willingness to cooperate. Collaborative development can be seen as entailing cooperation between different interest groups, versatility and crossing sector boundaries. This brings the street-level bureaucrat aspect to the middle of the picture, as we discussed earlier.

Three conceptual and theoretical discussion topics arise based on our research: (a) citizenship and the role of co-creation, (b) the role of reforms and development activities at the local level of governance and (c) performance monitoring and the question of accountability. We discuss these topics briefly as follows.

Firstly, we have underlined that a central perspective exists because an intelligent organisation builds its activities on certain types of knowledge management practices. Therefore, it is important to ask what forms of political and administrative agency this knowledge-intensive and service-user (i.e. patient)-centred approach offers, as seen from the citizens' point of view. The intelligent public organisation also contributes to how the knowledge produced by service users, citizens and inhabitants is acknowledged. At the same time, it is also a crucial condition for the forms and forums of administrative–political agency and the content of the concept of citizenship in encounters between citizens and public administration.

Secondly, it seems that the renewal of public organisations in the service space is very much context-dependent. It happens if certain favourable conditions exist—those being, for example, visionary leadership, the resilience of public organisations (manageable risk-taking in a chaotic and complex operating environment), political backup for public interventions, project management skills, adaptive capacity for sustainable innovations at the local government level, the development reputation of an organisation, flourishing cooperation networks, financing options and so on. We also found out that one challenge to development is the fact that the new modes of operations may give rise to new problems requiring development, in which case public administration development work can become a kind of perpetual motion machine. Continuous development of activities substantially complicates the assessment of individual development processes and projects, since new ways of thinking about activities never replace the previous ones as such, but rather mingle with them. Different interpretations within public administration and public healthcare services influence what kinds of participatory and co-creation modes of development are experienced as appropriate. Therefore it seems that renewal and development actions should not be taken for granted—they also ought to be implemented in an intelligent manner.

Thirdly, the current paradigm of performance measurement and evaluation in public policy and in the domain of public healthcare organisations is undoubtedly based on the assumption that societies can be governed by a rationalistic mode of thinking (and preferably by 'hard-nosed' economists), usually neglecting the social mechanisms incorporated in the measurement of accountability systems and procedures. Furthermore, current modes of performance evaluation rely excessively on the assumption of entity-based evaluation: the idea that it is possible to detect performances within clear-cut organisational boundaries and development projects. Based on our research, it would be equally important to understand performances within collaborative networks and in contexts where both public and private sector actors contribute to outcomes for citizens, service users, patients and inhabitants. There is an urgent need to solve the problem of 'multiple accountabilities disorder' in providing solid information on public sector performance (e.g. Koppell 2005). We feel that accountability is still a rather fuzzy concept and it needs to be rethought by describing it analytically using the dimensions of transparency, liability, controllability, responsibility and responsiveness, as Koppell (2005) has suggested. We think that the notion of organisational intelligence emphasising the role of consolidated performance management systems within the domain of public organisation renewal in a turbulent operating environment can offer a theoretical and conceptual framework for developing performance measurement in a setting where wicked policy problems exist and where they are tackled by multi-institutional service systems.

Finally, the intelligence factor of organisations—and most prominently knowledge-intensiveness and a service-user-centred operation model based on service science principles (e.g. Maglio and Spohrer 2013)—clearly represents a crucial element in any attempt to understand the changing roles and identities experienced by public healthcare organisations in the network environment and ecosystems at the local government level. The emergence of such hybrid organisations and their innovation networks within the public sector domain calls for a new understanding of public sector leadership and management. We feel that the management practices stemming from the era of New Public Governance, for instance (not to mention New Public Management), are today no longer valid in the world of open organisational systems. Moreover, it seems that leadership capacity, change management, knowledge management practices, service users and service design are key elements in the construction of new public sector service systems and the renewal of public healthcare organisations as a whole.

5.6 Synthesis

Organisational stupidity still exists. Alvesson and Spicer (2016: 97–98), to take one example from current evolving research literature, argue bluntly that organisational stupidity *abounds*—it is everywhere, and much of current corporate life seems to be about manufacturing organisational stupidity.

Consequently, according to Alvesson and Spicer (2016), functional organisational stupidity is today so widespread in organisations, both in the public and sectors as well as in the third sector, that it is simply seen as *normal*. According to our understanding, the field of healthcare has not been untouched in terms of organisational stupidity. The forms of organisational stupidity, according to Alvesson and Spicer (2016), are, for instance, unlimited wishful thinking, following leaders without appropriate scrutiny, unreasoning zeal for management fads and fashions, senseless imitation of other organisations (labelled as 'benchmarking'), change initiatives that actually do not lead anywhere and the use of clichés and hearsay instead of careful analysis.

So it definitely seems that stupidity exists in all kinds of organisations. Public organisations are in additional jeopardy when we bear in mind the financial constraints of today's societies. The development of intelligence in publicly financed organisations is therefore something that cannot be bypassed. This is because we believe that public services—and public healthcare services in particular—provide much of the raison d'être for public administration and public policy. They exist in the service space between the citizens and the service system in a framework constituted by public policy. By nature, the essence of healthcare is its service content. It provides care and treatment, which bring about its legitimacy.

Simultaneously, public healthcare services, operating in the service space, are also bastions of public administration in today's complex ubiquitously networked society, extending public authority to civil society and towards the domain of service users and their legitimacy claims. In this sense, we think Sennett (1992) was quite right in advocating the role of public life vis-á-vis the life of common people. Public healthcare services function as scenes and stages in the public domain. Thus, Sennett's quest to discover the reasons behind the impoverishment of civic life in modern society opens up fruitful new perspectives into the relationship between service users and the organisations that provide public services.

In this chapter, we have focused both on healthcare organisations and the service space (consisting of a plethora of interlinked and interconnected single service providers). We maintain that public healthcare services today are produced locally, regionally, nationally and globally by a multitude of institutions such as the state, local authorities, non-governmental organisations and private businesses. Old organisational boundaries have shifted and transformed into something new. In this service provider-related new setting and healthcare agenda, new challenges emerge consisting of reciprocal cooperation mechanisms, organisational learning and unlearning and competence building.

The service space affects single healthcare service organisations. The development of service culture and service attitudes becomes crucial in terms of an organisation's brand, reputation and image, which in turn affect its financial situation and positioning. We have argued that a new conceptualisation of organisational theory has to be there in order to understand the logic and dynamic of the service space. Classical organisation theories do not suffice anymore—at least those theories that only build upon single organisations and provide a treatise within the limits of single organisations. We have proposed an approach here that would bring together various single organisations as a network of service operators and providers. Therefore, the essence of organisational theory relates these days to the ways organisations behave with each other. To this end, we have deployed an idea that underlines the homogenisation of the field of healthcare services through isomorphic mechanisms.

Finally, we must take into account how society is changing. Since the 1970s and 1980s, we have witnessed the proliferation of academic and semi-academic discussions about the tenets of what comes after the post-industrial society. The post-industrial society definitely created new forms of service-related production and paved the way for becoming a service economy and information society (see, e.g. Bell 1973; Cameron and Sirianne 1996; Furco and Billig 2001; Schneider 1984).

We consider that the emergence of the service space and a new kind of patient-dominant logic is a natural consequence of this societal change. In this chapter, we also highlighted the street-level bureaucrats' role in shaping and reshaping healthcare strategies. The street-level bureaucrats in the field of health are personnel such as doctors, nurses, social workers, psychologists and other professional groups in the domain of health. This view holds that while it is important to acknowledge the patients' role in co-creating future healthcare services, it is equally important to understand the healthcare personnel's position between policy makers and patients as brokers in mediating and developing healthcare strategies.

Overall, the role played by the public healthcare service sector is at the heart of the next generation of New Public Management theories, which we propose in this book as the *New Public Integration*, simply because the provision of public services constitute the primary element of responsibility for the public administration across Europe and the OECD countries. Public healthcare services constitute an important interface between public administration and citizens. As such, to deploy the concepts used by current authors in the development of the notion of the 'intelligent public organisation', they delimit an intermediate boundary between the system and the service users (Virtanen and Stenvall 2014; Virtanen and Kaivo-oja 2015).

References

Alam I (2006) Removing the fuzziness from the fuzzy front-end of service innovations through customer interactions. Ind Mark Manag 35(4):468–480

Alam I, Perry C (2002) A customer-oriented new service development process. J Serv Mark 16 (6):515–534

Alvesson M, Spicer A (2016) The stupidity paradox. The power and pitfalls of functional stupidity at work. Profile Books, London

Argyris C (1993) Knowledge for action: a guide to overcoming barriers to organizational change. Jossey-Bass, San Francisco

Argyris C (2010) Organizational traps. Leadership, culture, organizational design. Oxford University Press, Oxford

Bell D (1973) The coming of post-industrial society. A venture in social forecasting. Basic Books, New York

Billis D (ed) (2010) Hybrid organizations and the third sector. Palgrave MacMillan, London

Bogers M, Afuah A, Bastian B (2010) Users as innovators: a review, critique, and future research directions. J Manag 36(4):857–875

Bouckaert G, Halligan J (2008) Managing performance: international comparisons. Routledge, London

Bourdieu P (1984) Distinction. A social critique of the judgement of taste. Harvard University Press, Cambridge, MA

Bourdieu P (2000) Pascalian meditations. Polity Press, Cambridge

Bourdieu P, Wacquant LJD (1992) An invitation to reflexive sociology. The University of Chigaco, Chicago

Bovard T (2007) Beyond engagement and participation – user and community co-production of public services. Public Adm Rev 67(5):846–860

Brodie RJ, Glynn MS, Little V (2006) The service brand and the service-dominant logic: missing fundamental premise or the need for stronger theory? Mark Theory 6(3):363–379

Brynjolfsson E, McAfee A (2014) The second machine age. Work, progress and prosperity in a time of brilliant technologies. W.W. Norton, New York

Cameron CR, Sirianne C (eds) (1996) Working in the service society. Temple University Press, Philadelphia

Checkland PB (1981) Systems thinking, systems practice. Wiley, Chichester

Chesbrough H (2006) Open innovation. The new imperative for creating and profiting from technology. Harvard Business Review Press, Boston, MA

Chesbrough H, Vanhaverbeke W, West J (2008) Open innovation: researching a new paradigm. Oxford University Press, Oxford

Chia R (2003) Organization theory as a postmodern science. In: Tsoukas H, Knudsen C (eds) The Oxford handbook of organization theory. Meta-theoretical perspectives. Oxford University Press, Oxford, pp 113–140

Cook LS, Bowen DE, Chase RB, Dasu S, Stewart DM, Tansik DA (2002) Human issues in service design. J Oper Manag 20(2):159–174

Currie C, White L (2012) Inter-professional barriers and knowledge brokering in an organizational context: the case of healthcare. Organization 33(10):1333–1361

DiMaggio PJ, Powell WW (2012) The iron cage revisited: institutional isomorphism and collective rationality in organizational fields. In: Calhoun C et al (eds) Contemporary sociological theory. Wiley, Chichester, pp 175–192 (Originally published in 1983)

Djellal F, Gallouj F, Miles I (2013) Two decades of research on innovation in services: which place for public services? Struct Chang Econ Dyn 27(4):98–117

Doz Y, Kosonen M (2010) Embedding strategic agility: a leadership agenda for accelerating business model renewal. Long Range Plan 43(2–3):370–382

Durand R, Vergne JP (2013) The pirate organization. Lessons from the fringes of capitalism. Harvard Business Review Press, Boston, MA

Ellis K, Davis A, Rummery K (1999) Needs assessment, street-level bureaucracy and the new community care. Soc Policy Adm 33(3):262–280

Evans T, Harris J (2004) Street-level bureaucracy, social work and the (exaggerated) death of discretion. Br J Soc Work 34(6):871–895

Fernandez S, Pitts DW (2007) Under what conditions do public managers favor and pursue organizational change? Am Rev Public Adm 37(3):324–341

Fernandez S, Rainey HG (2006) Managing successful organizational change in the public sector. Public Adm Rev 66(2):168–176

Fernandez S, Choo YJ, Perry JL (2010) Exploring the link between integrated leadership and public sector performance. Leadersh Q 21(2):308–323

Fournier M (2013) Émile Durkheim: a biography. Polity Press, Cambridge

Furco A, Billig SH (eds) (2001) Service learning: the essence of the pedagogy. Information Age Publishing, New York

Grönroos C (2011) Value co-creation in service logic: a critical analysis. Mark Theory 11(3):279–301

Haveri A (2008) Evaluation of change in local governance. The rhetoric wall and the politics of images. Evaluation 14(2):139–153

Hilgers M, Mangez E (eds) (2015) Bourdieu's theory of social fields. Concepts and applications'. Routledge, New York

Hood C (1991) A public management for all seasons? Public Adm 69(1):3–19

Hupe P, Buffat A (2014) A public service gap. Capturing contexts in a comparative approach of street level bureaucracy. Public Manag Rev 16(4):548–569

Ikeda N, Saito E, Inoue M, Ikeda S, Satoh T, Wada K, Stickley A, Katanoda K, Mizoue T, Noda M, Iso H, Fujino Y, Sobue T, Tsugane S, Naghavi M, Ezatti M, Shibuya K (2011) What has made the population of Japan healthy? Lancet 378(9796):1094–1105

Jansson A, Parding K (2011) Changed governance of public sector organisations – challenged conditions for intra-professional relations? Int J Public Sect Manag 24(3):177–186

Kaivo-oja J, Virtanen P, Jalonen H, Stenvall J (2015) The effects of the internet of things and big data to organizations and their knowledge management practices. In: Luden L et al (eds) Knowledge management in organizations, vol 224. Springer, Heidelberg, pp 495–513

Kaivo-oja J, Virtanen P, Stenvall J, Jalonen H, Wallin J (2016) Future prospects for knowledge management in the field of health. KMO 2016. In: Proceedings of the 11th international knowledge management in organizations, Article no. 40. https://doi.org/10.1145/2925995. 2926006, ACM, New York. http://dl.acm.org/icps.cfm

Kodner D (2009) All together now: a conceptual exploration of integrated care. Healthc Q 13 (4):6–15

Kolb D (1984) Experimental learning: experience as the source of learning and development. Prentice Hall, Englewood Cliffs

Koppell JGS (2005) Pathologies of accountability: ICANN and the challenge of "multiple accountabilities disorder". Public Adm Rev 65(1):94–108

Kurkela K, Virtanen P, Stenvall J, Tuurnas S (2016) Älykäs kokeilu- ja kehittämistoiminta kunnissa. Kuntien kokeilutoiminta älykkäiden kokonaisratkaisujen mahdollistajana. Loppuraportti (available in Finnish, Experiment and development activities in municipalities. Experimenting facilitating integrated intelligent solutions in municipalities. Final report.) Acta No. 263. The Association of Finnish Local and Regional Authorities, University of Tampere, Helsinki

Larsen P, Tonge R, Lewis A (2007) Strategic planning and design in the service sector. Manag Decis 45(2):180–195

Lipsky M (1980) Street-level bureaucracy. Dilemmas of individual in public service. Russell Sage Foundation, New York

Lyngsø AM, Godtfredsen NS, Høst D, Frølich A (2014) Instruments to assess integrated care: a systematic review. Int J Integr Care 14(3):1–15

Maglio P, Breidbach C (2014) Service science: toward systematic service system innovation. In: Newman A, Leung J (eds) Bridging data and decision. Tutorials in operations research, pp 161–170. http://pubsonline.informs.org/doi/book/10.1287/educ.2014

Maglio P, Spohrer J (2013) A service science perspective on business model innovation. Ind Mark Manag 42(5):665–670

March JG (1991) Exploration and exploitation in organizational learning. Organ Sci 2(1):71–87

Matthing J, Kristensson P, Gustafsson A, Parasuraman A (2006) Developing successful technology-based services: the issue of identifying and involving innovative users. J Serv Mark 20(5):288–297

Michel S, Brown SW, Gallan AS (2008) Service-logic innovations: how to innovate customers, not products. Calif Manag Rev 50(3):49–65

Molin MD, Masella C (2016) From fragmentation to comprehensiveness in network governance. Public Organ Rev 16(4):493–508

Nonaka I, Hirose A, Takeda Y (2016) Meso-foundations of dynamic capabilities: team-level synthesis and distributed leadership as the source of dynamic creativity. Glob Strateg J 6 (3):168–182

Normann R (1995) Service management: strategy and leadership in service business. Wiley, New York

North DC (2005) Understanding the process of economic change. Princeton University Press, Princetown, NJ

Osborne S (2010) Introduction. The (new) public governance: a suitable case for treatment? In: Osborne S (ed) The new public governance? Routledge, London, pp 1–16

Osborne S, Radnon Z, Nasi G (2013) A new theory for public service management? Towards a (public) service-dominant approach. Am Rev Public Adm 43(2):135–158

Pestoff V (2012) Co-production and third sector social services in Europe: some crucial conceptual issues. In: Pestoff V, Brandsen T, Vershuere B (eds) New public governance, the third sector and co-production. Routledge, London, pp 13–34

Pollitt C, Bouckaert G (2011) Public management reform: a comparative analysis. New public management, governance and the neo-Weberian state. Oxford University Press, Oxford

Praetorius T, Becker MC (2016) How to achieve care coordination inside health care organizations: insights from organization theory on coordination in theory and in actio. Int J Care Coord. Published online on 2.3.2016, https://doi.org/10.1177/2053434516634115

Prahalad CK, Ramaswamy V (2004) The future of competition. Co-creating unique value with customers. Harvard Business School Press, Boston

Pugh DS (2007) Introduction to the fifth edition. In: Pugh DS (ed) Organization theory. Classic readings. Penguin Books, London, pp xi–xiii

Rashman L, Withers E, Hartley J (2009) Organizational learning and knowledge in public service organizations: a systematic review of the literature. Int J Manag Rev 11(4):463–494

Saks M (2013) Regulating the English healthcare professions: zoos, circuses or safari parks? J Prof Organ. Published online on December 17, 2013, https://doi.org/10.1093/jpo/jot001

Schillemans T (2011) Does horizontal accountability work? Evaluating potential remedies for the accountability deficit of agencies. Adm Soc 43(3):387–416

Schneider B (1984) The service organization: climate is crucial. Organ Dyn 5(2):52–65

Schneier B (2015) Data and goliath. The hidden battles to collect your data and control your world. W.W. Norton & Company, London

Sennett R (1992) The fall of the public man. W.W. Norton, New York (Originally published in 1972)

Shostack GL (1977) Breaking free from product marketing. J Mark 41(2):73–80

Shultz M (2001) The uncertain relevance of newness: organizational learning and knowledge flows. Acad Manag J 44(6):661–681

Spohrer J, Freund LE (eds) (2013) Advances in the human side of service engineering. Taylor & Francis Group, Boca Raton

Spohrer J, Maglio P (2008) The emergence of service science: toward systematic service innovations to accelerate co-creation of value. Prod Oper Manag 17(3):238–246

Spohrer J, Maglio P, Bailey J, Gruhl D (2007) Steps towards a science of service systems. Computer 40(1):71–77

Stacey R (2010) Complexity and organizational reality: uncertainty and the need to rethink management after the collapse of investment capitalism. Routledge, London

Starbuck WH (2003) The origins of organization theory. In: Tsoukas H, Knudsen C (eds) The Oxford handbook of organization theory. Meta-theoretical perspectives. Oxford University Press, Oxford, pp 143–182

Tuurnas S (2016) The professional side of co-production. Acta Universitatis Tamperensis 2163, Tampere

Tuurnas S, Stenvall J, Rannisto PH (2015) The impact of co-production on frontline accountability: the case of conciliation service. Int Rev Adm Sci 82:131–149. https://doi.org/10.1177/0020852314566010, first published on July 2, 2015

Vargo SL, Lusch RF (2004) Evolving to a new dominant logic for marketing. J Mark 68(1):1–17

Vargo SL, Lusch RF (2008) Service-dominant logic: continuing the evolution. J Acad Mark Sci 36 (1):1–10

Virtanen P, Kaivo-oja J (2015) Public services and emergent systemic societal challenges. Int J Public Leadersh 11(2):77–91

Virtanen P, Stenvall J (2014) The evolution of public services from co-production to co-creation and beyond – an unfinished trajectory for the New Public Management? Int J Leadersh Public Serv 10(2):91–107

Virtanen P, Kaivo-oja J, Ishino Y, Stenvall J, Jalonen H (2016a) Ubiquitous revolution, customer needs and business intelligence. Empirical evidence from Japanese healthcare sector. Int J Web Eng Technol 11(3):259–283

Virtanen P, Laitinen I, Stenvall J (2016b) Street-level bureaucrats as strategy shapers in social and health service delivery: empirical evidence from six countries. Int Soc Work 16(3):1–14. https://doi.org/10.1177/0020872816660602

Virtanen P, Uusikylä P, Jalava J, Tiihonen S, Laitinen L, Noro K (2016c) Valtioneuvoston yhtenäisyys – kansainvälinen vertaileva tutkimus [available in only in Fiinish, The unity of government – an international comparative study]. Valtioneuvoston kanslia, Helsinki. Accessed at www.tietokauttoon.fi

Walker L, Gilson L (2004) We are bitter but we are satisfied: nurses as street-level bureaucrats in South Africa. Soc Sci Med 59(6):1251–1261

Weber M (1947) In: Henderson AM, Parsons T (eds) The theory of social and economic organization. The Free Press, New York. Originally published in 1924

Wright S (2006) The administration of transformation: a case study of implementing welfare reform in the UK. In: Henman P, Fenger M (eds) Administering welfare reform – international transformations in welfare governance. Policy Press, Bristol, pp 161–182

Chapter 6
Leadership and Human Resource Management

Abstract Leaders can be considered as artists who use intuition to navigate their way through chaos (Zalenzik, Harv Bus Rev 55:67–78, 1977). The content of this chapter is intelligent leadership in the field of healthcare. The basic argument in this chapter is that traditional leadership paradigms do not suffice anymore in intelligent healthcare organisations. Intelligent people—like doctors, nurses, psychologists, social workers and other healthcare professionals—are a unique breed. They, for instance, wish that leaders would appreciate their achievements and performance at work. Intelligent people quite often have the ability to find environments and challenges that motivate them. Intelligent organisations emphasise especially strategic personnel management, which is transformative and focusses on the growth of individual expertise, motivational aspects and continuous learning. Leading intelligent people is based on dynamic philosophy. The leader's role is to point the direction, act as a coach and develop the personnel. This approach challenges and confronts the contemporary models of clinical leadership of healthcare in multiple ways. Consequently, leadership in intelligent organisations demands the ability to build up collective trust in organisations. The working community is important for intelligent people. Through collective-based leadership actions, it is possible to strengthen the ability to work for common objectives. Trust, on the other hand, is necessary so that workers are ready to share their expertise and have the courage to develop their operations despite the possibility of errors. Intelligent healthcare organisations have the ability to make adaptive changes in complex environments. Leaders have an essential role in successful change management.

6.1 Intelligent People in Organisations

Without a doubt, the management of people can improve organisational outputs and outcome in intelligent organisations. The mechanisms through which human resources are managed can either hinder or enhance the capacity of intelligence.

Leading people includes two kinds of aspects. Leadership literature is littered with bold statements contrasting the two, such as managers 'do things right', while leaders 'do the right things', and 'the management works in the system; leadership works on the system' (Bolden et al. 2011, p. 23). From this perspective, management and leadership are different mindsets. In practice, however, the distinction

P. Virtanen, J. Stenvall, *Intelligent Health Policy*,
https://doi.org/10.1007/978-3-319-69596-9_6

between management and leadership is like a line drawn in water. It is very difficult to see any difference between them.

It is meaningful for intelligent people to use their talent and ability in their work. In this context, both management and leadership issues matter. For this reason, we move in this chapter away from the division between management and leadership. We concentrate generally on the issue of how to lead intelligent employees in organisations. It is necessary to take into consideration both the roles of leaders and the situational factors of organisations formulated by leading intelligent employees.

Over time, the leadership approach to management has grown, and it is now in full bloom. There are various ways in which the leading of people has been analysed and presented over the past century. Bolden et al. (2011) divide literature on leadership into three mainstreams:

1. Leadership as a property of leaders
2. Leadership as a relationship between leaders and followers
3. Leadership as a social process

Leadership as a property of leaders emphasises the viewpoint that leaders are the key group in managing people. The trait approach underlines the leader's character. The alternative approach is to consider how leaders behave or what kinds of leadership styles they have. Situational theories were developed to indicate that the style to be used is dependent upon situational factors, such as the nature of followers, tasks, the organisation and other environmental variables. This is an approach considering leadership as a property of leaders. It focusses especially on the skills and functions in people management. For instance, the classic model by Selznick (1957) sees that leaders have a role in the definition of missions, in building the organisation's social structure, in maintaining values and distinctive identity and in the settling of internal conflicts.

The second approach focusses on the relationship between leaders and followers. Traditional and conventional theories are based on the viewpoint that the leaders show the way for the followers. The leaders are positioned in the vanguard, guiding, directing, innovating and presenting a vision for change and making it become reality. The followers, on the other hand, conventionally track the leader, obey, report, implement innovations and accept the leaders' visions (Banks 2008). Leading employees was presented as a series of inputs and outputs that have an impact on performance. In response to this rather dry and analytic approach, Burns (1978, see also Bolden et al. 2011) developed the notion of transforming leadership. What really matters is the moral and reciprocal relationship between leaders and followers whereby one or more persons engage with others in such a way that leaders and followers raise one another to higher levels of motivation and morality.

The third mainstream approach sees the leading of people as a social process (Bolden et al. 2011). A shared perspective considers leadership as a dynamic, interactive influence process among individuals in groups for which the objective is to lead one another to the achievement of group or organisational goals or both (see Pearce and Conger 2003). Constitutive theories are interested in, for instance, that what the situation and the leader actually are is a consequence of various accounts and interpretations, all of which vie for domination.

In this chapter, our intention is to formulate what kinds of perspectives are possible to develop for managing people in intelligent healthcare organisations. This is something that is missing in the literature. Because our book is policy-oriented, our purpose is to design approaches for managing intelligent employees that support the adaptiveness of healthcare organisations. Before we present the approach, we will start with a discussion on technology and people management.

6.2 Robots and Big Data Take Over?

The core of intelligent organisations is not only human resources but also the deployment of technology. This combination means a lot of challenges for managing people in intelligent organisations. It is, for instance, obvious that people management will be faced with the impact of robotics in many ways in the future. Some management positions will be in danger of disappearing. It seems that robots are quite effective at, for instance, operational management, like formulating schedules of actions (Gombolay et al. 2014). Robots can make decisions rationally without feelings when they act as leaders. Hence, robots as leaders cannot recognise emotions. This means that people are willing to follow them (Hooman et al. 2012).

One of the key questions in robotisation is change management. For instance, intelligent organisations need a capacity to implement new kinds of technologies into practice. The second important issue is how people can work with technology in effective ways.

The tensions between technology and human resources can described using the concept of dilemmas. Dilemmas are mutually exclusive but desirable (or undesirable) options often resulting from conflicting or contradictory values held by individuals or organisations, and deciding between the options may result in tension and dispute (Kangaslahti 2007; Hampden-Turner 2009; Kuoppakangas 2015). The following dilemmas, which are based on our article on dilemmas and public services, are relevant for leading people in intelligent organisations (Stenvall et al. 2017):

- Repetitive continuity—radical change
- Risk-taking—security-seeking
- Individuality—communitarianism
- Technology-based developing—human-based developing
- Autopoietic—controlling

Repetitive continuity means a starting point where big data is implemented by changing the current practices as little as possible. For instance, dig data is utilised in existing practices by converting them to be technology-based. It is possible that data collecting is automated utilising new technology. It is also possible that intelligent organisations' purpose is to radically change working methods, managerial systems, etc. due to technological possibilities. Radical changes can, for instance, mean challenging people's meaningful work and values.

The second dilemma pair with technology is risk-taking—security-seeking. Risk-taking is a situation where the development of technology and the results to be gained involve plenty of insecurity. It may be uncertain where the implementation of technology is leading and what results it will bring about. In the security-seeking model, implementation is more cautious.

Individuality means that the implementation of technology is seen as being dependent on the individual actors. On the other hand, technology-based practices quite often presuppose some systematic and organised features in organisations as well as dedication to act under the conditions of the entity. For instance, in order to have big data as the way of operation, it may presuppose that every worker in the organisation uses technology in the same way for collecting information.

The implementation of technology might make it possible to strengthen autonomy and autopoiesis among workers. Workers and the teams they form could, for instance, plan their own work on the basis of information. On the other hand, it is possible that new technology—like big data practices—with its growing masses of information, makes it possible to have an increasingly strict control. Based on information, it would be, in principle, easier than ever before to monitor what the workers are doing and where and how are they working.

Technology development means that leaders have to lead the adaptability of employees. They have to find a balance between the human and technological aspects in leading people.

6.3 The Selection of Leadership Perspectives

How to lead intelligent people in organisations is an almost fundamental question (Nohria and Khurana 2011). As a part of NPM and NPG movements, an important trend in healthcare and in the public sector in general has been the growth of competence-based management. Instead of defining management according to broad job roles, competence-based management involves a detailed codification of what managers should know and be able to do and how they should behave at different levels of the management hierarchy (cf. McGurk 2013). This is our perspective on leading intelligent people.

We are convinced that leading intelligent people in health organisations requires a comprehensive approach. This means that the principles of leading people cover the whole organisation. We emphasise the importance of practices. We try to indicate how leading intelligent people is manifested in actions. Our framework is based on research concerning intelligent organisations and human resource management (Stenvall and Virtanen 2015; Laitinen et al. 2017a, b). There are different levels of human resource management:

Strategic human resource management in intelligent organisations: Strategic human resource management as choice and in action

Working community and intelligent organisations: How to create interactions between people and thereby increase intelligence in organisations

Leader–employee relations in intelligent organisations: How to lead people and thereby increase individual capacities of intelligence

Leadership perspectives have moved from rational and logic-argued management towards actions where personalities, emotions and empathy are in the centre (cf. Karp 2006). This is an important thing to notice because it means that human resources are not just a technical thing. In this chapter, our perspective is human resource management.

6.4 Strategic Human Resource Management

The strategic approach is a comprehensive approach to lead intelligent people in organisations. In this chapter, we especially make use of the discussion on strategic human resource management. Strategic management rests on two fundamentals: action logic and human aspiration. Strategy focusses on the first, and human resource management stresses the second (Leavy and Mckiernan 2009). Human resource management underlines the belief that people are the most important asset for any organisation.

The strategic approach places an emphasis on synergy (or, at least, congruence) among the various human resource management practices (internal fit or horizontal integration) and on ensuring that these practices are aligned with the needs of the business as a whole and the broader environment within which the organisation functions (external fit or vertical integration). It emphasises the role of human resource management systems as solutions to problems rather than individual human resource management practices in isolation (Bamberger et al. 2014; Becker and Huselid 2006)—the strategic and coherent approach to the management of people who individually and collectively contribute to the achievement of the organisation's objectives.

Talent management, especially, has an effect on the discussion of how organisations can develop their intelligence strategically. Actually, talent management has been one of the most debated themes in human resource management theory and practice in recent years. Hence, it is not clear what talent management really means in organisations' realities (Thunnissen et al. 2013a, b). Generally speaking, the talent management approach describes a strategy process in which organisations recognise and develop talented employees and their skills and knowledge (Silzer and Dowell 2010; Sparrow and Makram 2015). In existing research on healthcare management, the talent management approach has been rarely used and nurtured. Powell et al. (2012) have identified a strong focus on the private sector and on multinational companies in contemporary talent management literature. This might indicate that healthcare management has traditionally placed more emphasis on collective and collegial intelligence than on the importance of individual people.

Traditional approaches of human resource strategies are based on design thinking. This means that organisations have to concentrate on designing a suitable strategy that affects policy for treating and developing employees (cf. Boxall and Purcell 2003).

In this book, we approach human resource strategies from the perspective of strategy-as-practice. This means a shift from a static and possessive view of strategy (something that an organisation has) to a processual and performative definition of strategising (something that organisational actors do) (Jarzabkowski 2005; Vaara et al. 2010).

From our perspective, strategy-as-practice means that a meaningful human resource strategy is not necessarily planned or consciously formulated. Quite often, strategic practices can develop emergently in organisations. Individual problem-solving might be meaningful for human resource management. For instance, a hospital might recruit doctors for development tasks due to their knowledge of how to use new technology. This can create a culture of recruitment that has an effect on the success of the hospital.

Strategy-as-practice means the viewpoint that managers at all levels are all attributed a significant role concerning the human resource management strategy of intelligent employees. It is not just a special unit with the task of taking care of human resources like compensation or recruiting people.

Instead of this, the management of human resources is a responsibility for all leaders. There is coherent and incoherent human resource management in organisations. Human resource management is coherent if all leaders treat employees in the same way. It is incoherent if leaders have different approaches in treating people in the same organisation. The levels of coherence in human resource management tell us of the implementation capacity of organisations, for instance.

Human resource can be conceptualised as the pattern of decisions regarding the policies and practices associated with the human resource system and strategy. It means employing people, developing their resources, utilising, maintaining and compensating their services in tune with the individual, job and organisational requirements.

Using the literature, we consider the following subsystems are important in intelligent organisations (Beer et al. 1984; Dyer and Holder 1988; Bamberger et al. 2014):

- People flow subsystem. The subsystem incorporates human resource responsibilities such as recruitment, selection, placement and managing employee mobility.
- Competence management subsystem. This incorporates human resource practices in which organisations use and develop employees' intelligence.
- Engagement and employee's motivation subsystem. This subsystem covers rewards and practices that affect intellectual people's motivation and engagement.

- Performance management subsystem. This includes how organisations evaluate the outcomes of intelligent employees.

The *people flow subsystem* starts with the recruitment and selection of intelligent people. The first thing is to recognise what kind of intelligence the organisation needs. The criteria are likely to vary in terms of the degree to which organisations are focussed on certain core competences as opposed to the characteristics of single jobs (Snow and Snell 1993; Bamberger et al. 2014).

Strategic thinking and the vision of the organisation give criteria for analysing what kinds of intelligence—including competence and talent—will be needed in the future. Organisations analyse the current intelligence as well. The purpose is to recognise if there are gaps between the current intelligence and the intelligence organisations need in the future. This helps to develop intelligence at both individual and collective levels as well. For instance, a primary care organisation can prepare for the future by analysing the technological changes and intelligence that will be needed.

Talent management discussion has raised the question that an organisation has to make choices and what is their policy and methods to recruit intelligent employees. One challenge is to find the potentially intelligent people—a question that has been discussed a lot in talent management discourse. Implemented talent management strategy includes improved employee recruitment. Organisations must be increasingly strategic in their recruitment and selection because the intelligent people they find and attract are in almost every sense the key element to create value for the organisation (Schweyer 2004). One potential solution is to use head-hunting. Many organisations use web-based recruitment or professional social networking sites (Dineen and Noe 2009). In their selection processes, organisations can use different kinds of methods like tasks, interviews and tests.

One of the key issues is whether an organisation should recruit intelligent people from outside the organisation or should they support the high-potential or high-performing employees' careers inside of organisation (i.e. buy or make talent) (Cappelli 2008; Collings and Mellahi 2009; cf. Thunnissen et al. 2013a).

Career systems are a part of the people flow system. The key question is what kinds of possibilities do intelligent people see for their careers in organisations? They might ask if organisations give them possibilities to use or develop their intelligence in the future. A challenging question is also how we understand the normal careers of intelligent people. Scholars in the field of talent management, for instance, seem to assume that organisational–traditional careers are still the norm, i.e. careers characterised by upward mobility and long-term, full-time employment in one and the same organisation. However, organisational career systems might have witnessed major changes in recent decades even in healthcare organisations. The proactive role of the employee in shaping his or her own career (reflected in concepts such as the boundary-less career, the protean career and multidirectional career paths) is steadily gaining influence in the field of career management (Biemann et al. 2012; Thunnissen et al. 2013b).

The second subsystem is the *competence management system*. Organisations—including healthcare organisations—have various potential practices in which they can develop the employees' intelligence. Training, mentoring, education and rotating are examples of how organisations can develop their employees' competence.

There are two possible approaches to how organisations can develop a competence management subsystem in an intelligence approach. The first possibility is the so-called traditional competence management approach. It is based on the ideology of collective intelligence. According to the literature, organisations have quite often developed their competence and intelligence step by step. It is possible to recognise the following stages (Virtanen and Stenvall 2014):

• Training and developing competence without connection to strategies
• Recognising core competence and intelligence in organisations
• Comprehensive approach in developing competence and intelligence
• Developing competence and intelligence as a part of strategic approach

In many organisations, competence management has moved from the training to the strategic approach. One example is that when an organisation has strategic projects—like using big data in healthcare—it should take care of the development of intelligence.

The second possibility is that organisations invest in key intelligent people. This is a typical approach in talent management. It emphasises the viewpoint that an organisation's success depends on individual persons. The talent management approach incorporates the viewpoint of individual intelligence. Hence, it is important to think how talented and intelligent people can be useful from the perspective of organisations. Some researchers of talent management (Gallardo-Gallardo et al. 2013; Thunnissen et al. 2013a) make a distinction between inclusive (i.e. all employees) and exclusive (i.e. a specific employee group). The exclusive approach means that the organisation focusses on a select group of high-performing and/or high-potential employees. This might mean that a healthcare organisation that has a training programme with an inclusive approach encourages every employee to fulfil his or her potential.

The strategy-as-practice approach might even mean that organisations should be interested in the ways in which leaders act as coaches for their employees in their development of intelligence. Actually, managers make an enormous number of decisions in their daily work that show to the employees what kind of intelligence is important in the organisation.

On the basis of talent management, the *engagement and people's motivation subsystem* is a key challenge in the human resource management of intelligent employees. In a knowledge-intensive company, employee loyalty is almost as important as customer loyalty, and employees are not easily dispensable (Cunha 2002). In general, the engagement index slots people into one of three categories (Caplan 2013, p. 13):

1. Engaged employees work with passion and feel a profound connection with their organisation. They drive innovation and move the organisation forward.
2. Not engaged employees are essentially 'checked out'. They are sleepwalking through their waking day. They are putting in their time but not enough energy or passion into their work.
3. Actively disengaged employees aren't just unhappy at their work; they are busy acting out their unhappiness. Every day these workers undermine what their engaged co-workers accomplish.

Intelligent people's motivation and opportunities in organisations are critical aspects in human resource management. Motivation itself is made up of internal and external elements. Individuals are driven by their own inner motivation, but this also needs to be directed (Boxall and Purcell 2003). For instance, intelligent people—like doctors—might have purposes to do thing due to their abilities, which might be not useful for organisations. Hence, opportunities to use intelligence play an active role in engagement as well. Individuals are not able to exercise their abilities and motivation if the processes of their organisations are badly coordinated or poorly managed (Caplan 2013).

The strategic approach means that the development of intelligence is goal-oriented in organisations. Actually, there is a strong link between leading people and performance management.

The fourth subsystem is the *performance management subsystem*. Strategic human resource management especially has focussed on organisational performance rather than individual performance (Becker and Huselid 2006). Basically, this means that strategic human resource management is strengthening collective intelligence. Hence, human resource management practices, like compensation systems, affect individual intelligence as well.

Strategic aims can help to identify what kinds of performance measurements an intelligent organisation needs. For instance, it is possible that the level of a doctor's intelligence to utilise new technology affects the ability to get outcomes. The other strategic choice for making progress is to identify the kinds of aspects of managing people or human resource management that are amenable to measurement and then to estimate their effect on organisational outputs and outcomes (O'Toole et al. 2013).

There is a lot of critical discussion on human resource management's importance to healthcare organisations. One problem is that leaders do not take human resource management issues seriously. This is related to the issue that it is not easy to show what kind of value good human resource management produces for performance (Boudreau and Ramstad 2005). Hard times and cost-cutting in organisations may also result in an overall reduction in human resources and directing human resource activities to surviving.

All in all, the effectiveness of strategic human resource management is related to the issue of how organisations adopt, formulate and implement their strategies. For instance, implementation involves both execution and employee acceptance. That is, while strategy execution may be associated with a range of problems from technical glitches in associated human resource information systems to active resistance (Bamberger et al. 2014), implementation challenges can exist at both individual and organisational levels.

6.5   Trust Constitutes Work Community

Working conditions that facilitate employee control and support not only make significant contributions to the level of work satisfaction experienced by employees working in healthcare but also represent key features of high-performance work systems (Noblet et al. 2013). There is a lot of discussion that working conditions are an underestimated issue concerning intelligent organisations. The basic issue is providing the resources and space for intelligent employees in working communities. According to Goffee and Jones (2009, p. 49), the more astute leaders recognise that it is a balance between providing enough space to try out new things and creating a playground for the clever where they are not expected to deliver results.

Working conditions include people's well-being at work. This is especially important in intelligent organisations because mental work—including problem-solving, creativity, etc.—can be tough and stressful. In practice, it seems that quite often talented and intelligent organisations underestimate the importance of employees' well-being (Thunnissen et al. 2013a, b).

A part of well-being is that leaders might protect intelligent people from the rain. People make mistakes when they work with difficult problem-solving. Actually, any organisation that strives for high levels of innovation and creativity—exactly the area where intelligent people make a big difference—must recognise the necessity of failure (Goffee and Jones 2009).

An essential aspect in a working community is trust. It is a function of the intensity, quality and duration of human interaction (Harisalo and Stenvall 2004). Trust in interactive relationships is determined by the participants' impressions on the degree of trust experienced towards the other party in an indirectly or directly interactive relationship. The concept of trust is context-specific, multidimensional and a very complex interpersonal and organisational construct (Blind 2006; Nyhan 2000). According to Nyhan (2000, p. 89; see also Creed and Miles 1996), trust is often associated with situations involving personal conflict, outcome uncertainty and problem-solving. Mishra (1996, p. 265) states trust as one party's willingness to be valuable to another party based on the belief that the latter party is more competent, open, concerned and reliable.

Trust is an essential working condition in creating an environment for intelligent people to use their intelligence. The other important issue is human interaction. In the Chicago-school approach of human resource management, the essential thing is what kinds of meanings, definitions of situations and behavioural norms are formed in human interaction.

It is a quite typical phenomenon in organisations for different kinds of intelligent people to have their own perspectives on things and making decisions, etc. The challenge in leading people is to create human interaction that develops intelligence. In organisations, there are points of view that are interacting, possibly competing, and there are representations that may develop in dialogue with each other (Clegg et al. 2006).

There has been more and more discussion on inter-professional and cross-professional approaches in healthcare (Denton and Conron 2016; Marsilio et al. 2016). It seems that communication is especially important in healthcare if we think about how people can work effectively with each other. This is related to the issues of how people work when solving problems or how they share knowledge with each other.

According to Clegg et al. (2006, pp. 12–13; see Stenvall et al. 2014), the concept of polyphony came to organisation studies when this field of study became interested in language through its language-based approaches. As Clegg et al. (2006, p. 14) pointed out, to Bakhtin, the concept of polyphony meant not only the literary discourse itself but is 'a means of challenging an entire intellectual culture dominated by a monological conception of truth—a conception where a truth is regarded as having a singular existence'. Thus, an author or a leader is just one of the characters in an organisation.

Taking these definitions into account, polyphonous or polyphonic leadership is something that creates conclusions or decisions by listening to the multiple voices of the organisation. A polyphonic organisation is something where many, and possibly differentiated, dialogues occur simultaneously. The leaders or managers should have the ability to reconcile or to orchestrate the different views and interests by understanding that if there are disagreeing voices, there is no single voice that is right while others have made an error. Behind all voices, different rationales can be found, and this is why a manager should listen to a variety of voices in the decision-making processes. Managing by polyphony is to manage the plurality of values, ideas and aim systems and the heterogeneity of these differentiated communicative codes and incompatible values (Stenvall et al. 2014).

The essential role of leaders in intelligent organisations is to make dialogue, discourse as well as interaction possible—to enable them and find suitable means to encourage the personnel to share views, practices and values. What is meaningful is that passive hearing or understanding of the voices is not enough. It is more a question of whether there is a relevant amount of interaction between these voices. This requires arenas for discourse and interaction.

It is possible to argue that polyphonic leadership relates at least partly with the shared leadership approach. According to this, leadership in an organisation belongs to personnel and management (Jackson and Parry 2008). In the same way, polyphony can also be assimilated with transformational management. There, an organisation evolves and reaches its objectives through synergy between superiors and employees (Bass and Avolio 1994). Through interaction, room for different rationalities can be given, and this means that different voices in an organisation are considered equivalent.

At its best, polyphonic leadership increases the many-sidedness and scope of perspectives. In this sense, polyphonic leadership is connected to the viewpoint of leadership by an expert organisation (Sveiby 1997). Leaders understand that they are not necessarily the best experts in all matters. It is possible to utilise polyphony in a way that helps in creating an overall view of the operation of the organisation and of the characteristics affecting it.

Even in polyphonic leadership, leaders should assume the role of a leader of meanings (Podolny et al. 2010). This means that a superior must be able to manage polyphony so that the interpretations created in an interaction will be appropriate from the perspective of the whole organisation.

In this chapter, we have argued that human interaction, trust and well-being are especially important issues in creating working conditions in intelligent organisations. For this reason, those factors should be the starting points for leading intelligent people. Organisations and their culture might be unique. This means that leaders need the ability to analyse the individual cultural aspects that affect the working conditions.

6.6   Leaders and Employees Intertwined by Communication

The leader–employee relationship has been approached from the perspective of servant leadership, the discursive approach and the authentic leadership approach. There are several studies that have argued that human interaction between leaders and employees is the key issue.

Kaufman (2013) has argued that, taking the qualities of an intelligent organisation into account, the leader should have strong interactions with the followers, be aware of the uncertainties and probabilities, know the discontinuity of his/her leadership and know that the impact of his/her leadership depends on interaction. Sydänmaanlakka (2015) has noted that leadership is seen as a process, not a position in intelligent organisation. Intelligent leadership is shared and collaborative and therefore significantly different from the way leadership has been addressed in mainstream models. Therefore, it goes without saying that the proverbial followers are actively involved in this model and that they are also engaged in the phenomenon of leadership, not 'followership'. Goffee and Jones (2009, p. 43) have made notes that clever people do not like to be told what to do. Needing to be told seems to undermine their sense of self-esteem. The art of leadership begins with listening and talking.

There are a lot of discussions on the leader–employee relationship in healthcare research as well. Those studies have shown that different kinds of intelligence in healthcare professions have especially caused a lot of tensions between leaders and employees. This is related to values (Morgan and Ogbonna 2008; Nugus et al. 2010). It seems that the customer and professional aspects are especially important in healthcare concerning the leader–employee relationship (Syväjärvi and Stenvall 2006).

It is possible to think that leaders should be more intelligent than their followers in an intelligent organisation. In this context, a leader is the one who copes with and adapts to the rapid changes in conditions and the environment as well as uncertainty and the speed of access to data, information and knowledge to fulfil the objectives of the organisation. The key thing is to identify the situations and individual social factors that affect people's work.

Another possible way is to think that leaders have to act as the developers of their employees' intelligence in organisations. In this approach, adaptive leadership is another important framework concerning the leader–employee relationship in intelligent organisations. As Heifetz et al. (2009) underline, the concepts of adaptive leadership grew from efforts to understand organisations, leadership, systems and change. Thus, the concepts have been discussed by various theorists in complex adaptive systems (Laitinen et al. 2017a).

The starting point for adaptive leadership is that we are living in a complex and changing world. Leadership and change can be considered inseparable twins. Adaptive leadership is the practice of mobilising people to tackle tough challenges for which we need intelligence. One of the leader's roles is 'holding the environment', which means that they have to ensure that intelligent people solve purposeful problems from the perspective of the organisation. The adaptive leadership approach emphasises the importance of developing individual intelligence to strengthen individual people's ability to adapt to solving new kinds of problems. Hence, collective intelligence is important as well because adaptiveness needs human interaction in working places.

Heifetz (1994) defines leadership's role as mobilising employees' adaptive capacity to tackle wicked problems. The core of leadership comprises addressing adaptive challenges, a process known as adaptive work (Heifetz 1994; Hickman 2010; Laitinen et al. 2017a). The key challenge for the leader is to help people distinguish what is worthy of preservation from the past and what is expendable. Successful adaptations are thus both conservative and progressive.

According to Heifetz (1994, pp. 120–130), there are two types of challenges: adaptive and technical, and leadership requires addressing both. Technical challenges are those to which current knowledge may be applied and for which there are some tested answers that, typically, people in authority empower others with experience and knowledge to apply. These technical challenges vary and may be highly complicated, such as heart surgery or a broken arm, but the knowledge of what the outcome looks like already exists. Intelligent people—like doctors—know exactly how to fix problems. In this context, the leadership's challenge is that intelligent people are motivated to use their intelligence in solving problems. Technical problems reside in the head; solving them requires an appeal to the mind, to logic and to the intellect.

In contrast, adaptive challenges are those for which no known or ready solutions exist, and it is, therefore, vital to create and learn new approaches for addressing them. In such cases, those experiencing the problem or challenge are a part of the process of finding the best solution. Adaptive problems are often systemic problems with no ready answers. The solutions lie not in technical answers but rather in the people themselves. Adaptive situations are hard to define and resolve precisely because they demand the work and responsibility of managers and people throughout the organisation. They are not amenable to solutions provided by leaders; adaptive solutions require the members of the organisation to take responsibility for the problematic situations that are facing them.

Adaptive work narrows down the gap between aspiration and reality by demanding responses outside the repertoire, and learning is a vital part of adaptive work (Heifetz 1994). These adaptive challenges are murky, with no easy answers. Solving them requires the involvement of people throughout the organisation.

First, in order to make a change happen, executives have to break a long-standing behaviour pattern of their own: providing leadership in the form of solutions. Second, adaptive changes are distressing for the people going through them. They need to take on new roles, new relationships, new values, new behaviours and new approaches to work.

Adaptive work is counter-intuitive for leaders. Rather than providing solutions, you must ask tough questions and leverage employees' collective intelligence. Instead of maintaining norms, leaders must challenge the 'way we do business'. And rather than quelling conflict, leaders need to draw issues out and let people feel the sting of reality. In the adaptive approach, leaders are concerned with the creation of social capital. This increases mutual understanding, trust, commitment and obligation between managers to enhance cooperation and resource exchange in creating organisational value (Heifetz 1994).

Leadership requires a learning strategy in intelligent organisations. Adaptive organisations are characterised by learning interdependence, the critical elements of which are judgement, ethics, insight and creativity. Learning is seen as the key differentiator between adaptive and non-adaptive systems. The emphasis has moved to intelligent organisations, collective intelligence and information flows. Adaptive systems adapt through learning and self-organised responses to the current challenge.

A leader has to engage people in confronting the challenge, adjusting their values, changing perspectives and learning new habits. In this sense, the important issue is what Aldridge and Fraser (2000) described using the term 'minds-on' learning (Kinder et al. 2017). Vygotsky's (Kinder 2012) social learning theory centres upon cognition and emotions interrogating a learning activity system. Aligning this with the idea of sense-making, it is possible that individual learning connects to collective learning using distributed learning theory (Nardi 1996).

Adaptivity requires that leaders have the ability to contribute not only employees' learning but unlearning as well. Unlearning is not forgetting (like a dementia patient), suppressing negations (Freud) or restraining the use of knowledge (Ulysses) (Kinder et al. 2017). Unlearning is the implicit idea in Kurt Lewin's famous theory of change management—*freeze-change-refreeze*—which was brought to prominence by Hedberg (1981), who contests behavioural theory seeking to explain how organisations learn by stressing the importance of discarding old knowledge to make way for change. While accepting the idea of unlearning, conceived as eradicating barriers to new learning, arguing against a 'clean slate fallacy'. An alternative interpretation of unlearning by Klein (1989) disputes Hedberg's idea of overwriting old knowledge with new, suggesting that unlearning degrades old knowledge.

This bespeaks a new kind of leadership occurring in the face of adaptivity. Such challenges require learning, innovation and new roles and behaviour by leaders. Successful adaptive leadership requires patience, persistence, an eye for obstacles and a willingness to overcome them.

6.7   Synthesis

In this chapter, we have taken up factors that are important in leading intelligent employees. We have emphasised the strategy-as-practice approach. It means that it is decisive how human resource management affects intelligent people's behaviours in concrete ways. According to this approach, human resource management belongs to all leaders at the different levels of organisations. Even small-scale and emergent practices can lead to big changes in human resource management.

It is necessary to keep in mind that professional and intelligent people are at the centre in policy making. As Lipsky (1980) argued, the content of policy making depends in many ways on what kind of choices so-called street-level bureaucrats—people in charge of services—make in their work. In this sense, human resource management and practices have a meaningful influence on healthcare policy, not only in the implementation of policy, but in the formulation of policy as well.

In this chapter, we have presented that the strategic, working community and leader–employee relationship approaches constitute the core of leading intelligent people. Leaders should think about what the key human resource management practices are that affect the behaviour of intelligent people. Leaders need the ability to generate trust and well-being in working communities. Human interaction is the key to creating collective intelligence. Leadership has to be exercised every day and in all kinds of practices that have an effect on intelligent employees. In the best case, leaders encourage and push intelligent employees to work on difficult and constantly changing problems. In the worst case, leaders are the weakest links in the healthcare policy in intelligent organisations.

References

Aldridge J, Fraser B (2000) A cross-cultural study of classroom learning environments in Australia and Taiwan. Learn Environ Res 3:2101–2134

Bamberger PA, Biron M, Meshoulam I (2014) Human resource strategy. Formulation, implementation and impact. Routledge, New York

Banks S (2008) The troubles with leadership. In: Banks S (ed) Dissent and the failure of leadership. Edward Elgar, Cheltenham, pp 1–21

Bass B, Avolio B (1994) Improving organizational effectiveness through transformational leadership. Sage, Thousand Oaks, CA

Becker BE, Huselid MA (2006) Strategic human resources management: where do we go from here? J Manag 32(6):898–925

Beer M, Spector B, Lawrence PR, Mills DQ, Walton RE (1984) A conceptual view of HRM. Managing human assets. Free Press, New York

Biemann T, Zacher H, Feldmann D (2012) Career patterns: a twenty-year panel study. J Vocat Behav 81(2):159–170

Blind PK (2006) Building trust in government in the twenty first century: review of literature and emerging issues. Paper presented in 7th global forum on reinventing government building trust in government, 26–29 June 2007, Vienna, Austria

Bolden R, Hawkins B, Gosling J, Taylor S (2011) Exploring leadership: individual, organizational, and societal perspectives. Oxford University Press, Oxford

Boudreau JW, Ramstad PM (2005) Talentship, talent segmentation, and sustainability: a new HR decision science paradigm for a new strategy definition. Hum Resour Manag 44(2):129–136

Boxall P, Purcell J (2003) Strategy and HRM. Palgrave, London

Burns J (1978) Leadership. Harper & Row, New York

Caplan J (2013) Strategic talent development: develop and engage all your people for business success. Kogan Page, London

Cappelli P (2008) Talent management for the twenty-first century. Harv Bus Rev 86(3):74–80

Clegg SR, Kornberger M, Carter C, Rhodes C (2006) For management? Manag Learn 37(1):7–27

Collings DG, Mellahi K (2009) Strategic talent management: a review and research agenda. Hum Resour Manag Rev 19(4):304–313

Creed WED, Miles RE (1996) Trust in organization: a conceptual framework. In: Kramer RM, Tyler TR (eds) Trust in organizations: frontiers in theory and research. Sage, London, pp 302–330

Cunha MP (2002) The best place to be: managing control and employee loyalty in a knowledge-intensive company. J Appl Behav Sci 38(4):481–495

Denton E, Conron M (2016) Improving outcomes in lung cancer: the value of the multidisciplinary health care team. J Multidiscip Healthc 9:137–144

Dineen BR, Noe RA (2009) Effects of customization on application decisions and applicant pool char-labor-characteristic in a web-based recruitment context. J Appl Psychol 94:224–234

Dyer L, Holder GW (1988) A Strategic perspective of human resource management. In: Dyer L (ed) Human resource management – evolving roles and responsibilities, vol 1. Bna Books, Washington, DC, pp 1–45

Gallardo-Gallardo N, Dries T, González-Cruz T (2013) What is the meaning of 'talent' in the world of work? Hum Resour Manag Rev 23(4):290–300

Goffee R, Jones G (2009) Clever: leading your smartest, most creative people. Harvard Business Press, Boston

Gombolay M, Gutierrez RA, Sturla GF, Shah JA (2014) Decision-making authority, team efficiency and human worker satisfaction in mixed human-robot teams. Massachusetts Institute of Technology. http://people.csail.mit.edu/gombolay/Publications/Gombolay_RSS_2014.p

Hampden-Turner C (2009) Teaching innovation and entrepreneurship: Building on the Singapore experiment. Cambridge University Press, New York

Harisalo R, Stenvall J (2004) Trust as capital. The foundation of management. In: Huotari M-L, Iivonen M (eds) Trust in knowledge management and systems in organizations. Idea Group, Hershey, pp 51–81

Hedberg B (1981) How organizations learn and unlearn. In: Nystrom C, Starbuck W (eds) Handbook of organizational design. Oxford University Press, London, pp 18–27

Heifetz RA (1994) Leadership without easy answers, vol 465. Harvard University Press, Cambridge

Heifetz RA, Grashow A, Linsky M (2009) The practice of adaptive leadership: tools and tactics for changing your organization and the world. Harvard Business Press, Boston, MA

Hickman GR (2010) Leading change in multiple contexts: concepts and practices in organizational, community, social, and global change settings. Sage, Thousand Oaks, CA

Hooman S, Koh J, Tzu Valino K, Elham, S, Doros, P (2012) Lecture notes in computer science artificial intelligence and lecture notes in bioinformatics, vol 7197(2), pp 158–165

Jackson B, Parry K (2008) A very short, fairly interesting and reasonably cheap book about studying leadership. Sage, London

Jarzabkowski P (2005) Strategy as practice. Sage, London

Kangaslahti J (2007) Mapping the strategic leadership practices and dilemmas of a municipal educational organization. Department of Education, University of Turku, Turku

Karp T (2006) Transforming organisations for organic growth: the DNA of change leadership. J Chang Manag 6(1):3–20

Kaufman SB (2013) Ungifted: intelligence redefined. Basic Books, New York

Kinder T (2012) Learning, innovating and performance of locally delivered public services. Public Manag Rev 14(3):403–428

Kinder T, Stenvall J, Laitinen I (2017) Conceptualising unlearning by Finland's to civil servants. Manuscript. University Tampere, Finland

Klein JI (1989) Paranthetic learning in organisations toward the unlearning of the unlearning model. J Manag Stud 26(3):291–308

Kuoppakangas P (2015) Decision-making and choice in the adoption of a municipal enterprise form in public sector healthcare organisations – Reasoning, goals, legitimacy and core dilemmas. Turku School of Economics in the University of Turku, Doctoral dissertation A-9: 2015, Juvenes Print, Turku

Laitinen I, Piazza R, Stenvall J (2017a) Adaptive learning in smart cities – the cases of Catania and Helsinki. J Adult Contin Educ 23:119–137

Laitinen I, Kinder T, Stenvall J (2017b) Street-level new public governances in integrated services-as-a-system. Public Manag Rev:1–28. https://doi.org/10.1080/14719037.2017.1340506

Leavy B, McKiernan P (2009) Strategic leadership: governance and renewal. Palgrave Macmillan, Basingstoke, NY

Lewin K (1935) A dynamic theory of personality. McGraw-Hill, New York

Lipsky M (1980) Street-level bureaucracy. Dilemmas of individual in public service. Russell Sage Foundation, New York

Marsilio M, Torbica A, Villa S (2016) Health care multidisciplinary teams: the sociotechnical approach for an integrated system-wide perspective. Health Care Manag Rev 42:303–314

McGurk P (2013) Management and leadership development in public service organizations. Human resource management in the public sector, 153

Mishra AK (1996) Organizational responses to crisis. In: Kramer RM, Tyler TR (eds) Trust in organizations: frontiers of theory and research. Sage, Newbury Park, CA, pp 261–287

Morgan PI, Ogbonna E (2008) Subcultural dynamics in transformation: a multi-perspective study of healthcare professionals. Hum Relat 61(1):39–65

Nardi B (1996) Context and consciousness: activity theory and human-computer interaction. MIT Press, Cambridge, MA

Noblet A, Page K, Montagne T (2013) Building more supportive and inclusive public sector working environments: a case study from the Australian community health sector. In: Burke R, Noblet A, Cooper C (eds) Human resource management in the public sector. Edward Elgar, Chelteman, pp 90–108

Nohria N, Khurana R (2011) Advancing leadership theory and practice. In: Nohria N, Khurana R (eds) Handbook of leadership theory and practice. Harvard Business Press, Harvard

Nugus P, Greenfield D, Travaglia J, Westbrook J, Braithwaite B (2010) How and where clinicians exercise power: interprofessional relations in health care. Soc Sci Med 71(5):898–909

Nyhan RC (2000) Changing the paradigm: trust and its role in public sector organizations. Am Rev Public Adm 3(1):87–109

O'Toole LJ, Torenvlied R, Akkerman A, Meier K (2013) Human resource management and public organizational performance: educational outcomes in the Netherlands. In: Burke R, Noblet A,

Cooper C (eds) Human resource management in the public sector. Edward Elgar, Chelteman, pp 270–286

Pearce CL, Conger JA (2003) All those years ago. In: Shared leadership: reframing the hows and whys of leadership, pp 1–18

Podolny J, Khururana R, Besharov M (2010) Revisiting the meaning of leadership. In: Nohria N, Khurana R (eds) Handbook of leadership theory and practice. Harvard Business Press, Boston, MA, pp 65–106

Powell M, Durose J, Duberley J, Exworthy M, Fewtrell C, MacFarlane F, Moss P (2012) Talent management in the NHS managerial workforce. Final report, National Institute for Health Research, pp 1–216

Schweyer A (2004) Talent management systems: best practices in technology solutions for recruitment, retention and workforce planning. Wiley, Canada

Selznick P (1957) Leadership in administration: a sociological interpretation. University of California Press, Berkeley

Silzer R, Dowell BE (2010) Strategic talent management matters. In: Strategy-driven talent management: a leadership imperative. Jossey-Bass, San Francisco, CA, pp 3–72

Snow CC, Snell SA (1993) Staffing as strategy. In: Schmitt N, Borman WC (eds) Personnel selection in organizations. Jossey-Bass, San Francisco, pp 448–478

Sparrow PR, Makram H (2015) What is the value of talent management? Building value-driven processes within a talent management architecture. Hum Resour Manag Rev 25(3):249–263

Stenvall J, Virtanen P (2015) Intelligent public organizations? Public Organ Rev, published on-line 2.12.2015. https://doi.org/10.1007/s11115-015-0331-1

Stenvall J, Nyholm I, Rannisto PH (2014) Polyphonous leadership and middle managers. Int J Leadersh Public Serv 10(3):172–184

Stenvall J, Kuoppakangas P, Kinder T, Laitinen I (2017) Unlearning dilemmas – the case of big data. Manuscript. University of Tampere

Sveiby KE (1997) The new organizational wealth: managing and measuring knowledge-based assets. Berrett-Koehler, San Francisco

Sydänmaanlakka P (2015) Älykäs julkinen johtaminen: miten rakentaa älykäs verkostoyhteiskunta? (Intelligent public management). Talentum

Syväjärvi A, Stenvall J (2006) The eHealth: conceptualization, implementation and future possibilities. In: Anttiroiko A-V, Mälkiä M (eds) Encyclopedia of digital government. Idea Group Publishing, Hershey, PA, pp 244–250

Thunnissen M, Boselie P, Fruytier B (2013a) A review of talent management: infancy or adolescence? Int J HRM 24(9):1744–1761

Thunnissen M, Boselie P, Fruytier B (2013b) Talent management and the relevance of context: towards a pluralistic approach. Hum Resour Manag Rev 23(4):326–336

Vaara E, Sorsa V, Pälli P (2010) On the force potential of strategy texts: a critical discourse analysis of a strategic plan and its power effects in a city organization. Organization 17 (6):685–702

Virtanen P, Stenvall J (2014) The evolution of public services from co-production to co-creation and beyond – an unfinished trajectory for the New Public Management? Int J Leadersh Public Serv 10(2):91–107

Chapter 7
Intelligent Evaluation and Performance Measurement in Public Health Policy and Public Service Systems

Abstract Healthcare organisations are not immortal, far from it. The service science approach highlights the role of service users in the service process. Their success and failure are dependent on performance measurement and evaluation. This chapter analyses the role of performance measurement and evaluation in the domain of intelligent policy making in the field of health. Traditionally, the role of evaluation and performance measurement has been central in the management doctrines and practices of public policy and public organisations. Performance measurement and evaluation are important features in the public policy process since they provide feedback information on how public authorities have attained the goals set for them. In this chapter we discuss the role and definition of key evaluation concepts within the framework of intelligent public policy and link these key evaluation concepts into a time-wise three-dimensional model of intelligent evaluative inquiry (ex ante, ex nunc and ex post). We aim to make a strong case for more intelligent public policy evaluation by addressing the simple fact that even though the world is practically full of information today, only part of it converts to knowledge for decision-makers and public policy makers. This chapter builds upon the evaluation practice related to 'classical' evidence-based medicine, addressing the role of evidence (albeit always contested to a certain extent) in fostering and nurturing decision-making in public policy and public organisations, but goes further towards public policy and public organisations. To this end, we stress the importance of deploying the best ideas of evidence-based medicine to strengthen policy- and organisation-based performance judgement. This chapter also explores the implications of this transformation for evaluation, performance monitoring and accountability, underlining that horizontal accountability referencing a wide democratic footprint is likely to become more explicit. Consequently, this chapter develops the idea of transformation of public sector performance management from the viewpoint of organisational intelligence. This chapter concludes that 'hard nose' rationalistic models of performance and evaluation are no longer fit for purpose in the health sector.

P. Virtanen, J. Stenvall, *Intelligent Health Policy*,
https://doi.org/10.1007/978-3-319-69596-9_7

7.1   Are Public Healthcare Organisations Immortal?

Common wisdom probably holds that public sector organisations perform badly in terms of productivity, effectiveness and service quality and—even worse—in a neo-bureaucratic manner and for various reasons, topped with the aftermath of the ongoing financial crisis (e.g. Harrison and Smith 2013; Karanikolos et al. 2013). This section goes into these kinds of 'common wisdom' issues related to healthcare—and tries to open up the roots of the debate concerning these 'common wisdom facts'.

The title of this section is a paraphrase from Herbert Kaufman's (1976) famous book title from 40 years ago. Kaufman asked a rather startling question in a very pejorative manner in his book title: *Are Government Organizations Immortal?* His answer was '*sort of*', which was a nasty answer to a question addressed in the title of his book.

For the record, we read Kaufman as a representative of the old school meaning that currently public health policy and public organisations in the field of healthcare encounter multidimensional pressures in terms of performance and goal attainment than they used to back in the latter half of the twentieth century. Today, we think that the heyday is over for public healthcare organisations who perform badly in achieving goals to which they pay very little or no attention.

There is a growing discussion going on about the accountability function of public health policies as well as the role of value-based health including predictive, preventive, personalised and participatory approaches in the field of health (e.g. Hood and Flores 2012). This means—definitely—that public healthcare organisations have to be alerted in a sense about how it performs from the point of view of the service users, financially, in the eyes of their stakeholders and as an organisational member of society. In the business management literature, this kind of management and business leadership approach has gone under the title of 'balanced scorecard' since the mid-1990s (e.g. Kaplan and Norton 1996). The balanced scorecard received much attention a few decades ago as a management approach and tool incorporating a fruitful recipe for a management fad consisting of a rather convincing theoretical background as well as well-orchestrated and persuasive consultancy rhetoric (e.g. Nørreklit 2003).

Moreover, the days are over when there was no competition among health organisations. These days the transfer of resources from unproductive organisations to more productive organisations also takes place in the public sector domain. This relates to the development of more focussed and better calibre performance management models, which the public sector has put in place over the last 20 years. Given this, there is no extra mile to go for public health organisations in the public sector in terms of performance management, public finance management and the quality of performance in comparison with organisations from the private sector.

Dunleavy and Carrera (2013: 273) have made an interesting analogy between improving productivity in the public sector and dieting, a health-related topic. According to them, practically all of us agree that it would be an important thing to do. Good news ends here. There are multiple ranges of theoretically and conceptually plausible and noteworthy suggestions for making the actual change. Most of these suggestions have been proven either to not work or to be not as easy to implement as their proponents proclaim, as far as dieting is concerned. The same applies to a certain level with regard to productivity evaluation and performance measurement.

At the outset—and particularly in the private sector—productivity is a rather simple measurement procedure. It is calculated as the ratio of all the outputs produced by a given organisation divided by all the inputs (resources, including financial and human) deployed in the production of those given outputs. If this is the case, why has productivity measurement been so difficult in the public sector? To be more precise, why do we need more intelligence in collating, analysing and deploying performance data?

The problem arises precisely when entering the public sector domain—or the field of health policy in particular. The main reason for the problems related to productivity measurement is the lack of reliable productivity-oriented and price-related outputs. It is not easy to use prices to weigh the outputs produced by a public sector organisation. What is the price, for instance, of a doctor's output in a primary care organisation when he or she has consulted with a heavy user of health services who has a long-term illness?

Dunleavy and Carrera (2013: vii) argue that the lack of an appropriate output measurement was the fundamental deficiency in public sector productivity measurement until the late 1990s and the productivity measurement was based on input measurement rather than output measurement. Things started to change (probably the main reason for this was the rise of the NPM doctrine) at the turn of the millennium. Advanced methodologies in the field of public policy and health policy in particular allowed productivity measurement to be more consistent, concise and valid. Productivity measurement reached a new peak at this point because public services were tagged with a price note and this made it possible to weigh the outputs with the price.

Throughout this book, we try to break with the conventional wisdom that public policies and public sector healthcare services are worse—in terms of productivity and quality—than the business sector organisations. We believe that the domain of intelligent health policy creates a new forum and space for public, private and third-sector organisations in the field of health, which in turn creates new challenges in governing and leading this intelligence-based entity.

We argue instead that in the private sector, the measurement of productivity is grounded on a simple and straightforward index: the ratio of outputs divided by inputs. It is evident that the current performance measurement practices of the NPM and NPG era do not suffice anymore. Predominantly, health statistics and performance data are used to concern the value of inputs and—to certain extent—output indicators in the heyday of the NPM and NPG management doctrines, whereas the current landscape of healthcare presupposes a much more detailed approach in performance measurement.

The health 'philosophy' of current health policy calls for a new understanding of the value added by healthcare organisations from the patient's perspective. Today, much more emphasis is on the patient's side in terms of measuring the value the patient gains from healthcare. The role of the patient has changed radically because of societal changes and service ideology in particular. Today, a patient is more or less the producer of his or her own health (as the chronic care model presupposes) and not *just a service user* of healthcare services.

Consequently, we think it is important to ask why productivity is so important and why it is fundamentally important in the public sector. Another crucial question is why intelligence is important in interpreting productivity measures and performance metrics. The importance of productivity and performance measurement as a whole derives from the role of horizontal public policy and public organisation accountability. This argument holds the view that better information on public sector performance and productivity helps citizens and service users—patients in the field of health and well-being—to hold policy makers and public sector managers more accountable for the provision of public services (and healthcare services in the field of health policy).

Measuring productivity is thus a fundamental aspect in assessing public policy performance. Therefore, it is important to think about the genesis of public sector productivity measurement—and consequently think and rethink the role of intelligence in public sector performance management practices. As said, productivity measurement in the public sector has not been an easy task.

There are ways to overcome the theoretical and conceptual smog around the topic of public sector productivity. Dunleavy and Carrera (2013) suggest that productivity needs a wider framework for analysis. Their point, which is easy to agree with, is that public sector productivity rises somewhat automatically if one takes into account what happens in terms of digitalisation. Moreover, their suggestion is to make solid ground for organisational learning in public policy making as well as in public sector organisations. Both of these apply in all sectors of public policy and particularly in the specific sector of health and in sectors related to the well-being of the citizens.

Finally, we would like to stress that productivity change and improved performance are closely incorporated in innovation aspects. In this respect, we agree with Dunleavy and Carrera (2013: viii) that innovation-related advances in productivity can be a very positive approach for enhancing the continuous improvement of public sector organisations and public services. The need for intelligence enters into the picture here. One example of this is the measurement of productivity and performance of hybrid organisations. They are provided by multiple actors and institutions and are less standardised, and they often have remarkable variations in quality.

Finally, we would like to address the question posed in the title of this section: 'Are public healthcare organisations immortal?' To this question, we would answer: 'far from it'. If the question were rephrased as 'Are the public healthcare organisations immortal when we take into account the transformation process towards the service system ('service space') constituted by service organisations from public, private and non-governmental sectors', then we would have answered differently. In that case, we would have answered, 'No they are not, but they will be dead soon if they do not take the dynamics, competition and partnerships seriously'. Next, we turn to the 'world' of performance measurement and management with relation to healthcare service organisations and pinpoint key conceptual entities that are important to note in assessing the mechanisms of performance management.

7.2   The Links Between Accountability, Performance Measurement and Policy Evaluation

This chapter is grounded on the logic of value-based healthcare. This view holds that development of healthcare organisations is achievable when decisions by policy makers, healthcare managers, patients, service users and their families, and referring physicians and the planning of the healthcare agenda are based on an objective knowledge of results. According to Porter and Olmsted Teisberg (2006: 122–123), this knowledge management cycle covers medical and service outcomes and the costs of care and services over the full healthcare cycle.

According to Talbot (2005: 49), the discussions and debates on performance assessment in the public sector domain are as old as government itself. Rulers have voluntarily or involuntarily pursued legitimacy for their rule by showing how the acts of government have been beneficial to the citizens. The field of health is no exception here. Health concerns everyone, and it is definitely a topic that is in the interest of the rulers, regardless of the ruling mechanism, practice or ideology.

Talbot (2005: 496–501) makes a substantial point by addressing the fact that accountability is only one aspect of performance assessment: performance also relates to user choice, customer service, efficiency, results, effectiveness, resource allocation and creating public value, which are all important in running health and health-related public policies. Public value is of key interest in the field of health and in this book (discussed in Chap. 1). This view holds that public healthcare services are not merely about addressing market failures, but they have a more extended role in society by creating a value that is not made in the domain of private healthcare businesses. Public value is therefore an important aspect in thinking about the contents, limits and boundaries of accountability in healthcare services.

The world of performance management and public policy evaluation is definitely not without problems. We will deal with these problems later on in this chapter from many perspectives. They concern incomplete metrics, overcomplexity of measurement procedures, addressing various transaction costs, emerging attribution problems, methodological trivialities and debates about quantity vs. quality indicators and manipulation of performance reports, which are extensively reported in the academic literature on the subjects (e.g. Talbot 2005; Virtanen and Vakkuri 2016).

In addition, the role of unintended consequences of public health policy implementation, cyclical incompatibility (consistent measurement over long periods of time) and measurement degradation (i.e. the deterioration of measurement results over the course of time) are well-known problems in the discussions about the effects of health policy (e.g. Bauman et al. 2014; Cadilhac et al. 2012).

Traditionally, the role of public sector evaluation and performance measurement has been highly respected and appreciated. Weiss (1998), for instance, has argued that evaluation and performance measurement are important because they help increase the rationality of policy making. Therefore, it was not a big surprise that evaluation and performance management models and approaches had momentum in the public sector from the 1990s onwards. Management doctrines—predominantly New Public Management—incorporated evaluation and performance measurement as integral elements of a well-functioning public service. Greene, an eminent scholar in the domain of evaluation, anchored evaluation with even higher purposes in society. According to Greene, 'evaluators go beyond a value-relative stance, which acknowledges and engages the plurality of value that inhabit evaluation contexts, to a value-committed stance, through which evaluation purposefully advances particular values' (Greene 2006: 118). Evaluation and performance measurement became servants of society in terms of democracy and social change.

Since the end of the 1990s, dark clouds started to congregate in the clear sky of evaluation. The world of evaluation and performance measurement became puzzled. Rising problems were associated mainly with complex policy and public service environments and the existence of 'wicked' or 'nexus' policy problems (e.g. Head 2008; Weber and Khademian 2008; Ferlie et al. 2011; Peters 2005).

The more complex society became, the more profound were the methodological and conceptual problems of evaluation and performance measurement. In this chapter, we argue that intelligence embedded in public sector organisations requires a new understanding of seeing evaluation and performance measurement as mechanisms in distributed knowledge systems and sense-making communities.

It was no wonder that public sector performance management and policy evaluation have been under heavy criticism during the last few decades. This critique has reflected both the use of performance information—or its misuse or non-use, to be more precise—and the unintended institutional and behavioural effects of using performance information in public policy and public organisations (e.g. Heinrich 1999; Wholey and Hatry 1992; Patton 1997; van Helden et al. 2012).

Nevertheless, the evaluation of the outcomes of public policy and performance measurement of a public organisation's achievements are still key elements in a policy process (e.g. Birkland 2016). Professional evaluation and performance measurement should not be equated with the mere accumulation and summarising of data relevant for decision-making.

On the contrary, in a management context and in relation to public policies and services in particular, evaluation and performance measurement at its best serve multiple objectives and meanings. Both of them relate to the decision-making process. If this were not the case, we would effectively lack everything that qualifies as an evaluation and solid performance management (Scriven 1991: 5).

In addition, evaluation and performance measurement serve the purpose of accountability in multiple ways. For example, it can shed light on decision-making processes and on the activities of public organisations. This means that evaluation and performance measurement serve the democratic development of public policies and public organisations providing services for the citizens. This is precisely why the evaluation and performance measurement of public activities is so important.

Taking an argument by Bouckaert and Van Dooren (2009), Neely et al. (2006) and Bouckaert and Halligan (2008) as a starting point (all of whom conceive of the development of performance management models and public policy evaluation practices as an evolutionary process), this chapter concentrates on intelligent performance measurement and management. It develops the idea of the transformation of public sector performance management and public policy evaluation from the viewpoint of organisational intelligence. This chapter thus explores the implications of this transformation for evaluation, performance monitoring and accountability within the domain of health, underlining that horizontal accountability referencing a wide democratic footprint is likely to become more explicit (e.g. Schillemans 2011).

To synthesise, there are at least three major critical questions that relate to performance management and the evaluation of current health policies. (For more on these critical dilemmas and performance management contradictions, see Virtanen and Vakkuri 2015.) First, there are *systemic changes* as societal challenges—that is, globalisation, technological development and innovations, changes in social values and perceptions and climate change and ecological constraints.

We discussed the penetrating meaning of these systemic changes earlier in this book. From the performance management point of view, systemic changes represent a much broader theme than a mere economic issue. This is because it is a result of changes in the quality and number of human beings, the stock of human knowledge (particularly as applied to the human control of nature) and the institutional framework that defines that deliberative incentive structure of a society (North 2005). Public organisations ought to be resilient to these changes, and performance metrics ought to provide information on how this process proceeds (e.g. information about customer satisfaction, how public service delivery enhances service-user empowerment and the role of public service systems in the sphere of human life).

Secondly, *multilevel governance*—global, national, regional and local governance mechanisms—constitutes a form of vertical bureaucracy, coordination and division of labour. But in terms of planning and performance management, the decision-making process is far from completely rational or clear (e.g. Vakkuri 2010). Multilevel governance makes possible all sorts of problems in terms of overlapping decision-making, unclear division of labour and authority, distorted accountability order and overall complexity and interconnectedness in public policies. Consider the assessment of health-related policies in EU member states, for instance. It would be a tremendously difficult task, since the policies and practices in every EU member state vary a great deal.

Thirdly, *methodological problems* arise because of the complexity and interconnectedness of public policies and due to evolving intersections between the public and private sectors. With regard to health, problems arise when multiple healthcare organisations measure their performance in the same geographical area—the prevalence of certain diseases, for instance—and claim that they are the ones to thank for achieving the objectives. In this kind of measurement setting, there is the risk that goal attainment multiplies in every organisation's performance scoreboards.

The current paradigm of performance measurement and evaluation derives from the assumption that societies are governable by a rationalistic mode of thinking. This is definitely not the case, as we have argued earlier in this book. This is not the case because rationality in decision-making means neglecting the social mechanisms incorporated in the measurement of accountability systems and procedures and public policy evaluation.

Furthermore, current modes of performance measurement and evaluation rely excessively and extensively on the assumption of entity- or organisation-based evaluation—the idea that it is possible to detect performances within clear-cut organisational boundaries and to distinguish 'public' from 'private' and 'nongovernmental' performance in the field of health (Hodges 2012). In modern public administration practice, it would be equally important to understand performances within collaborative networks and in contexts where both public- and private-sector actors contribute to the 'final' outcomes for citizens as beneficiaries of public interventions in the field of health. This problem is labelled as 'multiple accountabilities disorder' in the current academic literature on the topic related to performance measurement and accountability (Koppell 2005; Bort et al. 2012).

7.3   The Composition of Intelligence in Policy Evaluation

The planning of public policy is not an easy task, and not very simple, because planning takes place in a complex society. This means that policy objectives are not easy to map out due to the complexity of societal problems and the lack of adequate policy analysis thereafter. No wonder then that the concept of the wicked or nexus problem in public policy has been taken up. New demands for public sector strategies have emerged. Innes and Booher (2016), to take one example, argue that classical modern planning mechanisms cannot solve wicked problems. As a consequence, a number of alternatives have been brought up to replace classical planning theories. For example, collaborative rationality (Innes and Booher 2016), system dynamics modelling (Bianchi 2015) and the deployment of public value theory (Geuijen et al. 2016) (ibid.) have been mentioned as possibilities to successfully tackle the dilemma of wicked problems in terms of planning.

The implementation of public health policy requires taxpayers' money. This is the main reason why the effects of policy delivery should be at the heart of the policy makers' agenda. Policy makers should be concerned about the delivery mechanism of policy (the organisational capacity of healthcare institutions, for instance), about how adopted policy really addresses the needs of the population and service users of policy and about the intended and unintended effects of the policy (also including opportunity costs and the possibility of reallocation of human and financial resources).

Moreover, as public policies should address societal values, it should be also taken into account what kind of health values health policies pursue. This being said, life is not easy for the person responsible for evaluating the overall usefulness of public policies—bearing in mind that health policies should be intelligent.

This leads to the essence of public policy evaluation. It should deal with various spheres of public policy—from simple input and output measures to the societal value and goals of public policy. This means that policy evaluation is like an onion. It can be peeled from one level to another, ending up in the core of the onion. Or it is like the famous souvenir from Russia, a wooden doll consisting of various wooden dolls of different sizes (the doll can be opened and on the inside you'll find another smaller doll...). Comprehensive public policy evaluation is more or less the same, reaching from the 'surface' towards the 'core'. One good example from this kind of policy evaluation thinking are the steps from input/output evaluation towards more complex levels of policy evaluation (e.g. the notion of societal verification of public policy and programme goals).

In terms of learning and evaluation, we start by sketching out the evolution of public policy evaluation. By doing this, we aim at providing a kind of 'big picture' of how the essence of public policy evaluation has developed over the years and decades. It is important to note that the development stages of public policy evaluation have occurred as a part of dominant public sector management doctrines (NPM and NPG). Overall, as we will propose, these paradigms—or waves, as Vedung (2010) has noted—differ substantially from each other in terms of motives, methodological approaches, reporting solutions and options as well as evaluator roles.

Those who have approached the literature about philosophy of science have most likely come across the concept of paradigm. Thomas Kuhn's influential book, *The Structure of Scientific Revolutions*, originally published in 1962 (see Kuhn 2012), canonised the concept of paradigm. For Kuhn, science develops cyclically—long periods of 'normal' science are punctuated by occasional violent 'revolutions' (think of the work of Copernicus in the sixteenth century and his revolutionary idea that the sun, not the earth, was at the heart of our universe). After a revolutionary phase, a new paradigm of science takes shape. This shaping and the form of the 'new' science is what Kuhn calls a paradigm (see Lewens 2015: 73–82).

We are well aware of the wise words of Lewens (2015: 77), who warns that the concept of paradigm has been used so widely that the concept has more or less become empty during the last decades. In our treatise in this section of the chapter, we deploy the concept of paradigm just to highlight the elementary differences in the evolution of public policy evaluation over the last 100 years or so. We think that the evaluation waves, which we will propose as follows, differ profoundly from each other and to certain extent also contain some revolutionary aspects in terms of how they incorporate public policy planning and delivery.

Vedung (1997: 3) advocates a view that puts public policy evaluation at the very heart of public policy. According to him, evaluation relates to analysing the outputs, outcomes and effects of public interventions in a systematic way in order to make explicit the merit of public interventions—policies, programmes, projects and organisation-level service delivery—and to make possible the reallocation of public resources. We think this a very solid working definition for evaluation since it links the idea of evaluation to the idea of learning from experience.

Next we ask how public policy evaluation has developed during the last 50 years or so and—to echo the concept Vedung (2010) has put forward—through what kind of waves has the idea of public policy evaluation evolved over the years since the 1960s.

First, a *science-based evaluation* wave became paradigmatic during the 1950s and 1960s. The main laboratory for this was the War on Poverty programme in the USA under the administration of President John F. Kennedy. The objective of the programme was to root out poverty in the USA, and this intervention brought about the need to harness economists and social scientists to provide information about the success of the programme (e.g. see Naples 2014; Zarefsky 1986). The whole idea about the programme was based on the assumption that poverty can be uprooted from society by rationalistic planning, adequate financial resources and appropriate knowledge about the outcomes of the programme. Science was harnessed to take part in this societal laboratory, and the form of science was policy evaluation.

Eventually there were a lot of criticism about the well-being indicators that were used in measuring the effects of the War on Poverty programme (e.g. Glennerster 2002) and about neglecting the race issue in assessing the merits of the policy (e.g. Heclo 1994). Another problem was that the measurement approach did not recognise the problem of the underclass, which was seen from the perspective of the 1980s and 1990s as predominantly a societal problem in the USA (e.g. Silver 1996).

In the end, the War on Poverty programme did not wipe out poverty in the USA, but it succeeded to a certain extent to create the requirements to alleviate the effects of poverty and social exclusion. Moreover, policy planners seem to have forgotten the fact (taking into account the scale of the federal programme) that there is always a time-related problem in assessing the effects of a policy. It simply takes time to map out the effects of a programme. This became a problem during the heyday of the War on Poverty programme since the measurement of the policy was anchored in the yearly budgetary process.

Second, a *dialogue-based evaluation* wave took place during the 1970s and the 1980s. It changed the world of evaluation at least in two aspects—the context (for evaluation) became very important as well as the qualitative methodology. These new perspectives meant that the focus of evaluation (policy, programme, project, organisation) was to be seen in a dialogue vis-á-vis the context which was the framework for public intervention.

According to Robson (2002), the 'real world' of society finally became the main focus for research and public policy evaluation. However, the 'flagship' of the constructive evaluation philosophy was Guba's and Lincoln's magnum opus *Fourth*

Generation Evaluation (Guba and Lincoln 1989), which was published in 1989 and gained an instant success among evaluation professionals and public policy planners. This book was very critical of the previous evaluation waves and science-based evaluation paradigm, which was conceived as having multiple methodological and practical problems. Methodologically, dialogue-based evaluation put qualitative methods at the centre of evaluation practice.

Third, a *new liberalistic evaluation* wave appears in Vedung's typology from the 1990s onwards, closely interlinked with the NPM tradition in public sector leadership. Vedung's argument goes as follows: once the public sector management paradigm changes (or rebuilds), the idea of public policy evaluation also changes. Many other scholars have shared this view when assessing the contents of public policy evaluation within the framework of New Public Management (Bouckaert and Van Dooren 2009; Bouckaert and Halligan 2008; Virtanen and Vakkuri 2016). In this setting, public policy evaluation was incorporated as a mechanism to enhance public sector performance management and vertical accountability functioning (subordinate agencies reporting upwards vertically to their principals and governing institutions). Thus public policy evaluation was harnessed as a tool to advocate the management principles of NPM. This task underlined policy evaluation's importance in terms of government decision-making, and it multiplied the number of evaluators working for the public sector throughout the OECD countries, either as government specialists or as the government's external evaluators.

Fourth, an *evidence-based evaluation* wave started to flourish at the end of the 1990s onwards, despite the fact that the evidence-based approach to public policy evaluation was introduced already in the 1960s in the works of Campbell in particular (e.g. see Campbell and Russo 1999). Campbell's merit was in bringing methodology, the varieties of randomised analysis settings, control groups and the idea of social experimentation to the centre of the public evaluation scene (e.g. see Shadish and Luellen 2004).

In Europe, evidence-based public policy evaluation gained a new impetus from the work of Pawson and Tilley in their *Realistic Evaluation* (Pawson and Tilley 1997), which gained immense popularity among evaluation professionals. Pawson and Tilley's groundbreaking idea was in fact rather simple. They underlined that in order to be trustworthy and legitimate, evaluators have to focus on the CMO principle (i.e. the connection between the interventions studied, the context of the intervention taking place and the outcomes of a given intervention).

This principle paved the way for new interpretations of case study generalisations, which is very important in terms of assessing health policy interventions and their effects (see also Pawson 2013). During the last 15 years, a plethora of books and articles have been published from evidence-based public policy and evidence-based decision-making in the domain of public policy (e.g. Aarons et al. 2011).

Overall, Vedung's typology can be criticised for oversimplifying reality. The distinctions between his evaluation waves are not clear, and they are not paradigms in the Kuhnian sense. However, we find Vedung's ideas inspiring because they provide clarity to the big picture in sketching out different forms and aspects of public policy evaluation. Vedung's typology brings about rather nicely the plethora of possibilities to judge and assess the role of public policy evaluation in the framework of planning, designing and delivering public policies.

In the following, we continue the analysis of Vedung by first making a distinction between auditing (carried out by an auditor), a performance audit (carried out by internal or external experts) and evaluation (implemented either as self-evaluation or by external experts). In the real organisational world, these conceptual entities pretty much interlink and overlap, which makes definite conceptual definitions hard to put forward. For the sake of clarity, we propose that all of these activities are needed in order for public health policy to be intelligent. This is because we consider that comprehensive monitoring and the evaluation framework of public policies, institutions and organisations consist of these three 'evaluation' functions—auditing, performance review and policy and organisational evaluation. They all serve somewhat different purposes—as Table 7.1 suggests—but all of them are needed to understand the comprehensive nature of evaluation intelligence within the public policy domain.

Our main point here is the application of existing evaluation models and approaches. Public policy designers in the field of health—as well as in other fields of public policy—ought to possess the competence to apply existing public policy evaluation approaches and models.

This is because evaluation approaches and models are always context-bound ('where and under what circumstances does the public intervention take place?'), related time-wise to the delivery of a given policy ('when does the public intervention take place and how should the reporting be organised?') and finally public policy and decision-maker related ('who are the decision-makers, what sort of information do they need in their decision-making process and what are the key evaluation criteria to judge the merits and misfortunes of a given programme?').

In Table 7.2, we provide a case example of the application of existing evaluation models and approaches. The example is from a healthcare service organisation, and it builds upon our previous work on the subject (Virtanen and Stenvall 2014). In the left column, there is reference to critical boundaries which we discussed earlier in Chap. 5 in this book.

Table 7.2 is based on service science logic building upon three conceptual entities—the service organisation, the service front-line staff and the service users. The *service performance* boundary exists between the service organisation and the service staff, the *service effectiveness* boundary between the service organisation and the service users and the service touchpoint boundary between the front-line service staff and the service users.

Our aim has been to bring attention to the fact that there are different ways to approach the practice of public policy evaluation. Our view is that in order to be intelligent, public policy evaluation should cover auditing of accounts, performance review and monitoring, as well as evaluating the actual health policies either internally or externally.

The logic behind our approach relates to two main aspects of intelligent policy making—the central role of the patients and the importance of decision-

Table 7.1   Three evaluation entities for intelligent health policy—auditing, performance review and audit and policy and organisational evaluation

	Objective	Information types and agency	Information reporting mode
Auditing of accounts	Accountability concerning the deployment and mobilisation of financial resources	Balance sheet analysis according to auditing standards addressing the question: 'Has public money been spent according to the laws and regulations?' *Agency:* Independent auditors, the State Audit Office	Independent auditors reporting to decision-makers how public institutions and organisations have used the resources allocated to them
Performance review and audit	Accountability for goal attainment of public institutions and organisations	Performance review reports according to performance review standards (e.g. INTOSAI) addressing the question: 'Have public policies, institutions and organisations reached the objectives which have seen as their targets?') *Agency:* Performance auditors at local and regional authorities, the State Audit Office http://www.intosai.org/issai-executive-summaries/4-auditing-guidelines/general-auditing-guidelines.html	Performance information about the goal attainment levels of public policies, institutions and organisations in the framework of performance management
Policy and organisational evaluation	Accountability for expected results and resource allocation (ex ante evaluation), policy delivery (ex nunc evaluation) and effectiveness (ex post evaluation) of public policies	Evaluation analysis according to national evaluation standards (e.g. AEA (American Evaluation Association) guiding principles for evaluation; see http://www.eval.org/p/cm/ld/fid=51) addressing the meta-question 'what has been the societal value added by public policy?' An important aspect to note is that policy and	Evaluation information for decision-makers about the performance of policy and organisational delivery, taking into account the intended and unintended goals of public institutions. Data collation, analysis and reporting take place in the framework of policy evaluation (e.g. see Vedung 1997)

(continued)

Table 7.1 (continued)

	Objective	Information types and agency	Information reporting mode
		organisational evaluation address intended goals of policies and, moreover, on unintended goals (i.e. unintended effects, deadweight effects, substitution effects and so on) *Agency:* Either in the form of self-evaluation (e.g. using CAF/EFQM frameworks) or by external evaluators deploying existing policy and programme evaluation standards	

making in the betterment of public services. These aspects help in understanding the dynamics of new service ecosystems and a new service, consisting of various forms of organising. And this also leads to question the role of accountability in the public policy cycle—in planning, designing and reorganising public policies. Another important question is how the accountability function is changing in terms of who is responsible for whom. Intelligent health policy making is not very intelligent if it does not build upon the idea of horizontal accountability.

7.4 Accountabilities

Assessing and managing performance is a conceptually multisided entity, comprised of many interrelated concepts and practices. One of those important concepts is accountability, which is under scrutiny in this section. The concept of accountability dates back centuries. The term relates to accounting, and it literally comes from the world of bookkeeping.

Today, accountability has gone far beyond its bookkeeping origins and has become a symbol for good governance. According to Bovens (2005: 182, 192–193), public accountability is the hallmark of modern democratic governance. In a word, accountability holds a strong promise of fair, trustworthy and equitable governance and public administration. This means that accountability is about democratic control of public organisations and public healthcare, and it is a

Table 7.2 Evaluation matrix for public healthcare services (Adapted from Virtanen and Stenvall 2014)

Service boundary/ evaluation sphere	Evaluation theme	Motives	Focus of analysis	Main actors of information dissemination
Boundary I Healthcare service performance	Productivity	• Utilisation of resources • Resource allocation • Betterment of health service delivery	Analysis of the effects of strategic HRM and the allocation of organisational resources	• Political decision-makers • Top management
	Employee (doctors, nurses, social workers, psychologists) satisfaction	• Employee feedback • Employer brand	Analysis on the sustainability of workplaces and well-being at work	• All vertical levels of organisational hierarchy
Boundary II Healthcare service effectiveness	Production supply	• Equilibrium between production means	Analysis on financial cash-flows and organisational agility and modes of service delivery	• Political decision-makers • Top management
	Customer satisfaction and prevalence levels of certain diseases	• Patient feedback • Legitimation of health services ('taxpayer' view)	Analysis of customer satisfaction (surveys and interviews), the prevalence of diseases	• All vertical levels of organisational hierarchy • Reporting to patients
Boundary III Healthcare service touchpoints	Deployment of capacities	• Work achievement • Learning by doing	Analysis on the deployment of competencies and innovation capacity	• All vertical levels of organisational hierarchy
	Empowerment of the patients	• Feeling of being served • Usefulness of services • Redesign of service	Participation in development actions; empowerment of service users	• Political decision-makers • Top management • Service personnel • Service users

mechanism to enhance the integrity of both public organisations and service users of public services. Moreover, it is a tool to improve the performance of public policy implementation and, at the end of the day, an operating instrument to maintain the legitimacy of public governance.

Public policy and management scholars (e.g. Bovens 2005, 2010; Schillemans 2011; Michels and Meijer 2008; Virtanen and Vakkuri 2016) have maintained over the years that public accountability has gradually shifted from vertical to horizontal accountability. It is important to note this transformation, since in practice it alters the service delivery logic of public services. In a word, this transformation is a change from bureaucratic *modus operandi* towards more service science-oriented logic of action in public administration. Service orientation eventually changes the organisation cultures of public organisations. Service users move at the heart of the public service delivery mechanism—they are incorporated in the planning and implementation of public services.

This view, which is related to the transformation from vertical to horizontal accountability, holds that the traditional accountability theorem be replaced more or less by one with more emphasis on horizontal organisational accountability, i.e. organisations operating in the service space (both competing with each other and collaborating). Our main argument in this book is that emerging horizontal accountability is two-dimensional by nature (e.g. Virtanen et al. 2016c). It also covers organisations; but not only that, service users are also affected. We consider our approach to be an extension in the current debate about public accountability, and it is important due to the fact that service users—and citizens—get an acknowledged position in the service process.

Let us continue with the concept of accountability. By definition, accountability is an elusive concept with many meanings, connotations, common view assumptions and pure misunderstandings. Bovens (2010), for instance, makes a distinction between accountability as a *virtue* and as a *mechanism*.

In the former case, according to Bovens (ibid.), accountability is a normative and moral-based concept. It constitutes a set of standards and criteria for the evaluation and assessment of the behaviour and actions of public actors. In this meaning, accountability is an indicator—positive or negative—for organisations in the public sphere. In this light, accountability measures the goal attainment of public organisations, i.e. how they have achieved their goals and how the public money has been used in achieving these goals. In addition, accountability is also a mechanism, and this definition leads to a narrower, more descriptive way to conceive the concept.

As a mechanism, accountability refers to a principal–agent structure, occurring in an institutional relation or arrangement in which an agent is held accountable for its actions to the principal. In this sense, accountability is a process more than a virtue—a process in which the agent reports to the principal. The components of the accountability process comprise of informing about the performance, debating, judging and specifying the consequences (sanctions or rewards, which can be formal or informal).

By definition, there are also multiple meanings of accountability when we think about the accountee in the accountability process (e.g. see Bovens 2005: 186–188; Bovens et al. 2014). We discuss these accountee roles briefly as follows:

Organisational accountability is perhaps the most known and discussed form of accountability in the public sector domain, and it is based on the so-called principal–agent theory (e.g. Lane 2005). Principals (hierarchical superiors in organisations) give their subordinate actors tasks and resources and require vertical bottom-up reporting about the performance that took place. This setting between the principal and the agent requires a hierarchical relationship.

Political accountability means that elected representatives and political party members are accountable for their actions towards the people that voted for them. There is a certain blurriness in political accountability, since it is not always easy to draw a clear line in public administration as to who is a political appointee and who is not. In parliamentary systems with clear ministerial responsibilities and a clear demarcation line between politically appointed public managers (e.g. political state secretaries), the 'name of the game' in political accountability is clearer. This means that ministers are responsible for their actions towards the cabinet of the government and towards the parliament.

Legal accountability means that a public manager's acts and operations have to follow existing law. Civil courts or specialised administrative courts can summon public managers for their acts. Hospitals, for instance, can be summoned by courts if they provide HIV-contaminated blood products to their patients or if medical operations are carried out in a way that harms a patient.

Administrative accountability relates to multiple actors that control and audit public sector activities and actions. In addition to audit institutions, there are also other kinds of forums that operate in the field of administrative accountability. Among these are European or national-level ombudsmen, who handle issues of bad quality in patient processes.

Regarding administrative control and auditing, Power (1994, 2005) has advocated a 'theory of audit explosion'. He says this audit explosion started in the 1990s in the wake of New Public Management, which brought about the emergence of new patterns and intensities of auditing, control and inspection in the public sector. This development also reached the shores of public healthcare. In the field of health, the intensification of performance monitoring and comparisons based on these performance reviews has become a normal routine in national healthcare policy planning and implementation during the last few decades (e.g. Papanicolas and Cylus 2015).

Professional accountability is about being accountable for one's professional peers (e.g. Flynn 2007). In the field of health, this aspect is important since the professions—doctors, nurses and psychologists—are rather strong, which consequently has led to questions such as who can lead healthcare organisations and what is the role of scientific backgrounds in each of the professions (e.g. Anderson and McDaniel 2000). Institutional bodies of professions often lay down ethical codes of conduct, which are supposed to be binding for members of the given professions. The problem with these ethical codes and standards is that they cannot cover all work-related activities and they leave room for interpretation (e.g. Virtanen and Laitinen 2004).

In summary, the content of accountability roles and procedures is definitely various. Still, we think that the discussion about accountability aspects is far from mature when we take into account the radical changes in the operating environment of public healthcare and the ongoing transformation from the single health service organisation to a more fractal hybrid service systems.

In this book, we would like to develop further the notion of horizontal account-ability by addressing two crucial dimensions of horizontal accountability—service provider horizontal accountability and service user/citizen horizontal accountability. We discuss these dimensions in the following paragraphs.

The dominant accountability relationships and configurations have traditionally been vertical in nature in most democracies. The management, audit and evaluation cultures of the NPM and NPG have strengthened this vertical line of accountability since the 1990s. However, the rise of quasi-autonomous or independent agencies within the service space (comprised of public, private and non-governmental service providers) does not fit well—or at all—within the classic top-down relation-ships based on principal–agent theory. In our treatise, *service providers' mutual accountability* is partly vertical—e.g. in terms of contracting out from principal actor to a service provider agent—but it is more or less becoming more horizontal by nature.

Horizontal accountability highlights service providers' relationships with each other. Shared information, joint cooperation mechanisms and a mutual innovation process bring about a new kind of horizontal accountability in the framework of the service space. This means that accountability for cooperation constitutes a major part of accountability. Consequently, this approach emphasises the role of trust as the key driver of accountability relationships.

Horizontal accountability covers organisational healthcare service organisations (organisation–organisation), but to a growing extent, it also covers the connection of service organisations vis-á-vis service users (i.e. the patients). In our treatise in this book, this is the second dimension of horizontal accountability, which we call *service-user/citizen horizontal accountability*. This approach highlights the role of service users as key actors in the healthcare service process. This means that accountabilities change as public organisations transform into service systems.

To date, the understanding of accountability has remained structural by nature (mainly vertical and to some extent horizontal, as we discussed earlier). Such is the case also for productivity and effectiveness measurement, but the shift from organisations towards services systems means that accountability ought to be considered as processual by nature. By processual, we mean that accountability is actually a flow within a service system. Seen from the service users' perspective, this flow between actors in the service space includes not only knowledge and awareness of the outputs of public services but also values, empathy and thus a multilayered understanding of accountability (see especially Virtanen et al. 2016c).

From the perspective of healthcare service managers and representatives of various healthcare professions, the ongoing change challenges the accountability systems deeply and comprehensively. In our earlier work (Stenvall and Virtanen 2015; Virtanen et al. 2016a), we have suggested that healthcare organisations in the emerging service space (operating at the local level of governance) are actually forums for an enhanced service ethos, and they simultaneously strengthen the democratic role of public services by adopting multiple co-creation mechanisms in particular. This happens as a form of hierarchy or extensively as networks by accepting a wider accountability footprint and investing in the remits, roles, responsibilities and relationships necessary for the next-generation healthcare services.

Service systems thus replace individual service organisations as the unit of analysis in the field of health. Adopting a service system perspective allows accountability to be viewed as a processual flow within the service system from services towards the patients.

Anchoring our approach of engaged citizens co-creating value with a consortium of public, private and third-sector agents invites a new perspective on the integration of local service design and delivery with centralised knowledge management, which supports continuous learning and opens up more sophisticated ways to serve patients.

To conclude, accountability is definitely an elusive concept and even more complex as a practice. Despite the semantics and conceptual blurriness, the accountability aspect is crucial in understanding the cooperation aspects of healthcare organisations active in the service space and in addressing the role of service users and patients—and all citizens—in current and future healthcare service delivery.

Overall, it is clear that the traditional understanding of classical, vertical and top-down accountability is no longer sufficient. The world, the operating environment and customer preferences in the public sector have changed so dramatically that accountability conceptions and practices must also change. This leads to the question about the criteria with which healthcare organisations' outputs, results and outcomes should be measured.

In the next section, we will take up the question of how different schools of thought exist in the public management domain. As we will show, the schools of thought in public sector evaluation and measurement have taken very different approaches to collating data for performance reviews, analysing data and reporting performance indicators.

7.5   The Key Concepts and Timescales of Intelligent Policy Evaluation

In Finland, there is a well-known 'old-school' ice hockey coach Juhani Tamminen who uses a slogan to motivate his team to beat their opponents—'keep the game simple and stupid'. This slogan reflects the fact that ice hockey is a rather simple game. You win games if you defend your goal efficiently and always attack when the opportunity arises. This philosophy also holds the view that players should try to score as much as possible.

We feel that it would be intelligent if the health policy evaluation should be kept as simple as possible. We maintain this view even though it might sound a bit naïve, bearing in mind the complexities of modern society and the contemporary constellation of public policies. This 'simplistic' argument basically requires a clear understanding of the objectives of the policy, measurable indicators and logical rationale to integrate performance information into the planning and implementation of public policy.

The words of relief are thus the evaluation of public policy is not rocket science. Evaluating health policy is no exception to this basic rule. Basically, public policy evaluation is grounded on certain key concepts. This is not to say that evaluating public interventions is easy. We are well aware by our own professional experience from multiple public policy evaluations that it takes time, effort and intelligence to decide how the evaluations should be carried out (Virtanen and Vakkuri 2015).

Even though public policy evaluation is not rocket science, we should bear in mind the warning by Lewens (2015: 174–175, 225–226), a professor of philosophy of science, who claims that the first step to untangling the confusing proliferation of common views about the achievements of public policies and public organisations requires that we get our concepts straight. This is important, since common sense and common views do not always correspond to reality. Therefore, we must deploy certain concepts to capture the success of public institutions in order to make judgements about accountability, which we discussed in the previous section of this chapter.

There are certain—relatively few—key concepts in evaluating health policy. In Fig. 7.1, we propose a distinction between first- and second-level health policy evaluation concepts. In doing so, we would like to highlight the procedural nature of evaluation concepts. Thus, by using the notion of first and second does not indicate a value or a ranking for the given concepts. Rather, this refers to the

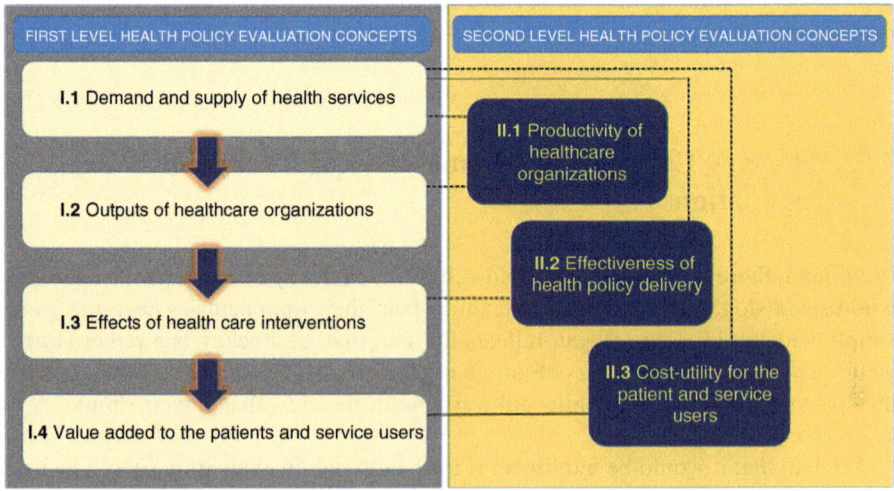

Fig. 7.1 The taxonomy of first- and second-level health policy evaluation concepts

sequence of how and when these concepts are deployed in the course of policy delivery.

By procedural, we maintain that first-level evaluation concepts are used *first* in the course of the policy evaluation, and second-level health policy concepts are used *secondly*. By saying this, we also explicitly argue that first-level evaluation concepts are prerequisites for putting into place the second-level evaluation concepts. This means, for example, that you cannot measure the effectiveness of healthcare interventions if you are not aware of the supply and demand (and objectives related to health policy) and the effects of the interventions.

As follows, we briefly explain the concepts made explicit in Fig. 7.1.

First-Level Health Policy Evaluation Concepts:

- I.1 *Demand* and *supply* of health services: demand and supply are interrelated concepts. The demand side of healthcare relates to the need for using health services. This can be explicated, for instance, by the prevalence of certain sickness cases within a certain population or by the intentions of service users to actually use services. The supply side, then, indicates the existence of healthcare services vis-á-vis explicit healthcare needs. This can be shown, for example, by indicating the number of healthcare facilities (of a certain kind) within certain geographical areas.
- I.2 *Outputs* of healthcare organisations: the outputs of healthcare service delivery is a measurable term for indicating, for instance, how many medical treatments of a certain kind have been delivered in certain areas for certain sicknesses and diseases. Output indicators are closely related to result indicators, which in our terminology refer to instant feedback from the service users after they have used the services. It is important to note that output indicators do not tell a lot about the effects and usefulness of the interventions—they merely reveal the production numbers of services in terms of how much (or how little) services actually have been delivered to the service users.
- I.3 *Effects* of healthcare interventions: public interventions aim at achieving objective-related effects—in practice this means figuring out the consequences for the citizens after receiving treatment. Improved health is a good example from the desired goals of healthcare. Treatment effects—or effects that are consequences of using the services from the perspective of service users—can be measured in multiple ways. Measurement can be based on individual (patient) judgement or based on medical evidence about the given disease. Effect indicators can cover individual service usage of certain healthcare services, or they can incorporate population-level information about the prevalence of a certain disease (e.g. by deploying pretest and posttest measurements).
- I.4 *Value added* for patients/service users using services provided by healthcare organisations: these criteria refer to the usefulness of the service deployed and analysed from the perspective of service users. Value added relates to cost–utility criteria (see below), but it does not mean that the financial aspect is the only aspect to take into account. Value-added can also relate to the enhanced well-being of the service user, which is not easy to present or measure in

financial terms. Well-being is a comprehensive attribution a human being possesses, and its improvement can also be conceived as a feeling, more or less at a psychological level. Thus, value added is a prominent example of an indicator that should be measured multidimensionally.

Second-Level Health Policy Evaluation Concepts:

- II.1 *Productivity* of healthcare organisations: this is the ratio between the outputs achieved by healthcare organisations and the inputs allocated (resources mobilised) in healthcare organisations (both financial and human resources).
- II.2 *Effectiveness* of health policy delivery: this is the ratio between the level of politically and socially desired outcomes achieved by healthcare organisations and the objectives set for health policy and healthcare organisations.
- II.3 *Cost–utility* for the patients/service users of using healthcare services: this relates to how patients and service users have benefited from using healthcare services. Porter and Olmsted Teisberg (2006: 98–101) argue that the right (and in our view, the only) objective for healthcare is to increase its value for patients, which is the quality that patients and service users receive relative to the financial resources expended during the treatment or service delivery. The cost–utility aspect is highly integrated with the idea of creating the value base of healthcare. In fact, this can be estimated by deploying the ratio between costs and achieved benefits assessed from the patients' perspective.

In public policy evaluation, key concepts postulate the focus of evaluation scrutiny. They constitute a framework for evaluation to judge the merits achieved by public policy delivery. Concepts and indicators relate to each other. This means that evaluation concepts more or less give direction to evaluators of policy, whereas indicators provide information (based on quantitative and/or qualitative data) on metrics for evaluation.

It is probably common sense that evaluation takes place only a posteriori, which is definitely flawed thinking. In order to be intelligent, public health policy evaluation takes place three-dimensionally time-wise—before, during and after the intervention. In the following (Fig. 7.2), we will describe these three-dimensional types of policy evaluation, their functions, how they address the decision-making process and how they differ from each other. Figure 7.2 illustrates the 'position' of these three dimension vis-á-vis key public policy evaluation concepts.

Ex Ante Evaluation of Health Policy:

- *Objective*: In terms of public policy, ex ante evaluation pertains to future actions. More specifically, it aims at evaluating the current situation vis-á-vis set objectives prior to the actual programme. Ex ante evaluation is the feasibility of planned interventions; it aims at nurturing knowledge about planned activities in the framework of the operating environment of a given policy. Ex ante evaluation addresses policy objectives, policy options, alternative scenarios and explicated resource allocation. Its main objective is to provide information

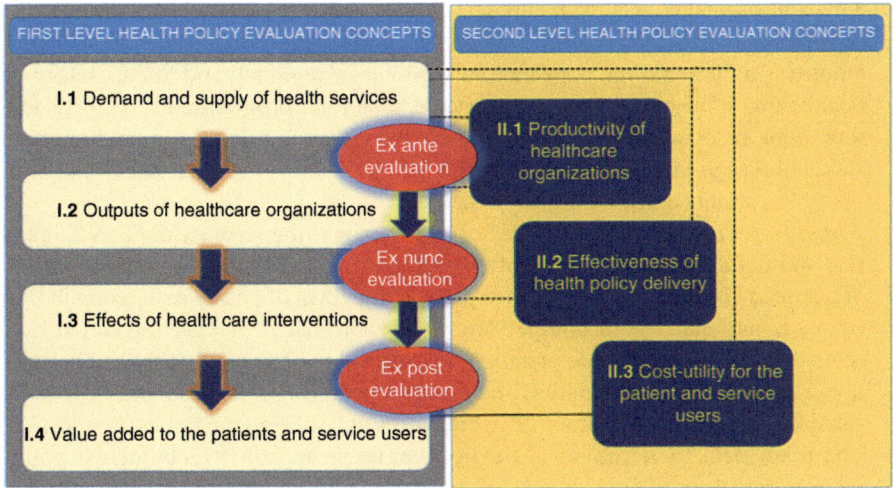

Fig. 7.2 The three timescales of public policy evaluation

about the usefulness of a policy in terms of its objectives and delivery mechanism.

- *Key stakeholders*: The key stakeholders of ex-ante evaluation include policy planners and decision-makers. Moreover (bearing in mind that we live in an open society), the media (TV, radio, the Internet and especially the social media) are important stakeholders in a democratic society.
- *Examples of approaches*: Methodologically, ex ante evaluation incorporates various evaluation and research techniques and methods. Content analysis and the Delphi method are concrete examples of how ex ante evaluation can be carried out methodically. The contextual framework of health policies can be addressed by the use of official statistics on the prevalence of certain diseases among the population.

Ex Nunc Evaluation of Health Policy:

- *Objective:* Ex nunc (or ongoing) policy evaluation takes place during the delivery of the policy. Its purpose is to ensure that the policy stays on the 'right track', which means that the policy delivery occurs according to objectives that have been set for the policy. Alternatively, ex nunc policy evaluation aims at bringing forth evidence for decision-makers on the appropriateness of the policy—meaning that if the policy objectives are not unclear or not for fit according to the aims of the policy, then the policy planners and decision-makers ought to adjust the policy and its subordinate programmes according to evidence made explicit by the evaluation. In terms of policy or organisational learning, the idea of ex nunc evaluation is thus to learn from experience and implement necessary adjustments to the policy.

- *Key stakeholders:* Key stakeholders for ex nunc evaluation include policy planners and decision-makers. Moreover, an important stakeholder agency constitutes (in national or transnational policies) regional and local actors in healthcare, consisting of local healthcare directors, programme directors, doctors, nurses, social workers and psychologists, among others. A very important stakeholder group is the beneficiaries of the policy—service-using patients, possible patients and all citizens in general.
- *Examples of approaches:* In terms of terminology, the term ex nunc evaluation (e.g. Winter and Lasch 2016) is often replaced by monitoring (e.g. Dahlgren and Whitehead 2007). Monitoring takes place in the form of policy management. For instance, national health policies are often coordinated by task forces led by a minister, a secretary of state or a director general in the field of health. According to our view, ex nunc evaluation and policy monitoring relate to more or less the same kind of evaluation practice, which aims at bettering the policy in question. The main data for ex nunc evaluation comes from policy documents, policy monitoring systems (indicator data), research literature and additional empirical forms of scientific inquiry (interviews, participant observation and so on). It should be noted that during the last few years, there has been growing interest in incorporating various forms of additional data into policy evaluation. These include, for example, using social media as empirical evidence (Mowery et al. 2016) and big data and the Internet of Things as a framework for policy and organisational decision-making (Kaivo-oja et al. 2015, 2016). Both of these require sophisticated knowledge management tools and approaches for policy evaluation.

Ex Post Evaluation of Health Policy:

- *Objective:* Ex post evaluation occurs when a given policy has been terminated. The aim of the ex post evaluation is to provide information about the successes and failures that took place during the delivery of the policy. Thus ex post evaluation deals distinctively with accountability (which was discussed earlier in this chapter). Ex post evaluation aims at determining the value added of a given health policy (and its subordinate programmes) and what should be learned from it for future policies on the same topic as the terminated policy. The main aim of the ex post evaluation is to form a bridge between effects and objectives of the policy under scrutiny. This bridge makes it possible to judge the effectiveness of the policy.
- *Key stakeholders:* The key stakeholders of the ex post data include policy planners and decision-makers. As in an ex ante evaluation, an ex post evaluation also addresses questions that are important to beneficiaries, citizens and patients. Bearing this in mind, the role of the media is very important because it provides channels from ex post evaluation for citizens.
- *Examples of approaches:* Ex post evaluation focusses on effects and outcomes of the delivered policy. This makes explicit the fact that the views of the

beneficiaries are very important in ex post evaluation. The effects of a given health policy can be addressed with statistical information, empirical research techniques (both qualitative and quantitative) and especially with case studies. In terms of drawing lessons learned from single public (health) policy, the use of appropriate research literature is highly recommended.

To summarise, in order to be intelligent, public policy evaluation has to fulfil three criteria. Firstly, performance information should be collated in a way that makes sense for decision-makers. It is of no use and intellectually stupid to gather all sorts of information that does not make any sense—the data can be biased, it can be too plentiful, or it can be too scarce. Secondly, performance evaluation and management requires conceptual cornerstones—i.e. key concepts. If the concepts are not clear, then the analysis from public health policy remains unclear. Concepts are more or less as lighthouses in the dark sea when you try to navigate ship safely to the harbour. Finally, the intelligence of public policy evaluation derives time-wise from three-dimensional entities. Policies and their subordinate programmes ought to be checked prior, during and after the policy delivery, which would guarantee a solid course for the policy in question.

Intelligent policy evaluation deals heavily with the principles of organisational learning, since it advocates timely intervention towards policy management if and when something goes wrong or if some results of the policy are not satisfactory. Without learning and unlearning, public policies remain stupid.

7.6 The World of Performance Evaluation Is Not Without Problems

So far, we have maintained that intelligent public policy evaluation is intelligent only if the evaluation approach is designed by application and only if it is based on certain key evaluation concepts and only if it is three-dimensional time-wise (taking place before, during and after the public intervention). All of these requirements have so far been discussed in this chapter. Next we turn to the problematic side of performance measurement and evaluation and relate our analysis to the work of Talbot (2005) and Virtanen and Vakkuri (2016). The downside of performance measurement and evaluation is important to note because if the information is wrong or misinterpreted, there is a huge risk of making wrong decisions at the top of the authority pyramids in the society. The downside of performance measurement and evaluation is brought about by the following factors:

- *The limited view of performance indicators.* This is a consequence of the complexity of society and partly due to the fact that healthcare organisations have traditionally only monitored their own organisation's performance. This has left out the service ecosystem of performance—the goals achieved by multiple organisations serving the same patient or patient groups.

- *The overcomplexity of performance information.* A set of key performance indicators easily becomes too complicated if it consists of too many subindicators. This problem also relates to difficulties in obtaining data for indicators. Once the process of collating information data for performance indicators becomes too arduous, it is a good point to ask the question: 'Is this indicator really so important that the workload in getting the data is reasonable?'

- *Attribution confusion.* Performance metrics seldom indicate exactly the link between cause and effect. Therefore, it is noteworthy to think very critically about what caused the effect and how the idea of intervention relates to the measured effect. For example, the well-being and health of the population in certain designated geographical areas do not necessarily coincide because of well-functioning healthcare services, but because of the fact that a number of people have fallen in love and thus improved their health status and experience of well-being. The basic problem in this respect is what caused the effect. There are number of means when trying to alleviate the effects of attribution problems, such as counterfactual reasoning (e.g. Yee 1996) and system logic modelling (e.g. Ghaffarzadegan et al. 2011; Leyland and Groenewegen 2003).

- *Performance measurement problems related to the quantitative and qualitative nature of information.* Many researchers we know take a rather strong position about the nature of data—there are advocates of quantitative data who think that qualitative data and methods are rubbish and vice versa. Our experience is that it is important to measure all critical aspects of health by using quantitative metrics. Qualitative information is also needed because it would be stupid to maintain that we make important things in the field of health and these interventions can be measured, because we cannot measure what is important. This is to say that it would be stupid to take only those policy options that are measurable in terms of quantifying the effects. A rule of thumb in this sense would rather be build a performance metrics system that is based on (a) an equilibrium between quantitative and qualitative metrics and (b) what is important with respect to the public intervention under scrutiny.

- *Manipulation of performance information.* The field of public health policy is not free from political or other manipulation. Decision-makers can be tempted to read evaluation reports through their 'political pair of glasses', or they just can neglect the information that appears to be unfavourable to them.

- *Hierarchical problems with performance indicators.* Sometimes performance indicators are not hierarchically very solid. This can be caused by various factors, but mainly it happens because the objectives of public policy are unclear and unanalytical. As an example, access to public health can be measured by counting how many patients the doctor sees during one day. Analytically, this does not have much to do with the health of patients, but the indicator certainly measures the wear on the hinges of the doctor's door.

- *Time-related problems in performance measurement.* Different societal phenomena require different analyses. This means that evaluation approaches should be adopted based on the information quality requirements. An additional problem stems from the fact that societal problems do not necessarily follow the annual logic of public policy planning and the budgeting cycle. This problem can be alleviated by explaining to the decision-makers these time-related problems and by introducing reporting models that occur during different parts of the annual policy cycle.
- *Annual volatility of performance metrics and indicators.* It is difficult to foresee your personal future, isn't it? Some use the help of a clairvoyant; the rest just decide to see what happens. The public policy strategy comes alive in the form of foresight. Foresight is a method or a mechanism that future studies deploy in analysing the options ahead of us. There is the volatility related to the existence of societal phenomena. It means that societal phenomena are not stable over time—they take different forms or become otherwise difficult to measure, depending on the topic the evaluation is focussing on. Consequently, this leads to the situation where decision-makers have to make extrapolations about what is really happening in society. Let's take loneliness as an example from the field of well-being. There is a plethora of indicators which indicate that loneliness is a crucial societal problem. The problem is that these indicators are more or less controversial, inconsistent and not available on an annual basis, depending on statistical studies taking place in respective years. This is not to say that loneliness is not an immense problem, but it definitely means that policy makers have to rely on very different sources of performance information from various policy agendas and various statistical sources (e.g. De Jong and Tesch Römer 2012). No wonder that it is really difficult to investigate mechanisms behind the puzzling differences between countries in social integration and loneliness, since many countries collate data on loneliness in a rather different way.
- *The overall uncertainty of decision-making in the domain of public policy.* The politics of public policies brings uncertainty to the planning, designing and redesigning of public policy. Incremental policy making, path dependency of decisions in public policy, contingency problems, political unrest—not to forget the populism and the post-fact type of politics that have been taken up in the UK (Brexit) and in the USA (the Trump presidency). These developments have proved to be non-rationalistic, and they have narrowed the possibility and the room for performance measurement (e.g. see Howlett and Migone 2011; Bendor 2015).

We hope that we have convinced our readers about the pitfalls of public policy performance measurement and evaluation. There are certain points which should be taken into account in developing intelligent solutions and agendas for performance analysis. We'll present these points as follows:

1. *Make sure that performance metrics and indicators can be defined exhaustively and profoundly.* In the framework of public policy, indicators should be defined

in a same manner throughout the policy delivery mechanism—i.e. in organisations delivering the policy for citizens and patients.

2. *Policy-level indicators should cover all aspects of the given policy.* Moreover, policy objectives should be broken down to a result chain, starting with the objectives themselves, making explicit the inputs and outputs and reaching expected effects. In terms of organisations, performance measurement should cover all relevant activities carried out in the organisations—that is, leadership, strategy and foresight, personnel policy, knowledge management and managerial aspects with regard to logistics, controlling economic resources as well as operational processes and various result areas (such as customer, personnel, societal and financial results). Comprehensiveness is essential because the simple fact is: 'what gets measured, gets also done' (e.g. Patton 1997). It should be noted here that comprehensiveness and a balanced approach in organisations' performance information systems proliferated from the mid-1990s onwards, based on the works by Kaplan and Norton (1996) in particular. Their publications related to balanced scorecards gained immense popularity, not only in private business organisations but also in public and non-governmental sectors of society (e.g. Niven 2011; Nørreklit 2003).

3. *Organisation and programme-level indicators should be geared in a way that makes possible the generic collation of information vertically.* This enables summative information, based on similar indicators, at the policy level. For instance, healthcare organisations should collate same kind of information about their performance with regard to heavy users of healthcare services. Aggregating results from the service organisation level towards policy gives policy planners and decision-makers a kind of overall picture of the phenomena of heavy usage of services, which in turn helps policy planners to pinpoint the reasons and causes for this kind of behaviour. From a policy perspective, it would be reasonable to look at other factors, such as the role of chronic diseases in certain age cohorts (e.g. Lee et al. 2015), rather than just old age as key determinants affecting the heavy use of services (e.g. see Hudson and Nolan 2015).

4. *Performance indicators at the policy, programme and organisational levels should be linked to the means of intervention.* This principle highlights the idea that indicators should relate to the policy contents. This helps to understand the causal link between the activities (carried out within the framework of given policy) and the effects (achieved by the activities). In practice, policy planners and evaluation designers should determine the specific cause–effect question being addressed. According to Mayne (2008), a variety of questions about causes and effects can be asked about most policies and programmes. A reasonable question is: To what extent has the policy or programme caused the outcome? Or is it reasonable to conclude that the policy or programme has made a difference to the problem? A good example is Japan. According to Ikeda et al. (2011), the improvement in population health in Japan became evident after the mid-1960s through the implementation of primary and secondary preventive community public health measures as well as through an increased use of advanced medical technologies and a universal insurance scheme. As a

result, disparities in health across regions and socioeconomic groups in Japan have narrowed in this homogenous and egalitarian society over time, and the average population health has increased. However, a very appropriate question is whether the latest achievements with regard to the health level of the total population is a result of the fact that the Japanese pay a lot of attention to personal hygiene and they are eager to use health-related technology to improve their well-being (e.g. Virtanen et al. 2016a).

5. *Performance measurement and monitoring systems should be realistic.* We believe that managerial creativity is practically endless when it comes to putting forward all sorts of performance indicators. Another question is: do these indicators really make sense—or is the measurement system cost-effective? Indicators produce useless information for decision-making if the data is not valid or reliable. If the data is corrupt, then we suggest that it not be collated. The public policy domain is complex enough without corrupted data involved in decision-making.

In this chapter section, we have tried to present a case for intelligent performance measurement and policy evaluation. To put it in a nutshell, we feel it would be important to note that evaluation in an intelligent manner is not nuclear science, so to say. Far from it. It is really about thinking critically about the nature of the policy under scrutiny and about the evaluation mechanism that is orchestrated to capture the essence from this policy. In the following, we focus on the engineering logic of evaluation—something you must reach beyond in order to reach the level of smart performance measurement and evaluation.

7.7 Engineering Logic of Performance Measurement Is Passé

So far, we have learned in this chapter that the evaluation of the outcomes of public health policy and public healthcare organisations is one of the key elements in the policy process (e.g. Weiss 1998; Vedung 1997; Dahler-Larsen 2006). At first glance, the task of evaluation and performance management is clear-cut and easy to define. It is the process of determining the merit, worth and value of things, and performance information is the product of that decision-making process (see Scriven 1991: 1).

However, professional evaluation and performance measurement should not 'only' be equated with the accumulation and summarising of the data relevant for decision-making. This is because the process of transforming information, based on performance indicators, relates to foresight, leadership and interpretation of knowledge. Before using performance 'numbers', you have to understand the logic of what performance information consists of and how it is deployable.

Take the example of traditional logic models in evaluation research (e.g. Newcomer et al. 2015). It is tempting and suggested to use logic models when sketching, planning and implementing policies, programmes or projects. Who would resist the idea of captivating the crucial links between programme inputs, operations, outputs, results and impacts? From experience, we know that politicians and public sector managers are in favour of finding logical links between public activities and their presumed effects.

Bad news enters the picture here. We consider that the world and societies today are too complex for logic models. Policy and programme evaluation calls for different levels of intellectual synthesis. Fischer (1995), for instance, makes a distinction between programme verification, situational validation (coming very close to the idea of realistic evaluation, coined by Pawson and Tilley 1997), societal-level vindication and social choice. Both of the examples mentioned here, Fischer and Pawson and Tilley, take at least a couple steps away from the clear view of the logic models of evaluation.

In this chapter we read Fischer (1995) mainly from the point of view of social mechanisms, which we admit is a rather specific angle. The idea is not to look straightforwardly at performance 'numbers', but to search for the social mechanisms behind the performance management and evaluation systems. This view helps researchers and public managers pinpoint methodological flaws, which in performance monitoring and evaluation relate to the lack of understanding of social mechanisms that produce outcomes and to understanding the contextual factors that work under certain circumstances but might not produce the desired effect under circumstances (e.g. see Hedström and Swedberg 1998; Virtanen and Uusikylä 2004).

Social mechanisms reveal additional problems in current performance management practices. These problems concern the difficulties in finding reliable monitoring and evaluation indicators, aggregating data from outputs to outcomes and long-term impacts, proving the attribution and net effect of a particular policy, programme and project interventions and finally utilising evaluation findings in reformulating policies from the perspective of the learning/unlearning organisation. These are limitations in current performance systems and metrics.

Figure 7.2 illustrates the problem of the rationalistic mode of thinking, which we call the engineering logic of performance. The main problem with this type of performance logic concerns the fact that this does not take into account the human aspect of planning and implementing public policies and delivering public services (March 1978). Figure 7.3 highlights the fact that public health policies or programmes are fields of action where societal actors base the courses of their actions on interpretations of the expected logic of a policy or a programme (cf. Vakkuri 2010, 2013). Actions in an organisational, policy-programme context are always socially constructed rather than objectively derived from abstract policy/ programme logic.

Consequently, all public policies interfere with an intervention field of social actors whose reactions actually produce the final 'version' of the policy—and thus create the framework for performance reporting and the evaluation of the actual outcomes and effects of the policy. This means that evaluation shapes public policy from the social point of view, as a social construction.

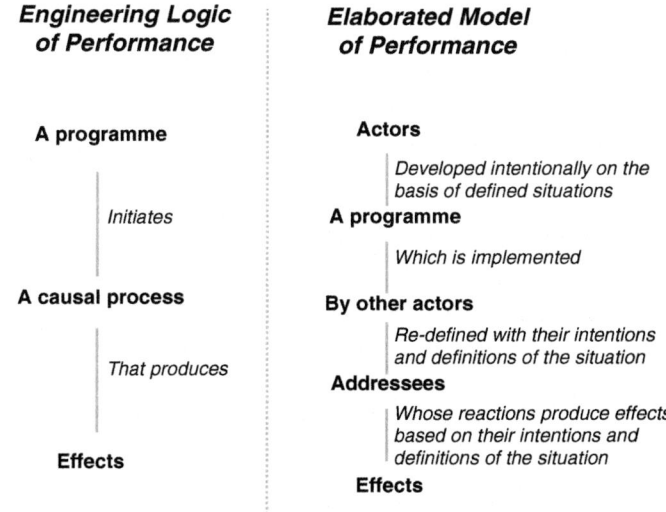

Fig. 7.3 Two logics in understanding performance: the engineering model and the elaborated model (Adapted from Virtanen and Uusikylä 2004; cf. March 1978)

To summarise, in Fig. 7.3—and grounding our idea on Kaufmann (1987) in particular—*the elaborated model* (i.e. the mechanism-based explanation) begins with the idea that policies are always socially constructed. In practice, this means that certain agents develop and elaborate policies, which thereafter are delivered by other actors who might (and most often do) have their own interpretations of policy logic and its situational validation. The process described in Fig. 7.2 indicates that the role of performance systems begins at the ex ante stage of policy delivery. This notion is important in ensuring the validity and reliability of performance metrics.

There is an obvious need for systemic performance measurement and evaluation models, based on social mechanisms incorporated in policy/programme/ organisational planning by public sector institutions. This would tackle various methodological flaws in policy, programme and project delivery as well as under-standing the results and effects of public sector organisations.

The elaborated model described in Fig. 7.3 opens up a new research agenda: how ambiguous strategy objectives really are, how different interpretations of effects exist with regard to public interventions (those being policies, organisations' activities or service-delivery outputs), how different views of performance are weighed and what causal relation exists between the cause and the effect. It is important to develop further insights into complex dynamic systems, uncertainty and nonlinearity, particularly in respect of their emergence in the domain of public policies, programmes, services and organisations.

Next we turn our gaze to evidence-based aspects of healthcare and try to pinpoint the link between evidence-based medicine and the management of organisations.

7.8 Hard Facts, Dangerous Half-Truths or Total Nonsense?

So far, we have approached the question of public performance measurement system and public policy evaluation from a rather generic perspective. Next we focus more thoroughly on performance measurement and evaluation specific to the field of health.

Evaluation has a long history in the health service sector. According to Long (2006), four interconnected topics have been priorities in the evaluation debates concerning the field of health services—the 'what works' agenda (what is the role of evidence in health interventions), the role of theory in evaluating health services (matching method to the purpose of evaluation), the consumer/patient/service-user movement (addressing the role of patients in evaluation practices) and the overall purpose of deploying evaluation methods in the field of health services to judge the merit of service delivery activities (how evaluation results are disseminated, if any).

At the core of the evaluation of health service practices has thus been the *evidence* of what has happened. Thus, the major challenges for health services evaluation are the issue of health system complexity, attribution problems (with regard to evidence and intervention) and the breadth of the stakeholder perspective (Long 2006: 479–480).

The title of this section derives from Pfeffer and Sutton's (2006) famous book a decade ago. In writing their book, Pfeffer and Sutton were worried that many business and public sector leaders built their actions on flimsy information, 'miracle cure' hype and flawed thinking about best practices, whatever those might be. Pfeffer and Sutton's recipe for success was evidence-based management, an approach that has taken hold in medicine (for ages) and which is spreading to all sectors of public policies.

It is of course true that the practice of the medical doctor has changed dramatically over time. Not until about 100 years ago could a typical patient expect to benefit from the medical care provided by a typical physician. Today most patients benefit from medical care, but all patients could benefit more if clinicians routinely provided care consistent with the latest scientific knowledge. This is the domain of evidence-based medicine (e.g. Shortell et al. 2007). Greenhalgh et al. (2014) concluded recently that '. . . Evidence-based medicine quickly became an energetic intellectual community committed to making clinical practice more scientific and empirically grounded and thereby achieving safer, more consistent, and more cost effective care. . .'.

The 'what works' agenda, proposed by Long (2006: 462–464), relates to evidence-based medicine. At the practice level, evidence-based medicine aims to demonstrate the value and benefit of current and future service delivery. The emphasis on evidence-based medicine lies on clinical, treatment-based and policy-oriented decision-making deriving from sound evidence.

The 'what works' agenda is not without problems, though. The problems relate, first, to what counts as evidence in certain decision-making frameworks. Secondly, there is the problem with regard to the dominance of randomised controlled trials (RCT). The RCT's limitations include doubts over the ethical feasibility of the approach (i.e. who is included in the treatment group), focussing on short-term health effects, and the narrowness of the eligibility criteria (which may cause severe limitations on the generalisability of findings from a single RCT).

The achievements of evidence-based medicine have been noteworthy, despite all of the criticism and method limitations. They included, for instance, establishing the Cochrane Collaboration to collate and summarise evidence from clinical trials, setting methodological and publication standards for primary and secondary research, building national and international infrastructures for developing and updating clinical practice guidelines, developing resources and courses for teaching critical appraisal and building the knowledge base for implementation and knowledge translation (Greenhalgh et al. 2014).

We now change our focus from evaluation traditions in health services and evidence-based medicine to the performance management point of view. As a matter of fact, this transformation is important to notice and acknowledge, since evidence-based medicine constitutes an important phase in developing intelligence in performance management systems in today's healthcare organisations.

By definition, evidence-based medicine incorporates several procedural steps. In Table 7.3, we demonstrate that the same kind of steps also exists when we take a look at the management aspects of the healthcare service organisation. From the

Table 7.3 Procedural steps of inquiry in evidence-based medicine and in the management of the organisation (Clarke 2006: 561–562; Kaivo-oja et al. 2015; Stenvall and Virtanen 2015)

Procedural steps	Evidence-based medicine	Managing healthcare organisations by deploying performance management techniques
Step 1. Problem formulation	A clinical question concerning the patient's problem with his/her health	A managerial question concerning the organisation doing the right things and doing them correctly
Step 2. Collating evidence	Consulting the existing scientific literature on medicine	Using performance metrics to obtain data from the organisation's performance
Step 3. Making judgement	Making judgement about the treatment of the patient and taking into account the validity and usefulness of the evidence	The management of single-loop learning: Is the organisation achieving its objectives?
Step 4. Disseminating practice	Collated evidence is deployed during clinical practice	The management of double-loop learning: If the organisation is not achieving its objectives, what should be done to change the situation?
Step 5. Evaluating the outcome of the intervention	Assessing the usefulness of the treatment from the point of view of the patient and his/her health	Evaluating the productivity and effectiveness of the organisation with special emphasis on service culture metrics

healthcare organisation's point of view, these procedural steps are sketched by using performance measurement and management as an analytical framework.

What is important in the work of Pfeffer and Sutton (2006) is their treatise on what brings about management decisions in public policies and public organisations. Pfeffer and Sutton approach the question of evidence-based decision-making from the management point of view, and their approach differs greatly from the proponents of evidence-based medicine. Even though there has been some discussions about combining evidence-based medicine with evidence-based management in the field of healthcare (e.g. Walshe and Rundall 2001), the role of evidence-based management and policy making is far from mature even in academic terms. For example, evidence-based management is not an indexed key concept in the recent *Palgrave International Handbook of Healthcare Policy and Governance* (Kuhlmann et al. 2015a, b).

Pfeffer and Sutton (2006: 6–12) list three major reasons for poor decisions from the point of view of management. (We believe that this list is also valid in the realm of public policy.) The three reasons are causal benchmarking, focussing on what (seems to have) worked in the past and uncritically and deeply following unexamined ideologies.

In essence, *benchmarking* is very useful, and there is definitely nothing wrong with learning from others' experience. But it becomes a burden when it is mindless imitation, and, as such, benchmarking does not make a lot of sense. Pfeffer and Sutton are right in arguing that benchmarking does make sense only if we copy how the organisations think instead of copying what others do.

Secondly, the worst scenario is to look *how things used to be in the past*. As an example, consider this: what would you think about the doctor if he or she does an appendectomy on you. Then if you ask 'why', the doctor tells you that this is because he or she did the same thing for the previous patient. In organisational and public policy terms, this means that problems arise when the upcoming situation is very or somewhat different from the past and when what we learned in the past may have been right at the time the decision was made, but it might be very wrong at the present time.

Thirdly, *unexamined ideologies and truths* are the most dangerous ones for organisations and public policies. Accepted truths or conventional wisdom often guide decisions and actions in public policy and public organisations—and healthcare is no exception. Rooted in organisational culture and past management wisdom and anomalies, unexamined ideologies are often hard to pinpoint. Then you should ask whether my preference, as a leader, for a certain management practice is solely or mostly because it happens to fit my intuitions about people, service users, performance and organisation.

Competent crime scene detectives focus on evidence. What evidence do we have for the crime, whether it be a murder or a less dramatic crime? This attitude is also valid for managers in healthcare and decision-makers in health policy. In management terms, this means that first, we should not copy the ways organisations do things but rather copy the way the management of organisations think. Managers in healthcare should therefore 'go inside' the minds of neighbouring organisations.

Secondly, they should look to the future, not at the past. If your leadership mentality is only backward-looking, you'll definitely miss the future. Finally, beware of the conventional wisdom. It always lurks behind the corner and is ready to keep you unaware of the plethora of rational possibilities.

Conventional wisdom—or unexamined ideologies, to use the phrase of Pfeffer and Sutton (2006)—hassles with your mind and distorts your decision-making. One example of this—a controversial one—is the role of patients in the treatment process. A critical question is: Are the patients really involved in the treatment process or are they just passive followers of whatever guidance they get from the doctor? Another example of conventional wisdom in the domain of healthcare is the assumption that public sector organisations always perform badly in terms of efficiency.

7.9 Synthesis

Organisational intelligence, at first glance, would seem to be more related to 'engineering logic', which we discussed in this chapter, as it is traditionally and primarily understood as the organisation's ability to produce, process, store, retrieve, utilise and share knowledge relevant and instrumental to its purpose. Our argument is actually somewhat opposite to this presumption.

If we accept the view that social mechanisms prevail in all phases of the performance management processes, then the question of organisational intelligence arises, and knowledge-based leadership enters into the picture. We have argued (Virtanen and Stenvall 2014) that the intelligence of a public organisation refers to two dimensions—to knowledge-based decision-making (including the constructionist way to build performance systems, management and metrics) and customer-centred thinking, emphasising the role of service-dominant logic in organising public service delivery. This view holds that an intelligent public organisation—and public policy making as well—develops consolidated knowledge management systems which take the whole planning process into account, from strategy to implementation and from implementation to the evaluation of the effects of public interventions.

We would like to underline that public service delivery has matured during the last 10–15 years or so—and now there is an urgent need to look for new directions for performance measurement and evaluation. Namely, the new planning ideology has been built upon the *New Public Governance* principles: management has conveyed the idea that society, public policies and organisations cannot be governed without the capacity of managing networks and cooperation (e.g. Greve 2015). These networks exist at all levels of governance—that is, at the local, regional, national and global levels. Consequently, the time-frame logic of planning has also changed radically. Planning cycles are now shorter and service ecosystems more complex, and this calls for a new kind of reflexivity in terms of both the agility of the public organisations and their performance systems.

Organisational intelligence is thus a process determining the most appropriate performance monitoring systems, the most valid performance indicators and the most efficient use of performance information in decision-making. This calls for new kinds of competencies in public organisations to understand performance management systems' logic in terms of how information metrics are linked to target-setting in the strategy process, how retrospective and prospective types of performance indicators are deployed in performance metrics and how to make sure that outcome indicators really measure the effects of a specific public organisation.

Targeting performance indicators and enhancing decision-making leadership capacity, however, are only limited solutions to performance management dilemmas within the framework of intelligent public organisations. Research evidence suggests that resilience is one key feature of intelligent public policy making, programme implementation and 'business intelligence' of public organisations, and this underlines the role of solid and trustworthy performance management models and metrics to ensure resilience.

Resilience often relates to emergency management issues, which is not the case when we look at it from the intelligent-public-organisation point of view. In organisational terms, it refers to the capacity of making decisions based on valid performance information. Furthermore, resilience refers to an organisation's capacity to anticipate disruptions, adapt to disruptive events and create lasting service-user value in a turbulent environment.

Finally, from the organisational perspective, it is apparent that resilience does not occur by accident or by chance. On the contrary, it is the effect of intelligent actions, decision-making and leadership as well as converting organisational processes towards the mode of organisational learning and adjustment (e.g. Hernes 2014).

Two challenges are at the top of the agenda when summarising the role of productivity and performance in public health policy and public healthcare organisations. The first challenge concerns digitalisation as a driver to renew patient processes, and the second challenge relates to the practices of organisational learning. Digitalisation will be a drastic change—for itself as a societal phenomenon, for how people behave, for how individuals connect to society, for how people use publicly financed health services and for how communities of people form innovation policies from the bottom up. Until now–and we agree with Dunleavy and Carrera (2013: 273–274)—the digital waves have only crossed the boundaries and outer shores of public sector bureaucracies and their customer-driven processes.

So far, organisational learning processes also remain vague. Public health organisations can definitely learn, but their learning occurs (to convey the idea of Argyris (2005, 2010)) at the level of single-loop learning (*why understand what we are not performing well*). The problem or challenge is to enhance the capability of raising the organisational learning to the level of double-loop learning (*we understand why we perform badly and we know how to fix the problem*). Developing an organisation's learning culture is of course much easier to explicate as an objective than doing it in practice. From the research literature in organisational learning, we know that this development activity consists of renewing the organisation's culture, introducing a knowledge management leadership system and building effective organisational learning systems. This latter component refers to individual learning processes, collective learning capacities, structural learning capacities, cultural learning capacities and the capacity of organisational leadership per se. All of these subcomponents of an organisational learning system indicate the challenges healthcare organisations are facing—due to multiple reasons, such as the strong roles of different professions and professional groups in the field of healthcare.

It is clear that performance management and evaluation provide much of the raison d'être for public policies and public administration. We have argued that the role of systemic changes in society and the role of intelligence in public organisations should be properly addressed in discussing performance management and evaluation. Much of the current doctrine originates from rationalistic performance management and evaluation models and is therefore reluctant or unable to see the social mechanisms incorporated in the mechanisms of accountability (March 1978). Moreover, it seems that the academic discourse on performance measurement and policy evaluation—within the framework of public administration, policy analysis and management studies, economics, accounting and finance—has perhaps been rich in content but to date still largely relies on the simple rationalistic engineering logic of performance (van Helden et al. 2012).

Two conclusions can be drawn here.

First, it seems that 'hard-nosed' rationalistic models of performance and evaluation are no longer fit for purpose. To be measured by traditional performance metrics, society is far too complex, constructed by various social networks and retrospective interlinkages, and constituted of public service systems. There is an urgent need for further scientific research on how performance measurement and evaluation models are designed and implemented, how performance information is used in organisational decision-making processes and how performance information affects organisations, service users, citizens and stakeholders. In such research efforts, performance logic should not only be that of engineering logic, but it could incorporate more fully the features of various elaborated models. Therefore, the role of the human or social aspect in the service of programme-delivery planning is of special interest here.

Second, as we have argued throughout this book, as the context for public sector organisations becomes more complex, the need for intelligence in organisational knowledge management and decision-making processes ought to be addressed more systematically. Many important perspectives, such as the organisational intelligence point of view that we have addressed, are therefore underutilised.

We think that the notion of organisational intelligence emphasising the role of consolidated performance-measurement systems with changing environments can offer a theoretical and conceptual framework to develop performance measurement in a setting where wicked policy problems exist and where they are tackled by multi-institutional service systems in the policy domain of health. It is noteworthy to think that technologies related to knowledge management—such as the Internet of Things, the Internet of Intelligent Things, big data, robotics and nanotechnology—will be upgraded in the future. This process paves the way for improved knowledge processes with public organisations. The issue at stake here is not in fact how to manage and control the technological possibilities but rather to understand their interlinkages to performance monitoring, evaluation and smart leadership. Taking disruptive and advanced technologies seriously may lead towards the revolution of digitalisation, with a profound effect on management processes, service delivery and performance measurement in public organisations.

References

Aarons GA, Hurlburt M, McCue Horwitz S (2011) Advancing a conceptual model of evidence-based practice implementation in public service sectors. Adm Policy Ment Health 38(1):4–23

Anderson RA, McDaniel RR Jr (2000) Managing healthcare organizations: where professionalism meets complexity science. Healthc Manag Rev 25(1):83–92

Argyris C (2005) Double-loop learning in organizations. A theory of action perspective. In: Smith KG, Hitt MA (eds) Great minds in management. The process of theory development. Oxford University Press, Oxford, pp 261–279

Argyris C (2010) Organizational traps. Leadership, culture, organizational design. Oxford University Press, Oxford

Bauman AE, King L, Nutbeam D (2014) Rethinking the evaluation and measurement of health in all policies. Health Promot Int 29(1):143–151

Bendor J (2015) Incrementalism: dead yet flourishing. Public Adm Rev 75(2):194–205

Bianchi C (2015) Enhancing joined-up government and outcome-based performance management through system dynamics modelling to deal with wicked problems: the case of societal ageing. Syst Res Behav Sci 32:502–505. https://doi.org/10.1002/sres.2341

Birkland TA (2016) An introduction to the policy process. Theories, concepts and models of public policy making. Routledge, New York

Bort E, McAlpine R, Morgan G (2012) The silent crisis: failure and revival in local democracy in Scotland. The Jimmy Reid Foundation, Glasgow

Bouckaert G, Halligan J (2008) Managing performance: international comparisons. Routledge, London

Bouckaert G, Van Dooren W (2009) Performance measurement and management in public sector organizations. In: Bovaird T, Löffler E (eds) Public management and governance. Routledge, London, pp 151–164

Bovens M (2005) Public accountability. In: Ferlie E et al (eds) The Oxford handbook of public management. Oxford University Press, Oxford, pp 182–209

Bovens M (2010) Two concepts of accountability: accountability as a virtue and as a mechanism. West Eur Polit 33(5):946–967

Bovens M, Goodin RE, Schillemans T (eds) (2014) The Oxford handbook of public accountability. Oxford University Press, Oxford

Cadilhac DA, Amatya B, Lalor E, Rudd A, Lindsay P, Asplund K (2012) Is there evidence that performance measurement in stroke has influenced health policy and changes to health systems? Stroke 43(12):3413–3420

Campbell DT, Russo MJ (1999) Social experimentation. Sage, Newbury Park

Clarke A (2006) Evidence-based evaluation in different professional domains: similarities, differences and challenges. In: Shaw IF et al (eds) The SAGE handbook of evaluation: policies, programs and practices. Sage, London, pp 559–581

Dahler-Larsen P (2006) Evaluation after disenchantment? Five issues shaping the role of evaluation in society. In: Shaw IF et al (eds) The SAGE handbook of evaluation. Sage, Thousand Oaks, CA, pp 141–160

Dahlgren D, Whitehead M (2007) European strategies for tackling social inequalities in health: levelling up part 2 [Online]. http://www.thehealthwell.info/node/91930. Accessed 23 Dec 2016

De Jong GJ, Tesch Römer C (2012) Loneliness in old age in Eastern and Western European societies: theoretical perspectives. Eur J Ageing 9(4):285–295

Dunleavy P, Carrera L (2013) Growing the productivity of government services. Edward Elgar, Cheltenham

Ferlie EL, Fitzgerald G, McGivern DS, Bennett C (2011) Public policy networks and 'wicked problems': a nascent solution? Public Adm 89(2):307–324

Flynn N (2007) Public sector management. Sage, London

Geuijen K, Moore M, Cederqvist A, Ronning R, van Twist M (2016) Creating public value in global wicked problems. Public Manag Rev, published online 25.8.2016. https://doi.org/10.1080/14719037.2016.1192163. Accessed 27 Dec 2016

Ghaffarzadegan D, Lyneisb J, Richardson GP (2011) How small system dynamics models can help the public policy process. Syst Dyn Rev 27(1):22–44

Glennerster H (2002) United States poverty studies and poverty measurement: the past twenty-five years. Soc Serv Rev 76(1):83–107

Greene JC (2006) Evaluation, democracy and social change. In: Shaw IF et al (eds) The SAGE handbook of evaluation. Policies, programs and practices. Sage, London, pp 118–140

Greenhalgh T, Howick J, Maskrey N (2014) Evidence based medicine: a movement in crisis? BMJ 348:g3725 (published online 13.6.2014, Accessed 5 Nov 2016)

Greve C (2015) Ideas in public management reform for the 2010s: digitalization, value creation and involvement. Public Organ Rev 15(1):49–65

Guba EG, Lincoln YS (1989) Fourth generation evaluation. Sage, Newbury Park

Harrison S, Smith C (2013) Neo-bureaucracy and public management: the case of medicine in the National Health Service. Compet Chang 7(4):243–254

Head BW (2008) Wicked policy problems. Public Policy 3(2):101–118

Heclo H (1994) Poverty politics. In: Danziger SH et al (eds) Confronting poverty. Prescriptions for change. The Russell Sage Foundation/Harvard University Press, Cambridge, pp 396–437

Hedström P, Swedberg R (eds) (1998) Social mechanisms: an analytical approach to social theory. Cambridge University Press, Cambridge

Heinrich CJ (1999) Do government bureaucrats make effective use of performance management information? J Public Adm Res Theory 9(3):363–394

Hernes T (2014) A process theory of organization. Oxford University Press, Oxford

Hodges R (2012) Joined-up government and the challenges to accounting and accountability researchers. Financ Account Manag 28(1):26–51

Hood L, Flores M (2012) A personal view on systems medicine and the emergence of proactive P4 medicine: predictive, preventive, personalized and participatory. New Biotechnol 29 (6):613–624

Howlett M, Migone A (2011) Charles Lindblom is alive and well and living in punctuated equilibrium land. Policy Soc 30(1):53–62

Hudson E, Nolan A (2015) Public healthcare eligibility and the utilisation of GP services by older people in Ireland. J Econ Ageing 6(4):24–43

Ikeda N, Saito E, Inoue M, Ikeda S, Satoh T, Wada K, Stickley A, Katanoda K, Mizoue T, Noda M, Iso H, Fujino Y, Sobue T, Tsugane S, Naghavi M, Ezatti M, Shibuya K (2011) What has made the population of Japan healthy? Lancet 378(9796):1094–1105

Innes JE, Booher DE (2016) Collaborative rationality as a strategy for working with wicked problems. Landsc Urban Plan 154(5):8–10

Kaivo-oja J, Virtanen P, Jalonen H, Stenvall J (2015) The effects of the internet of things and big data to organizations and their knowledge management practices. In: Luden L et al (eds) Knowledge management in organizations, vol 224. Springer, Heidelberg, pp 495–513

Kaivo-oja J, Virtanen P, Stenvall J, Jalonen H, Wallin J (2016) Future prospects for knowledge management in the field of health. KMO 2016. In: Proceedings of the 11th international knowledge management in organizations, Article no. 40. https://doi.org/10.1145/2925995. 2926006, ACM, New York. http://dl.acm.org/icps.cfm

Kaplan RS, Norton DP (1996) The balanced scorecard. Translating strategy into action. Harvard Business School Press, Boston, MA

Karanikolos M, Mladovsky P, Cylus J, Thomson S, Basu S, Stuckler D, Mackenbach JP, McKee M (2013) Financial crisis, austerity and health in Europe. Lancet 381(9874):1323–1331

Kaufman H (1976) Are government organizations immortal? Brookings Institution Press, Washington, DC

Kaufmann X-F (1987) Prevention and intervention in the analytical perspective of guidance. In: Hurrelmann K et al (eds) Social intervention: chances and constraints. Walter de Gruyter, New York, pp 3–20

Koppell JGS (2005) Pathologies of accountability: ICANN and the challenge of "multiple accountabilities disorder". Public Adm Rev 65(1):94–108

Kuhlmann E, Blank RH, Bourgeault IL, Wendt C (2015a) Healthcare policy and governance in international perspective. In: Kuhlmann E et al (eds) The Palgrave international handbook of healthcare policy and governance. Palgrave MacMillan, New York, pp 3–19

Kuhlmann E, Blank RH, Bourgeault IL, Wendt C (eds) (2015b) The Palgrave international handbook of healthcare policy and governance. Palgrave MacMillan, New York

Kuhn T (2012) The structure of scientific revolutions. Chicago University Press, Chicago (originally published in 1962)

Lane J-E (2005) Public administration and public management: the principal-agent perspective. Routledge, London

Lee G, Park JY, Shin S-Y, Hwang JS, Jeong Ryu H, Lee JH, Bates DW (2015) Which users should be the focus of mobile personal health records? Analysis of user characteristics influencing usage of a tethered mobile personal health record. Telemed E-Health 22(5):419–428

Lewens T (2015) The meaning of science. Pelican Books, London

Leyland AH, Groenewegen PP (2003) Multilevel modelling and public health policy. Scand J Public Health 31(4):267–274

Long A (2006) Evaluation of health services: reflections on practice. In: Shaw IF et al (eds) The SAGE handbook of evaluation. Policies, programs and practices. Sage, London, pp 461–485

March JG (1978) Bounded rationality, ambiguity and the engineering of choice. Bell J Econ 9 (2):587–608

Mayne J (2008) Contribution analysis: an approach to exploring cause and effect. ILAC Brief 16 (May 2008). www.cgiar-ilac.org

Michels A, Meijer A (2008) Safeguarding public accountability in horizontal government. Public Manag Rev 10(2):165–173

Mowery D, Smith HA, Cheney T, Bryan C, Conway M (2016) Identifying depression-related tweets from Twitter for public health monitoring. Online J Public Health Inf 8(1), https://doi.org/10.5210/ojphi.v8i1.6561. Accessed 23 Dec 2016

Naples NA (2014) Grassroots warriors. Activist mothering, community work, and the war on poverty. Routledge, London

Neely A, Kennerly M, Walters A (2006) Performance measurement and management: public and private. Cranfield School of Management, Cranfield

Newcomer KE, Hatry HP, Wholey JS (eds) (2015) Handbook of practical program evaluation. Jossey-Bass, New Jersey

Niven PR (2011) Balanced scorecard. Step by step for government and non-profit agencies. Wiley, New Jersey

Nørreklit H (2003) The balanced scorecard: what is the score? A rhetorical analysis of the balanced scorecard. Acc Organ Soc 28(6):591–619

North DC (2005) Understanding the process of economic change. Princeton University Press, Princetown, NJ

Papanicolas I, Cylus J (2015) Comparison of healthcare systems performance. In: Kuhlmann E et al (eds) The Palgrave international handbook of healthcare policy and governance. Palgrave MacMillan, New York, pp 116–132

Patton MQ (1997) Utilization-focused evaluation: the new century text. Sage, Thousand Oaks, CA

Pawson R (2013) The science of evaluation. A realist manifesto. Sage, London

Pawson R, Tilley N (1997) Realistic evaluation. Sage, London

Peters GB (2005) The problem of policy problems. J Comp Policy Anal Res Pract 7(4):349–370

Pfeffer J, Sutton RI (2006) Hard facts, dangerous half-truths and total nonsense. Profiting from evidence-based management. Harvard Business School Press, Boston, MA

Porter ME, Olmsted Teisberg E (2006) Redefining health care. Creating value-based competition on results. Harvard Business School Press, Boston, MA

Power M (1994) The audit explosion. Demos, London

Power M (2005) The theory of audit explosion. In: Ferlie E et al (eds) The Oxford handbook of public management. Oxford University Press, Oxford, pp 326–344

Robson C (2002) Real world research. Blackwell, Oxford

Schillemans T (2011) Does horizontal accountability work? Evaluating potential remedies for the accountability deficit of agencies. Adm Soc 43(3):387–416

Scriven M (1991) Evaluation thesaurus. Sage, Newbury Park

Shadish WR, Luellen JK (2004) Donald Campbell: the accidental evaluator. In: Alkin MC (ed) Evaluation roots: tracing theorists' views and influences. Sage, London, pp 80–87

Shortell SM, Rundall TG, Hsu J (2007) Improving patient care by linking evidence based medicine and evidence-based management. JAMA 298(6):673–676

Silver H (1996) Culture, politics, and national discourses of the new urban poverty. In: Mingione E (ed) Urban poverty and the underclass. Blackwell, Oxford, pp 105–138

Stenvall J, Virtanen P (2015) Intelligent public organizations? Public Organ Rev, published on-line 2.12.2015. https://doi.org/10.1007/s11115-015-0331-1

Talbot C (2005) Performance management. In: Ferlie E et al (eds) The Oxford handbook of public management. Oxford University Press, Oxford, pp 491–517

Vakkuri J (2010) Struggling with ambiguity: public managers as users of NPM-oriented management instruments. Public Adm 88(4):999–1024

Vakkuri J (2013) Interpretive schemes in public sector performance: measurements creating managerial problems in local government. Int J Public Sect Perform Manag 2(2):156–174

Van Helden GJ, Johnsen Å, Vakkuri J (2012) Evaluating public sector performance management: the life cycle approach. Evaluation 18(2):159–175

Vedung E (1997) Public policy and program evaluation. Transaction, New Brunswick

Vedung E (2010) Four waves of evaluation diffusion. Evaluation 16(3):263–277

Virtanen P, Laitinen I (2004) Beyond evaluation standards? Eur J Spat Dev (http:/www.nordregio.se/EJSD). ISSN 1650-9544-Refereed articles Oct 2004 no 13

Virtanen P, Stenvall J (2014) The evolution of public services from co-production to co-creation and beyond – an unfinished trajectory for the New Public Management? Int J Leadersh Public Serv 10(2):91–107

Virtanen P, Uusikylä P (2004) Exploring the missing links between cause and effect. A conceptual framework for understanding micro-macro conversions in programme evaluation. Evaluation 1(10):77–91

Virtanen P, Vakkuri J (2015) Searching for organizational intelligence in the evolution of public sector performance management. NISPAcee J Public Adm Policy 8(2):89–99

Virtanen P, Vakkuri J (2016) Julkisen toiminnan tuloksellisuusarviointi [Public sector performance assessment and management, in Finnish]. Tietosanoma, Helsinki

Virtanen P, Kaivo-oja J, Ishino Y, Stenvall J, Jalonen H (2016a) Ubiquitous revolution, customer needs and business intelligence. Empirical evidence from Japanese healthcare sector. Int J Web Eng Technol 11(3):259–283

Virtanen P, Uusikylä P, Jalava J, Tiihonen S, Laitinen L, Noro K (2016c) Valtioneuvoston yhtenäisyys – kansainvälinen vertaileva tutkimus [available in only in Fiinish, The unity of government – an international comparative study]. Valtioneuvoston kanslia, Helsinki. Accessed at www.tietokauttoon.fi

Walshe K, Rundall TG (2001) Evidence-based management: from theory to practice in health care. Milbank Q 79(3):429–457

Weber EP, Khademian AN (2008) Wicked problems, knowledge challenges, and collaborative capacity builders in network settings. Public Adm Rev 68(2):334–349

Weiss C (1998) Evaluation. Prentice-Hall, New Jersey

Wholey JS, Hatry HP (1992) The case for performance monitoring. Public Adm Rev 52 (6):604–610

Winter S, Lasch R (2016) Recommendations for supplier innovation evaluation from literature and practice. Int J Oper Prod Manag 36(6):643–664

Yee AS (1996) The causal effects of ideas on policies. Int Organ 50(1):69–108

Zarefsky D (1986) President Johnson's war on poverty. Rhetoric and history. The University of Alabama Press, Tuscaloosa

Chapter 8
The Fundaments of Intelligence in the Future Health Policy

Abstract This concluding chapter summarises the main contents of this book. It presents, in short, the main ten fundaments of the intelligence of health policy—deployable to other fields of public policies as well—divided in four cohorts of fundaments. These cohorts are orchestrated as contextual, conceptual, service-related and leadership-related fundaments. By fundament, we refer here to theoretical cornerstones—axioms or established principles if you like—of why and how we think intelligence will be rooted in the public policies of today and especially in the future. In our approach, contextual fundaments (i.e. the complexity of the society and societal change, the evolution of institutions, horizontal accountability and the value of increased public value in terms of legitimation of public policies) shape the societal setting for planning, running and evaluating health policy; conceptual fundaments (i.e. systems thinking, loosely coupled systems, open innovations, knowledge and agency) create and regulate the structure and the functioning logic of the public policy system; service-related fundaments (i.e. the service dominant—logic and value co-creation) reframe the production logic of public goods and services and heighten the role of service users in the heart of the health policy; and leadership-related fundaments (i.e. knowledge sharing and policy integration and new forms of public sector leadership) provide the practical functioning logic for the health policy actors and interventions. This final chapter of this book outlines these fundaments, providing short commentaries for each of the fundaments (and their sub-criteria) addressed.

8.1 Contextual Fundaments of Policy Intelligence

8.1.1 Fundament 1: Complexity of Society and Societal Change Trajectories

The operating environment of health policies throughout OECD countries has radically changed over the last few decades. For instance, Doz et al. (2017) have recently discussed in lengthy detail the nature of this change, and they came to the conclusion that, first, the world itself has radically changed due to demographic changes, technology and radical controversies in real politics (i.e. Brexit, the rise of populistic political movements and so on). Additional changes have been caused by the vulnerability of the

© Springer International Publishing AG 2018   177
P. Virtanen, J. Stenvall, *Intelligent Health Policy*,
https://doi.org/10.1007/978-3-319-69596-9_8

financial systems and financial shocks at both the national and supranational levels, leading to unsustainable levels of public spending and borrowing.

Moreover, existing public policies are meeting their limits simply because they are not able to solve longstanding wicked problems in society—problems that fall into in-between zones in existing public policy categories. Public policies and public administration institutions and organisations are not able to find solutions to societal problems with management doctrines that have prevailed since the 1990s. It is clear that the NPM and NPG models were well fitted to situations in which policy areas were independent, policy problems could be reduced to fit single policy areas and there was no pressure to think about the question of unified government and collaboration in between public sector organisations. Finally, there is the question of democracy linked with the evolutionary stage of political parties and representative democracy. Historically, political strategies have been motivated by ideologies, but the confrontation with reality has eroded and exhausted ideologies in favour of greater pragmatism and—to certain extent—narrow-minded political populism. Constant (social) media attention makes politics and policy planning different than they used to be. The attention span of public opinion these days is driven by media hype, social networks and opinion polls.

Today's society is full of complexity, which causes noteworthy trouble to the advocates of rationalistic policy planning. First, societal problems that need to be addressed do not necessarily—if ever—fall into a category or typology of existing public policies. The ever-growing complexities in society affect public policies in many ways—societal problems are more or less always interrelated, and their respective solutions are more than often path-dependent. However, we are convinced that it would be very naïve to think that the complexity in society can be lessened because it simply cannot be accomplished. The only possibility is to manage this complexity in an intelligent way.

Building upon from Ashby (1991) and Boisot and McKelvey (2011), this (the intelligent way to do it) can be addressed by nurturing organisational diversity in the public sector domain, bearing in mind the two critical aspects of diversity: cognitive and structural. Cognitive diversity refers here to broad-scale professional training (concerning all healthcare personnel but particularly persons in leadership possessions); cross-boundary collaboration in between stakeholders in government, public administration, business and non-governmental organisations and joint learning forums and initiatives; as well as multilevel dialogue within public sector authorities.

Organisational diversity, then, can be maintained and developed by new forms of public–private–people partnerships, decentralising collective decision-making; by adopting the experimental approach to pursue public sector reforms and develop public institutions; by new horizontal coordination mechanisms; by network collaboration; and by introducing new dialogue elements to public policy formulation and implementation.

The complexities of society constitute a shift from a simple (linear) policy system to a complex policy system. The differences between linear and complex ways of policy making are essential, and they concern the nature, the context and the role of public policy making. The complexity model sees government and public institutions more or less as self-organising entities that implement emerging and complex policies, countered by entropic tendencies towards chaotic policy disorder. It should be mentioned that a recent OECD 'Public Governance Committee Report' (OECD 2017) advocated the view that governments should find new systemic solutions to complex—or wicked societal challenges—to build more resilient and adaptive government and public administration structures that incorporate, rather than filter out, complexity. In the OECD report, this argument was made because of the increasing complexity of societies.

8.1.2 Fundament 2: The Evolution of Agile Government and Public Administration Institutions

Doz and Kosonen (2008) and Doz et al. (2017) have advocated the view that governments and their public organisations should be developed in a manner that would make them more agile. We think this is an important step towards how health policy and publicly financed healthcare services should be developed and renewed. The main argument, which this view is based upon, relates to the complex nature of society that was discussed above. According to this view, the strategic agility of an organisation (public or private) results from the interplay of three capabilities: strategic sensitivity (the capability for superior foresight and insight and for real-time strategic sense-making), resource fluidity (the capability to reallocate resources to new opportunities and emerging challenges in a timely fashion) and collective commitment (the capability to make and implement decisions that mobilise multiple subunits towards sustained integrated action).

In terms of governance, public policies and public organisations, strategic sensitivity requires early perception and recognition of emerging trends, a combination of foresight and insight, high-quality dialogue with internal and external key stakeholders and an ability to frame strategic issues in a fresh and insightful way. Resource fluidity, then, refers to the reallocation of financial resources and people—and especially the rotation of top leaders and managers within public organisations from one organisation to another. This is not always possible because, to take an example, of different salary and track development systems public sector institutions have adopted in different sectors. Budgetary processes in the public sector do not necessarily make life easy for those public sector leaders and managers who would like to implement the idea of reallocation of financial resources. The lack of clear value comparisons of the expected net benefits of alternative policies emphasises the role of common priority-setting rules and shared ambition in resource allocation. And it is not always the case that this is how things go in health policy formulation and implementation. Finally, collective commitment to joint government and public administration action results from a deep cognitive and emotional sense of unity. Beyond principles and policies, this emerges only from experimentation from repeated successful collaboration around implementing integrated policy formulation, implementation and evaluation across and in between different stakeholders (Doz and Kosonen 2008, 2010, 2014; Doz et al. 2017).

8.1.3 Fundament 3: The Accountability of Public Actions and the Public Value Perspective

Accountability evaluation and reporting bring about the success stories and failures of public authorities. This aspect relates accountability to governmental and public sector learning and unlearning. This value-for-money view holds that it is necessary to learn how public authorities in the field of health have succeeded to reach the goals set for them. We would like to stress that public policies are not always triumphs seen from the point of view of taxpayers. For instance, King and Crewe (2013) have maintained that governments quite often fail in their purposes to deliver their public policies. Their conclusion is that 'they [public policy makers] screw up more than most people seem to realise. Our strong impression [from the British case during 1979–2010] is that, while a majority of Britons know about this, that or the other cock-up, they are by no means aware of the full range of them [policy failures]' (King and Crewe 2013, p. ix).

No wonder, then, that the accountability aspect is perhaps one of the most important ingredients of public policy making, although quite often rather neglected. It is important to notice the transformation of accountability from a vertical towards a more horizontal accountability, which means, in practice, that the citizens' and service users' roles in the accountability process become crucial. This shift means that publicly financed healthcare service providers in public, private and non-governmental sectors are predominantly accountable for their patients in addition to their superior authorities and to those institutions that purchase services. This shift underlines the public value perspective for healthcare and strengthens the idea that service providers ought to maintain a very clear public value aspect in their activities and service delivery.

Box 1 Intelligent Health Policy: Practical Implications Concerning the Evolving Nature of Health Policy

The practical implications of the *contextual fundaments* with regard to health policy and healthcare services are as follows:

1. Changes in society affect health policy in multiple ways. Strategic sensitivity, resource reallocation and shared commitment are key elements of agile and intelligent policy making in the field of health.
2. Cognitive and structural diversity are the key factors for healthcare organisations to adapt to in the current societal changes. The main element of future health policy making rests upon collaboration and dialogue between various policy stakeholders at all vertical and horizontal levels.
3. The complexities of society continue to reshape the contents of the current domain of health policy. Also, the production logic of healthcare services continues to evolve towards a service ecosystem model, which is the healthcare service space where public, private and non-governmental organisations operate to fulfil the service needs made explicit by various forms of data.

(continued)

Box 1 (continued)

4. The legitimation of health policy and healthcare services is based on horizontal accountability. The public value perspective and various co-creation models enhance the importance of citizens and service users in the process of policy making and service development.

8.2 Conceptual Fundaments of Policy Intelligence

8.2.1 Fundament 4: Systems Thinking, Loosely Coupled Systems and Open Innovation Processes

Our commitment to complexity theory (and to service science) relates our analysis to systems thinking and especially to MST. We have treated public policies in this book as a policy system—a system constituted by various public policies interwoven together. The policy system orchestrates the healthcare service ecosystem, which is, borrowing from Green et al. 'a relatively self-contained, self-adjusting system of resource-integrating [service organisation] entities that are connected by shared institutional logics and mutual value creation through service exchange' (2016; see also Virtanen et al. 2016a). This statement means that the boundaries between single public policies and single healthcare service organisations are blurred, and no single public policy maker, policy planner nor service provider is in charge or controls the policy system and service ecosystem that provides services. This means bad news for those who think a single public policy can be singularly planned or designed. Primary examples of future healthcare service organisations are those that are non-hierarchical, flat, collaborative subsystems of the service ecosystem, collaborating and networking with each other in terms of shared vision, resource integration and process integration.

Policy systems and the service ecosystems are, by their nature, flexible and loosely coupled. By loosely coupled, we mean the situation where policy systems and service ecosystems can be temporary in nature depending on, for instance, the market situation with regard to the service delivery of healthcare services. The demand for strategic sensitivity is very important in the realm of loosely coupled systems since the alliances and rivalries in the market are shaped and reshaped constantly. The idea of loosely coupled policy systems is relevant also in terms of wicked policy problems since the ties among entities in the loosely coupled policy systems and service ecosystem are not permanently fixed, allowing flexibility and resource reallocation when necessary.

Systems thinking, loosely coupled policy systems and service ecosystems set out a framework for an ecosystem approach to innovation. Innovations take place in markets, which, in our case, refer to a service space that is constituted by variously financed service providers from the public, private and non-governmental sectors, forming a loosely coupled service ecosystem. Vargo et al. (2016) have recently advocated the view that market innovations do not automatically occur when actors or groups of actors introduce shared-value propositions but only when new innovative solutions are institutionally produced and their ownership described. In terms of the health sector, the challenge is how to make innovation processes nonlinear, collaborative, continuous and co-created by various stakeholders.

8.2.2   Fundament 5: Knowledge Intensity and Agency Perspective

Knowledge intensity is at the heart of intelligent policy making for at least two reasons. First, without knowledge there is no action, or the activities implemented are at worst stupid and wrong vis-á-vis the articulated needs with regard to the policy design. Second, in the world of multiple as well as alternative truths, data becomes knowledge only through proper analysis carried out by systematic analytical diagnostics. In terms of health, it is essential that policy makers have adequate knowledge time-wise from two dimensions: from the past (the retrospective view about, for instance, how patients have used the services provided for them) and from the future (insights about what service preferences are for service users, the emergent diseases, the future causes of morbidity and so on).

A policy system approach enables involved decision-makers to zoom out to the larger policy constellation, a network of interlinked public policies. From this broader perspective, they are more likely to consider all agency groups—the policy designers, policy implementers, service providers and service users—as elementary stakeholder entities embedded within public health policy process.

> **Box 2 Intelligent Health Policy: Practical Implications Concerning Healthcare Organisations and Healthcare Ecosystems**
> The practical implications of the *conceptual fundaments* with regard to health policy and healthcare services are as follows:
>
> 1. The adopted policy system—and healthcare service ecosystem—approach profoundly affects the role of policy making and service delivery. This approach means that the service needs of service users are at the heart of the policy planning and implementation as well as in the service delivery. In practice, this demands reorganising the operational processes from the service delivery constituencies. Service organisations should be process-oriented, and processes should be based on articulated patient and service-user needs.
> 2. The ownership of institutionalised innovation processes in the field of health needs clarification. There should be a distinct model for healthcare service innovations, and stakeholders of the policy should set a framework

(continued)

Box 2 (continued)

for clear division of labour with regard to innovation activities in between actors from the local, regional, national and supranational levels of governance.

3. In terms of resource allocation and reallocation, the effectiveness of policy and service delivery constitutes an essential element. In practice, healthcare services need to develop new analytics for effectiveness measurement which would partly replace old models of performance measurement and monitoring.

4. Relevant and accessible data is necessary for effectiveness measurement. The process of data analytics consists of data collation, data analysis and data reporting. In this process, a clear distinction between data, conclusions and recommendations helps decision-makers at the policy level to make decisions with regard to policy (planning, target setting, performance reviewing and so on).

8.3 Service-Related Fundaments of Policy Intelligence

8.3.1 Fundament 6: Service-Dominant Logic

In the domain of marketing science, the dynamic nature of service-dominant logic has attracted growing interest for over a decade now. To echo what Vargo and Lusch (2015) have quite recently put forward, the narrative and process of service-dominant logic consist of service exchange (as a fundamental basis of exchange in society), institutional arrangements, functional service ecosystems, involved actors taking part in the service ecosystem and, finally, resource integration (addressing the fact that knowledge and operant resources are the essential source of competitive advantage).

Service-dominant logic has replaced goods-dominant logic of the past. Take, for instance, the fast-food conglomerate McDonald's, who became famous and dominant decades ago by focussing on a high division of labour, homogeneous goods as outputs, efficiency and selling units of outputs at market prices to maximise company profits (Ritzer and Dean 2015; Ritzer 2015). The critics of 'McDonaldisation' (Dorsey and Ritzer 2016) have argued that if there are no measures and profound service-oriented thinking to counter McDonaldisation, healthcare's most cherished and defining values, including care for the individual and meaningful patient-physician relationships, will be threatened.

Our point in this book has been to take up service-dominant logic in the domain of public policies and public administration. In the realm of public administration, our approach has been to replace the 'old days' of bureaucracy-dominant logic with a refreshed view of seeing public interventions as services by definition and by underlining the role of citizens and service users per se. In the case of healthcare, our aim has been to underline the shift from output-related healthcare services towards a more service-oriented manner emphasising the aspect of health improvement as the core of service in healthcare. We have argued this on the assumption that there is plenty of evidence that the service perspective can be embedded to public policies and in the wider public administration domain (addressed in Osborne et al. 2013; Virtanen and Stenvall 2014). Moreover, these elements of service-dominant logic have been taken up in developing governments and public administration institutions in a more strategically agile manner (Doz and Kosonen 2010; Doz et al. 2017).

8.3.2   Fundament 7: Joint Value Co-creation in the Field of Health

Today, there is a transformation going on from service co-production towards co-creation of value. This is happening also in the field of healthcare. By definition, co-production and co-creation are conceptually different things. Co-production refers to designing, defining and producing services in a way such that authorities in service delivery work together with service users to improve existing services and to innovate new solutions for healthcare (in our book's case). Value co-creation, then, refers to activities of multiple actors within the health policy domain, often unaware of each other, contributing to each other's well-being, profitability (individual and institutional motive) and the betterment of public health policy strategies (societal motive).

Value creation does not just take place based on the activities of a single policy actor, but it is rather created by reciprocal dialogue among various actors and through joint resource (human and financial) integration. Service science scholars' important notion is that the beneficiary should always be included in the value creation process, whatever the case might be (Vargo and Lusch 2015). In the field of health, this refers to the citizens as a whole, service users and patients in particular.

> **Box 3 Intelligent Health Policy: Practical Implications Concerning Service-Dominant Logic and Service User Perspective in Healthcare Services**
> The practical implications of the *service-related fundaments* with regard to health policy and healthcare services are as follows:
>
> 1. In the field of healthcare, the service science–perspective approach offers a fresh view to understand the logic of health policy. In the past, healthcare organisations and healthcare service have contributed in the wealth of societies by delivering healthcare interventions that were mainly planned

(continued)

Box 3 (continued)

top-down and delivered in the output mode as a measurement logic (the clerks and audit authorities as well as the policy makers have been interested to see how many patients a doctor can take during 1 day at the healthcare centre). In the future, we foresee the goods-dominant logic will be replaced with service-dominant logic that addresses the improvement of community and individual health as the key ingredient in healthcare service provision. This pretty much demands a new mindset in the healthcare professions.

2. In the future, co-creation of healthcare value will be dependent on how health policy actors can and will be mobilised. This requires collaboration, coordination and cooperation both at the local, regional, national and supranational levels of governance. This would open up new possibilities for service integration in healthcare and would give new opportunities for gathering and combining all relevant actors of the health policy and healthcare services as potential resource integrators.

3. Joint policy and organisational strategies and experimentation are the nexus of the future integrated health policy and collaboration-based healthcare service delivery. Joint policy making alleviates siloed policy delivery and requires new forms of strategic sensitivity. Societal experimentations offer new perspectives to develop and to reorganise healthcare services (Mulgan 2009). Quite often, it would make more sense to experiment with societal innovations first rather than put forward full-scale systemic changes in society. Policy makers every now and then forget this useful and appropriate idea.

4. The service user and patient are always, as beneficiaries, the key co-creators of value in the chain of designing, planning and evaluating health policy as well as in the healthcare service delivery. A service-centred view holds that healthcare services are inherently service user-oriented and relational (e.g. the reciprocal connection in between the patient and the medical personnel).

5. In the field of healthcare, co-creation models with service users and patients exist, but the lessons learned from co-creation experiments and projects should be mainstreamed and analytically disseminated. Co-creation models call for new kinds of expertise in the field of healthcare service, such as service design, service architects and change management know-how.

8.4   Leadership-Related Fundaments of Policy Intelligence

8.4.1   Fundament 8: Knowledge Sharing and Policy Integration

As Greer et al. advocated, there are several well-known barriers to knowledge sharing, such as structural obstacles, communication structure, physical distance and managerial biases. From the point of view of healthcare, the confidentiality of patient records can be added to the list. This sounds a bit naïve perhaps, but we think the service perspective and collaborative co-creation of value approach might help with these knowledge-sharing obstacles because of a simple fact: looking at healthcare from the service perspective, the main aim of the network of the policy and service actors is to improve policy making and achieve better service delivery.

In terms of public policy, we maintain the view that knowledge sharing is a form of service exchange. This is due to the fact that—bearing in mind the relational nature of service exchange (Vargo and Lusch 2015)—enables knowledge that stimulates strategic sensitivity, resource integration and reallocation as well as innovations. We feel that the success of future health policy is dependent on how innovative aspects are integrated in the policy formulation and design. We think—controversially—that existing financial- and human-capacity resources for health are enough and renewing the service portfolios for healthcare does not necessary need additional (new) resources. Instead of additional resources, a new mindset is needed in healthcare service delivery—a mindset of healthcare professionals, which is based on unlearning and seeing new possibilities for policy and service integration and innovation (Stenvall and Virtanen 2012).

Complex society is about profound and pervasive challenges to traditional knowledge management practices in health policy and healthcare services as well as to policy integration in regard to health. From the point of view of complexity theory, traditional policy making has come to the end of the road. Policy planning based on reductionism is not only flawed, but it makes no sense from a wider societal perspective. The solution to wicked problems of health—such as obesity, mental problems and multi-diagnosed problems of health—cannot be solved in a single policy domain but in collaboration with input from multiple policy sectors.

8.4.2   Fundament 9: Trust, Inspirational and Entrepreneurial Leadership

Leadership know-how embedded with healthcare service delivery is under pressure, both from within the system (policy makers demand better performance) and from outside of the system (service users want better and more efficient services). We foresee a paradigm shift to take place in the leadership practices in the field of healthcare resulting from the changes in policy-level decision-making (from representative democracy and rational policy making towards digitalised, ad hoc democracy based on social media and 'garbage can' decision-making at the level of policy), the role of public administration (from regulator roles and vertical accountability towards creator-of-possibilities roles and horizontal accountability functions), the modus operandi of public governance (from government for the people and stability towards government by the people and experimentation) and overall public sector leadership (from controlling and leading single organisations towards change-adaptive mindsets and leading service ecosystems).

Additionally, we are convinced that the service perspective forces healthcare service managers to rethink their leadership practices. In this process, complementary aspects are integrated into the traditional public service motivations that healthcare service managers possess. Rational views of leadership and commitment to public good, norm-based desires to serve the public interest, loyalty to public duty and effective mindsets to run healthcare services with a genuine conviction about services' societal importance with the addition of benevolent patriotism are challenged by various ingredients of new leadership elements (Perry and Wise 1990; Kim et al. 2013). These include, for instance, the role of entrepreneurial dimensions in managing the healthcare services at the local level of governance. As the traditional, goods-dominant logic of leadership underlined the role of efficiency in the manufacturing of healthcare services, the service-dominant logic of future healthcare services emanates the idea of entrepreneurial activity in leadership as the rule, rather than the exception. To echo what Vargo and Lusch have written, value creation in services is '...an unfolding process, for which there is no end state to optimise or toward which to move. Rather this [value creation in collaboration with all relevant stakeholders] is an emergent process within an everchanging [health market–related] context, including ever-changing resources [and resource integration]; it is, by necessity, and entrepreneurial process' (2014, p. 242).

Box 4 Intelligent Health Policy: Practical Implications Concerning Knowledge Management and Leadership in Healthcare Services
The practical implications of the *leadership-related fundaments* with regard to health policy and healthcare services are as follows:

1. Future health policy is essentially based on knowledge sharing among politicians (from all levels of politics), policy makers, academia, innovation agencies, healthcare professionals, service users and patients. This is, of course, easier said than actually achieved. Politics and policy making are somewhat different things. Politics include bargaining, negotiating, consultation and hidden agendas, and this applies partly to policy making also if we consider policy making as the domain for the ruling political group(s). We are convinced, however, that knowledge sharing is possible at all levels of governance—at the local, regional, national and

(continued)

Box 4 (continued)

supranational levels of governance. The latest development of classical policy instruments (steering based on legislation, financial measures and information/knowledge) with an emphasis on information practices and agendas back this development towards a more integrated knowledge base for healthcare.

2. Intensive knowledge sharing and intelligent policy integration are Siamese twins. Without the existence of both of these elements, there is no intelligence in policy making in the field of health. Our point is policy integration does not take place only at the policy level of governance, but it is the ultimate character of public policy and public administration that prevails at all levels of governance—local, regional, national and supranational. Planning and performance management practices need to be developed in a way such that policy integration really takes place. Service delivery is, of course, very important in this respect. Without broad-view-centric leadership, this service integration would not succeed.

3. Even today, healthcare is a good example of a sector where various professions predominantly regulate the service practices at all levels. We foresee that a profound change will take place in the future, and leadership will be at the top of the agenda in this transformation process. In the future, more generic leadership competencies will evolve in the domain of healthcare leadership because of the service perspective. In practical terms, this means that leadership competencies are what counts in service delivery. Doctors can lead healthcare personnel—but so can nurses and psychologists and representatives from all other health professions as well. We are convinced that strategic human resource management and the service-integration view will constitute the core of the future's leadership curricula in the field of health. This will cause overwhelming challenges for the professional training of the future healthcare personnel at universities, at polytechnics and at low-educational training institutions. If the strategic human resource perspective and service integration mindset are not nurtured in the professional training curricula, then the efforts to develop healthcare systems and services in a more intelligent manner are of no use.

References

Ashby RW (1991) Requisite variety and its implications for the control of complex systems. In: Klir GJ (ed) Facets of systems science. Kluwer, New York, pp 405–417 (originally published in 1958)

Boisot M, McKelvey B (2011) Connectivity, extremes, and adaptation: a power-law perspective of organizational effectiveness. Organ Inq 20(2):119–133

Dorsey ER, Ritzer G (2016) The Mcdonaldization of medicine. JAMA Neurol 73(1):15–16

Doz Y, Kosonen M (2008) Fast strategy: how strategic agility will help you to stay ahead of the game. Wharton School Publishing, Harlow

Doz Y, Kosonen M (2010) Embedding strategic agility: a leadership agenda for accelerating business model renewal. Long Range Plan 43(2–3):370–382

Doz Y, Kosonen M (2014) Governments for the future. Building an agile and strategic state. Sitra, Helsinki, p 80

Doz Y, Kosonen M, Virtanen P (2017) Agile government and public administration? Article manuscript (In press)

Greer CR, Lusch RF, Vargo SL (2016) A service perspective: key managerial insights from service-dominant (S-D) logic. Organ Dyn. https://doi.org/10.1016/j.orgdyn (published online in December 2015)

Kim S, Vandenabeele W, Wright BE, Bøgh Andersen L, Cerase FB, Christensen RK, Desmarais C, Koumenta M, Leisink P, Liu B (2013) Investigating the structure and meaning of public service motivation across populations: developing an international instrument and addressing the issues pf measurement invariance. J Public Adm Resour Theory 23(1):79–102

King A, Crewe I (2013) The blunders of our governments. Oneworld, London

Mulgan G (2009) The art of public strategy: mobilizing power and knowledge for the common good. Oxford University Press, Oxford

OECD (2017) Working with change: systems approaches to public sector challenges. GOV/PGC 2017/2. OECD Publishing, Paris

Osborne S, Radnon Z, Nasi G (2013) A new theory for public service management? Towards a (public) service-dominant approach. Am Rev Public Adm 43(2):135–158

Perry JL, Wise LR (1990) The motivational bases of public service. Public Adm Rev 50 (3):367–373

Ritzer G (2015) The dehumanized consumer: does the prosumer offer some hope? In: García Martínez AN (ed) Being human in a consumer society. Ashgate, New York, pp 25–40

Ritzer G, Dean P (2015) Globalisation. A basic text. Wiley, New York

Stenvall J, Virtanen P (2012) Sosiaali- ja terveyspalvelujen uudistaminen [available only in Finnish, The development of social and healthcare services]. Tietosanoma, Helsinki

Vargo SL, Lusch RF (2014) Inversions of service-dominant logic. Mark Theory 14(3):239–248

Vargo SL, Lusch RF (2015) Institutions and axioms: an extension and update of service-dominant logic. J Acad Mark Sci 44(1):5–23

Vargo SL, Wieland H, Akaka M (2016) Innovation in service ecosystems. J Serviceol 1(1):1–5

Virtanen P, Stenvall J (2014) The evolution of public services from co-production to co-creation and beyond – an unfinished trajectory for the New Public Management? Int J Leadersh Public Serv 10(2):91–107

Virtanen P, Kaivo-oja J, Ishino Y, Stenvall J, Jalonen H (2016a) Ubiquitous revolution, customer needs and business intelligence. Empirical evidence from Japanese healthcare sector. Int J Web Eng Technol 11(3):259–283

Bibliography

Cairney P, Geyer R (2016) Introduction. In: Geyer R, Cairney P (eds) Complexity and public policy. Edward Elgar, Cheltenham, pp 1–15

De Walle S, Groeneweld S (eds) (2016) Theory and practice of public sector reform. Routledge, Oxford

Greenwood R, Hinings CR (1993) Understanding strategic change: the contribution of archetypes. Acad Manag J 36(5):1052–1081

Moran M, Rein M, Goodin RE (eds) (2008) The Oxford handbook of public policy. Oxford University Press, Oxford

Nystrom PC, Starbuck WH (1984) To avoid organizational crises, unlearn. Organ Dyn 12:53–65

Piketty T (2013) Le capital au XX1 siécle. Editions de Seuikl, Paris

Reed M (2006) Organizational theorizing: a historically contested terrain. In: Clegg S et al (eds) The Sage handbook of organization studies. Sage, Thousand Oaks, CA, pp 19–54

© Springer International Publishing AG 2018
P. Virtanen, J. Stenvall, *Intelligent Health Policy*,
https://doi.org/10.1007/978-3-319-69596-9

Printed by Printforce, the Netherlands